The Reconstruction of Religious T
by Allama.Mohammad Iqbal

Editor's Introduction

In the present edition of Allama Iqbal's *The Reconstruction of Religious Thought in Islam*, an attempt has been made at providing references to many authors cited in it and, more particularly, to the passages quoted from their works. The titles of these works have not always been given by the Allama and, in a few cases, even the names of the authors have to be worked out from some such general descriptions about them as 'the great mystic poet of Islam', 'a modern historian of civilization', and the like.

The work, however, referred to more often than any other, and quoted most, is the Qur'«n. Of a large number of passages quoted from it, about seventy-seven, generally set apart from the main text, carry numbered references to the Quranic Su'rahs and verses. The unnumbered passages from the Qur'«n, about fifty or so, given within the text are comparatively briefer - sometimes very brief, merely calling attention to a unique expression of the Qur'«n. References to these as well as to many Quranic ideas and quite a few Quranic subjects, alluded to especially in the first five Lectures, have been supplied in the Notes and later also in the Index of Quranic References. A numerical scanning of this Index shows quite significantly that the number of verses bearing on the subjects of 'man', 'Quranic empiricism' and the 'phenomenon of change' (mostly in terms of alternation of the night and the day and also in a wider sense) in each case, is comparatively larger than the number of verses on any other single subject. This may as well be noted in the clustering of such verses or of references to them on quite a few pages of the *Reconstruction*.

Added to the verses quoted from the Qur'«n and references to them, in the present work, are a good number of quite significant observations and statements embodying Allama's rare insight into the Qur'«n born of his peculiarly perceptive and deep study of it. These are to be found scattered all over the work, except in Lecture VII, where one would notice just one observation and complete absence of passages from the Qur'«n, possibly because it was originally addressed to a non-Muslim audience. About sixty-five of these observations and statements have been listed in the general Index under: 'observations and statements based on' as a sub-entry of the 'Qur'«n'.

Of the other works quoted from in the *Reconstruction*, forty-nine that I could work out and later list in the Index, about fifteen are by Muslim authors, mostly mystics and mystic poets. Passages from these Muslim works, originally in Arabic, Persian or Turkish, have been given, with the single exception of Rëmâ's *Mathnawi*, in their first-ever English translation by Allama Iqbal. Notable among these are passages from Fakhr al-Dân al-R«zâ's *Al-Mab«hith al-Mashriqâyah* and Shaikh Ahmad Sirhindi`'s *Maktëb«t* and, above all, Ziya Gokalp's Turkish poems, which the Allama was able to render into English from their German version by August Fischer in his *Aus der religiö sen Reformbewegung in der Tü rkei* (Leipzig, 1922).

Equally important and perhaps more are Allama's condensed English versions of considerably longer passages or sections from Ibn Maskawaih's *al-Fauz al-Asghar* (on evolutionary hypothesis in both the biological and the spiritual sense), Sh«h Walâ'ullah magnum opus *al-Hujjat All«h al-B«lighah* (on the prophetic method of building up a universal *Sharâ'ah*) and *'Ir«qâ's Gh«yat al-Imk«n fâ`Dir«yat al-Mak«n* (on the plurality of space-orders and time-orders). This last, the longest of all the summarized translations from works in Arabic or Persian, was originally prepared by Allama Iqbal from the, then a rare, Manuscript for his Sectional Presidential Address: 'A Plea for Deeper Study of the Muslim Scientists' presented at the Fifth Oriental Conference, Lahore: 20-22 November 1928. The translation of the passage from Sh«h Walâ 'All«h's *Al-Hujjat All«h al-B«lighah* however, seems to belong to a still later date. There is a clear reference to this significant passage in Allama Iqbal's letter addressed to Sayyid Sulaim«n Nadvâon 22 September 1929, i.e. a month before he delivered the first six Lectures at the Aligarh Muslim University. All these summarized translations, it may be added, from parts of the main text of Lectures III, V and VI.

As to Rěmâ's *Mathnawâ*, quoted very extensively (six of its verses are quoted even in the original Persian), one is to note that the translations of all the passages from it are not by Allama Iqbal himself but by others: Whinfield, Nicholson (with certain modifications) and Thadani, only in one case has the Allama given his own translation of a verse from Rěmâ (p. 88); but, unbelievable though it is, this verse, according to the Persian translator of the *Reconstruction*, is to be found neither in the *Mathnawânor* in the *Kulliy«t-i Shams*. This certainly needs further research. However, almost every time a passage is quoted from the *Mathnawâor* even a reference is made to it, the reader is reminded of 'the beautiful words of Rěmâ' and of his being 'far more true to the spirit of Islam than', says, 'Ghazz«`lâ'.

Of about thirty-four Western writers from whose works the Allama has quoted, as many as twenty-five were his contemporaries and among these one is to underline the names of Whitehead, Eddington, Wildon Carr, Louis Rougier, and certainly also of Spengler. One is also to note that the works of these and other contemporaries quoted from happen to be mostly those which were published between 1920 and 1928. This is not at all to minimize the importance of quite significant passages quoted from the works of Bergson, James, Hocking and even Aghnides, all published before 1920, but only to refer to the fact of there being a greater number of quotations in the *Reconstruction* from Western works published within a certain period of time.

The year 1920, in fact, happens to be the year of the publication of Einstein's epoch-making *Relativity: The Special and the General Theory: A Popular Exposition*. And it is the year also of the publication of Eddington's *Space, Time and Gravitation* and Wildon Carr's *General Principle of Relativity in Its Philosophical and Historical Aspect*, perhaps the earliest expository works on Relativity by English writers. Passages from both these works are to be found in the *Reconstruction*. Einstein's own work is catalogued in Allama's personal library along with a dozen others bearing on Relativity-Physics.

Mention must also be made here of Alexander's peculiarly difficult two-volume *Space, Time and Deity*, which on its appearance in 1920 was hailed as 'a philosophical event of the first rank'. This is perhaps the first contemporary work which received Allama's immediate professional comments, even though brief, embodying his significant admission: 'Alexander's thought is much bolder than mine'. Despite Alexander's pronounced realistic (and thereby also naturalistic-empiric tic and so scientific) metaphysics, the Allama seems to have found in his supreme 'principle of emergence' a kind of empirical confirmation of Bergson's creative evolution. It was verily in terms of the principle of emergence that he explained to Nicholson his idea of Perfect Man in contradistinction to that of Nietzsche's Superman in his long, perhaps the longest, letter addressed to him on 24 January 1921.

Allama Iqbal's assessment of the works of Western writers, especially of those which received his closest attention, seems to be characterized by the ambivalence of admiration and dissatisfaction, or acceptance and rejection. This is also reflected in one of his most valuable dicta addressed to Muslims: 'Approach modern knowledge with a respectful but independent attitude' (p. 78). Nowhere is this ambivalence perhaps better exemplified than in Allama's treatment of Spengler's *Decline of the West*; two volumes published in April 1926 and November 1928. He readily accepts some of Spengler's pronouncements such as these: 'The history of Western knowledge is thus one of progressive emancipation from classical thought'; 'The symbol of the West . . . is the (mathematical) idea of function'; 'Not until the theory of functions was evolved' could it become possible for us to have 'our dynamic Western physics'. But the Allama was completely dissatisfied with the very central thesis of The *Decline of the West* 'that cultures, as organic structures, are completely alien to one another'. In his Address at the Oriental Conference, he pointedly observed that facts 'tend to falsify Spengler's thesis'. It was this thesis or doctrine of 'mutual alienation of cultures' or cultural isolationism, the Allama strongly felt, that blinded Spengler to the undeniable Muslim influences or ingredients in the development of European culture. There is no mention in his otherwise 'extremely learned work' of such known facts of history as the anti-classicism of the Muslim thinkers, which found its clearest expression in the work of the very brilliant Ibn Khaldën - Spengler's Muslim counterpart in many ways. Nor is there any reference, in The *Decline of the West*, to Al-Bârënâ's 'theory of functions', clearly enunciated in his al-Q«nên al-Mas'ëdâ, six hundred years before Fermat and Descartes - a fact which Spengler had every right to know for he was so well versed in mathematics, and even as a historian of cultures.

Again, while referring to Spengler's allegation that 'the culture of Islam is thoroughly Magian in spirit and character' Allama Iqbal candidly observes: 'That a Magian crust has grown over Islam, I do not deny'. And he adds quite importantly for us: 'Indeed, my main purpose in these lectures has been to secure a vision of the spirit of Islam as emancipated from its Magian overlayings' (p. 114). However, Spengler's vision of Islam as a cultural movement, according to Allama, was completely perverted by his thesis of 'mutual alienation of cultures' and also by his morphological approach to history, which led him to group Islam as a culture with the manifestly Magian cultures of Judaism, Zoroastrianism and others. Allama Iqbal did recognize the historical fact that Islam imported some concepts and a 'religious experience' - as reflected, for instance, in some esoteric traditions in Muslim theology and in certain theosophical and occultistic tendencies in Sufism - from these earlier cultures in the period of its expansion as also in later periods especially when the conquered became conquerors culturally. But these importations, the Allama insisted, remained all along the husk of Islam, its Magian crust or its Magian overlayings. Spengler's capital error is obvious.

Moreover, Spengler failed to perceive in the idea of finality of prophethood in Islam, 'a psychological cure for the Magian attitude of constant expectation'. It should be clear to any body that with the 'revelation' of this idea of finality, one of the greatest that dawned upon the prophetic consciousness, 'all personal authority claiming a supernatural origin came to an end in the history of man'. Spengler also failed to appreciate the cultural value of this idea in Islam. With all his 'overwhelming learning', it perhaps did not become possible for him to comprehend the all-important truth that 'the constant appeal to reason and experience in the Qur'«n, and the emphasis that it lays on Nature and History as sources of human knowledge are . . . different aspects of the same idea of finality'. It is these aspects of the idea of finality which bring to man, indeed, a keen awareness of the 'birth' of a new epoch with Islam, the epoch 'of inductive intellect'.

The fact that none of the works of the Western writers quoted from in the *Reconstruction* crosses 1928 as its date of publication does not make much of a problem so far as the first six Lectures are concerned. One has only to recall that the first three Lectures were written or finally re-written in 1928, and the next three in 1929, mostly perhaps during the summer vacations of the Courts. It is quite likely that at the time of writing the second set of three lectures in 1929, Allama Iqbal did not come across many works published in the West the same year, or did not find anything in them to quote from in his Lectures. But the last Lecture in the present work: 'Is Religion Possible?' was delivered in a session of the Aristotelian Society, London, in December 1932; and yet all the six Western works quoted from, even in this Lecture, happen to have been published within 1928. How is one to understand Allama's not keeping up his usual keenly perceptive and reportedly avid reading of the Western philosophers?

Why this almost an ascetic self-denial of philosophy? There could be many reasons for this. Among these, due allowance has to be made for his preoccupation of two different orders: one which suited his superb poetic genius most; and the other, of more practical nature, which increasingly took possession of his time and attention towards guiding and helping the Muslims of India in their great struggle for an autonomous homeland. Allama Iqbal all along keenly felt that Islam was to have an opportunity 'to mobilize its law, its education, its culture, and to bring them into closer contact with its own original spirit and with the spirit of modern times' (*Speeches, Writings and Statements of Iqbal*, p. 11). From the depth of these feelings there emerged a prophetic vision of a geographical form - now called Pakistan.

As stated above Allama's avowed main purpose in his Lectures is 'to secure a vision of the spirit of Islam as emancipated from its Magian overlayings' (p. 114). There is, however, not much mention of Magianism, nor of the specific Magian overlayings of Islam, in the *Reconstruction*. In all there is a brief reference to Magian culture in the opening section of Lecture IV and to Magian idea or thought in the concluding passage of Lecture V. In the latter case Allama's statement that Ibn Khaldën has 'finally demolished the alleged revelational basis in Islam of an idea similar . . . to the original Magian idea' (p. 115) is an implied and may be somewhat suppressed reference to his view that 'all prophetic traditions relating to mahdâ, *masihiyat* and *mujaddidiyyat* are Magian in both provenance and spirit' (Iqb«l N«mah, II, 231). It may be rightly said that Allama's whole *Weltanschauung* is so completely anti-Magian that he does not always have to name Magianism whenever he says something which implies anti-Magianism. A good instance of this, perhaps, would be his observation in Lecture VII on the 'technique' of medieval mysticism in the Muslim East. 'Far from reintegrating the forces of the average man's inner life, and thus preparing him for participation in the march of history', this Muslim mysticism, he tells us, 'has taught man a false renunciation and made him perfectly contented with his ignorance and spiritual thraldom' (pp. 148-49).

It remains, however, true that there are not very many statements in the *Reconstruction* even with Allama's implied anti-Magianism, unless we understand the expressions 'implied' and 'implication' in a different and deeper sense, and go to the very starting-point or genesis of his anti-Magianism. As is the case with most of his other great and rare insights - generally couched in a language different from that of Bergsonian-Whiteheadian metaphysics, Allama owes his anti-Magianism to his uniquely perceptive reading of the Qur'«n. It essentially emanates from his keen understanding of the profound significance of the supreme idea of finality of prophethood looked at from the point of view of religious and cultural growth of man in history, and even thus, looked at also from the point of view of 'man's achieving full self-consciousness' as bearer of the 'Divine trust' of 'personality' (ego) and of the 'Divine promise' of a complete subjugation of all this immensity of space and time'. With this Prophetic idea of the perfection and thereby the completion of the chain of all Divinely-revealed religions in Islam, says Allama: 'all personal authority, claiming a supernatural origin, has come to an end in the history of man' (p. 101). But then from the same supreme idea also emanates the keen awareness of the epochal 'birth of inductive intellect', summed up in Allama's well-known aphorism. 'Birth of Islam is the birth of inductive intellect' (p. 101). Added to this is his observation, characterized by the same simplicity and directness of 'perception': 'In the Prophet of Islam, life discovers other sources of knowledge suitable to its new direction' (p. 101). Thus, 'abolition of all Magian claims' and 'the birth of inductive intellect', within the logic of Islamic experience, are two co-implicant ideas, for they owe their origin to the same supreme idea of finality and from it they draw their common inspiration.

Because of the veritable inner unity of the Qur'«n, man's new awareness of himself with regard to both his place in Nature and his position in History awakened by 'the idea of finality' is already clearly reflected in 'the emphasis that the Qur'«n lays on Nature and History as sources of human knowledge'. The latter, according to the Allama, is only one of the other aspects of the former; as is also 'the constant appeal to reason and experience in the Qur'«n'. Thus, 'the birth of inductive intellect' is to be found in the Qur'«n in more than one way; and, therefore, in as many ways is to be found also the repudiation of Magianism inherently implied by it. This explains largely, perhaps, Allama's having taken up in the *Reconstruction* the methodological device of removing the Magian crust from Islam by promoting, from within Islam, its own intrinsic awareness of the birth of inductive intellect. This is borne out by many of the brightest parts of the present work.

Some of the perceptive Western readers of the *Reconstruction* have correctly noticed in Allama's idea of 'the birth or awakening of inductive intellect' a middle term between 'Islam' and 'modern science', even as one is also to notice Allama's bracketing 'science' with 'God-consciousness' - more precious than mere belief in God, in some of his extraordinary pronouncements. These appear sometimes, suddenly as if, in the concluding part of an argument as spontaneous expressions of an essential aspect of that argument's inner impulse, which seems to have become a little more heightened in the end. Such are the pronouncements, for instance, in which the Allama equates the scientist's observation of Nature with someone's 'virtually seeking a kind of intimacy with the Absolute Ego' (p. 45) or where he calls 'the scientific observer of Nature,' 'a kind of mystic seeker in the act of prayer' (p. 73). Making this matter of 'God-consciousness-through-science' more explicit, he tells us that 'scientific observation of Nature keeps us in close contact with the behaviour of Reality, and thus sharpens our inner perception for a deeper vision of it' (p. 72), or that 'one indirect way of establishing connexions with the reality that confronts us is reflective observation and control of its symbols as they reveal themselves to sense-perception' (p. 12). So sure is Allama of the near at hand possibilities of the scientific observer's 'establishing connexions with Reality' through his following the 'modest' ways of inductive intellect that he significantly concludes: 'This alone will add to his power over Nature and give him that vision of the total-infinite which philosophy seeks but cannot find' (p. 73).

The *Reconstruction*, however, cannot be said to be a critique of Magian supernaturalism, nor, perhaps, is it altogether a dissertation on Islamic awareness of inductive intellect, or on Islam's saying 'yes' to the world of matter and the unique emphasis that it lays on the empirical aspect of Reality, and thence on science and on power over Nature. All these do get their due place in Allama's work, but they also get their share of criticism in the philosophically conceived total religio-moral synthesis of Islam. In fact, the exigency of the writing of the major part of the *Reconstruction* seems to have arisen, among other things, out of a state of despair into which Muslim religio-philosophic tradition had fallen, apparently, out of sheer neglect over the ages. Muslims in the end were, thus, left with what the Allama has described 'a worn-out' or 'practically a dead metaphysics' with its peculiar thought-forms and set phraseology producing manifestly 'a deadening effect on the modern mind' (pp. 72, 78). The need for writing a new Muslim metaphysics could not be overemphasized; and the Allama wrote one in the *Reconstruction* in terms of contemporary developments in science and philosophy. This he hoped would 'be helpful towards a proper understanding of the meaning of Islam as a message to humanity' (p. 7). Allama's hope came true. The *Reconstruction* is one of the very few precious Muslim works available today for a meaningful discourse on Islam at the international forum of learning. Even thus it is unique in promoting effective interreligious dialogue, provided the 'metaphysics' at least of the major world religions are got similarly translated into the common idiom and metaphor of today. The *Reconstruction* certainly also aims at greatly facilitating the much-needed inner communication between Islam and 'some of the most important phases of its culture, on its intellectual side' (p. 6), which now, with the passage of time, have come to be manifested in many human disciplines rapidly progressing all over the world. Promotion of Islam's communication with its own manifestations elsewhere is, perhaps, today, historically speaking, an indispensable part of Muslims' own 'proper understanding of the meaning of Islam'.

While preparing the script of the *Reconstruction* for its present edition I have used basically its Oxford University Press edition of 1934. The few misprints of the proper names like Maimmonides, Rongier, Tawfâk Fitrat - which seem to have been transferred to the Oxford edition of the *Reconstruction* from its poorly printed original Lahore (Kapur Art Printing Works) edition of 1930 - were pointed out by some of the earlier Western reviewers. None of these misprints, however, posed much of a problem except one, which, I confess, put me on real hard work. I mean: 'Sarkashâ of the tenth century of the Hijrah, a misprint of composite nature relating to both name and date. The French, the Urdu and the Persian translators of the *Reconstruction* have noted it as a misprint for 'Sarakhsi' of the fifth century of the Hijrah' - a bit too commonly known a name and date to steal into a composite misprint in the *Reconstruction*; and then the date certainly a bit anachronistic for the passage where it is meant to go. After arriving at, what I may be allowed to call, my foolproof reasons and authenticated evidence with regard to this misprint in name and date, I decided to change it into Zarkashâ of the eighth century of the Hijrah with a long note to this name.

As to my primary task of tracing the passages quoted in the *Reconstruction* to their originals in the Muslim or Western writers, I am to say that I did finally succeed in finding them out except four, i.e. those quoted from Horten, Hurgronje, von Kremer and Said Halâm P«sh«. All these passages belong to Lecture VI. This Lecture, as I have adduced some evidence to show in my Notes, is justly believed to be the revised and enlarged form of a paper on *Ijtih«d* read by Allama Iqbal in December 1924. After all my search for the so far four untraced passages in the possible works which could become available to me, I am inclined to assume that they are Allama's own translations from German works. Allama's translation of two passages from Friedrich Naumann's *Briefe ü ber Religion* and five passages from August Fischer's *Aus der religiö sen Reformbewegung in der Tü rke*i in Lecture VI, earlier paper on Ijtih«d and his past practice of quoting from German works in *The Development of*

Metaphysics in Persia as well as his correspondence with some of the noted German and other orientalists are among the additional reasons for this assumption.

As to the passages which have been quoted in Lecture VI and could be traced to their originals, there are good reasons to believe that all the three passages quoted from Nicolas Aghnides' *Mohammedan Theories of Finance* (a copy of which was presented to the Allama in March-April 1923), in the latter part of this Lecture, belong to the period of Allama's writing his paper on the 'Idea of *Ijtih«d*' in the Law of Islam' in 1924. This also seems to be true of Ziya Gö kalp's poems translated by the Allama from *Aus der religiö sen Reformbewegung in der Turkei* (1922) a copy of which he did receive in April 1924 from the author, August Fischer, then also the editor of *Islamica*. In one of his letters to Sayyid Sulaim«n Nadvâ, the Allama clearly refers to his having made use of Ziya Gö kalp's poems in his paper on *Ijtih«d*. There are, however, at least two passages which, with some good measure of certainty, can be said to belong to later dates. I mean the passage in the beginning of Lecture VI from Denison's *Emotion as the Basis of Civilization*, published in 1928; and, secondly, the passage from *al-Àujjat All«h al-B«lighah* which, as stated earlier, is to be linked with Allama's letter to Sayyid Sulaim«n Nadvâ on 22 September 1929.

Composition of Lecture VI, thus, appears to be spread over a longer period of time than is the case with other Lectures; even as Allama's interest in the 'idea of *Ijtih«d* in the Law of Islam' and thereby in the entire methodology of Muslim jurisprudence - recurrently visible in the last fifteen years of his life - is much more sustained than his interest in many other subjects, including a good many that he came across in his avid and vast reading of the great Western philosophers.

In a press interview, a little before the second Round Table Conference, the Allama expressed his intention of writing a book on 'the system of *fiqh* in the light of modern knowledge', another 'work of *reconstruction*' on the legal aspect of Islam, much more important than its purely theological aspect. To this second work of reconstruction, his present work of reconstruction on the philosophical aspect of Islam, he added with his usual modesty, was 'necessary as a prelude'. The much cherished book: '*The Reconstruction of Legal Thought in Islam*' was, however, not written: but the bare fact that the Allama wanted to write it and the great importance that he attached to the writing of it, signifies, perhaps, his will to posterity.

In working out references to the views of many authors - Islamic or Western, medieval or modern - cited in the present work, or in providing notes to some of the points raised or names and terms mentioned in it, I sincerely believe that, though I have reaped a rich academic harvest of my work, I have done only what any other admirer and lover of Allama Iqbal would have done, and done it better.

From an almost encyclopedic range of views and facts covered in the *Reconstruction* as also from the pre-eminently towering intellectual and spiritual stature of Allama Iqbal, it should not be difficult to imagine that the production of an annotated edition of this work could not have become possible for me without the kindly assistance and advice of many friends and scholars both in Pakistan and abroad. I most sincerely acknowledge my debt to them all.

I owe a special debt of gratitude to Chief Justice Dr. J«vid Iqbal for his kindly agreeing to the proposal of bringing out an annotated edition of the *Reconstruction* and also for granting permission for its publication. I am also grateful to the members of the Board of Directors of the Institute of Islamic Culture, Lahore, for their approval of my undertaking this work as one of my academic assignments in partial fulfilment of my duties as Director of the Institute, and especially to Dr. M. Afzal, Minister for Education, for his kind encouragement and sustained keen interest in its publication.

It is my most pleasant duty to thank Professor M. Âiddâq of Islamia College, Lahore, for his many courtesies and generous assistance in the use of Allama Iqbal's personal library and particularly for his expert advice in the matter of locating and reading Allama's marginal and other marks and notes in his personal copies of many important works.

My grateful thanks are also due to Dr. AÁmad Nabâ Kh«n, Director: Archaeology, and his junior colleague Mr. M. H. Khokhar, Curator: Allama Iqbal Museum, Lahore, for their special courtesy which made it possible for me to examine and study some of the important MSS and books preserved in this Museum and especially the letters of the orientalists. This did help me solve some of my riddles.

I am gratefully indebted to Q«zâ Mahmëdul Haq of the British Library, London, for his kindly sending me the photostat of Allama Iqbal's article published in the first issue of *Sociological Review* (1908), and also of sections from Denison's, now a rare book, *Emotion as the Basis of Civilization*. In addition Mr. Haq very kindly arranged to send to me microfilms of certain MSS in Cairo including the unique MSS of Khw«jah Muhammad P«rsa's *Ris«lah dar Zam«n-o-Mak«n*. Thus alone did it become possible for me to work out some difficult, if not impossible, references in the *Reconstruction*.

I also wish to express my gratitude to Mlle Mauricette Levasseur of Bibliothè que Nationale, Paris, for her kindly supplying me the requested information on Andrè Servier, and more importantly for her detailed notes on Louis Rougier (earlier Rongier) which helped me work through a somewhat tangled problem of names and titles.

My very grateful thanks are due to the two Dutch friends: the Reverend Dr. Jan Slomp and Mr. Harry Mintjes. The former was never tired of translating for me passages from articles and books in German or French, for the information requested by me sometimes was to become available only in these languages. And it was Mr. Mintjes who finally made it possible for me to have the photostat of the passages from Naumann's *Briefe ü ber Religion* quoted in the *Reconstruction*.

I must also thank my nephew, Professor Dr. Mustansir Mir of the University of Michigan, Ann Arbor, for his ready supply of photostats of this or that article, or of parts of books, or more importantly of a new dissertation on Allama Iqbal in the States.

Of the many more friends and scholars who have kindly helped me in my work or from whose views I have benefited in one way or the other, mention must be made of Maul«n«M. Àanâf Nadvâ and Maul«n« M. Ish«q Bhattâ`. I met them almost daily in the office of the Institute of Islamic Culture, and it was always so convenient to take some significant Arabic texts to them and enter into a lively discussion on this or that Islamic issue touched upon in the *Reconstruction*. I am ever so grateful to them for all these discussions.

I must also acknowledge my great indebtedness to Mr. M. Ashraf D«r, Secretary and Publication Adviser of the Institute, for his kindly preparing the entire manuscript for press, for his many valuable suggestions and technical assistance in the difficult task of preparing the two Indexes - particularly the second, which, in fact, has grown unto index-cum-concordance - and finally for reading and correcting proofs of the latter part of the work, i.e. the editor's part starting with his Notes and References.

Nobody is more conscious of the many drawbacks in this latter part than I, and, for that very reason, none so eager to welcome the suggestions of the worthy reader to improve upon it, for the next edition.

Even so, I would like to dedicate this part of the work by the editor to the memories of the late Chief Justice S. A. Rahman and the late Maul«n« Sa'âd Ahmad Akbar«b«dâ, the two Iqbalites, who helped me understand 'the great synthesis, the greatest in the modern Muslim world' that Allama Iqbal is. May their souls rest in eternal peace!

Lahore: 1984 M.S.S.

PREFACE

The Qur'«n is a book which emphasizes 'deed' rather than 'idea'. There are, however, men to whom it is not possible organically to assimilate an alien universe by re-living, as a vital process, that special type of inner experience on which religious faith ultimately rests. Moreover, the modern man, by developing habits of concrete thought - habits which Islam itself fostered at least in the earlier stages of its cultural career - has rendered himself less capable of that experience which he further suspects because of its liability to illusion. The more genuine schools of Sufism have, no doubt, done good work in shaping and directing the evolution of religious experience in Islam; but their latter-day representatives, owing to their ignorance of the modern mind, have become absolutely incapable of receiving any fresh inspiration from modern thought and experience. They are perpetuating methods which were created for generations possessing a cultural outlook differing, in important respects, from our own. 'Your creation and resurrection,' says the Qur'«n, 'are like the creation and resurrection of a single soul.' A living experience of the kind of biological unity, embodied in this verse, requires today a method physiologically less violent and psychologically more suitable to a concrete type of mind. In the absence of such a method the demand for a scientific form of religious knowledge is only natural. In these Lectures, which were undertaken at the request of the Madras Muslim Association and delivered at Madras, Hyderabad, and Aligarh, I have tried to meet, even though partially, this urgent demand by attempting to reconstruct Muslim religious philosophy with due regard to the philosophical traditions of Islam and the more recent developments in the various domains of human knowledge. And the present moment is quite favourable for such an undertaking. Classical Physics has learned to criticize its own foundations. As a result of this criticism the kind of materialism, which it originally necessitated, is rapidly disappearing; and the day is not far off when Religion and Science may discover hitherto unsuspected mutual harmonies. It must, however, be remembered that there is no such thing as finality in philosophical thinking. As knowledge advances and fresh avenues of thought are opened, other views, and probably sounder views than those set forth in these Lectures, are possible. Our duty is carefully to watch the progress of human thought, and to maintain an independent critical attitude towards it.

Knowledge and Religious Experience

by Dr. Muhammad Iqbal

What is the character and general structure of the universe in which we live? Is there a permanent element in the constitution of this universe? How are we related to it? What place do we occupy in it, and what is the kind of conduct that befits the place we occupy? These questions are common to religion, philosophy, and higher poetry. But the kind of knowledge that poetic inspiration brings is essentially individual in its character; it is figurative, vague, and indefinite. Religion, in its more advanced forms, rises higher than poetry. It moves from individual to society. In its attitude towards the Ultimate Reality it is opposed to the limitations of man; it enlarges his claims and holds out the prospect of nothing less than a direct vision of Reality. Is it then possible to apply the purely rational method of philosophy to religion? The spirit of philosophy is one of free inquiry. It suspects all authority. Its function is to trace the uncritical assumptions of human thought to their hiding places, and in this pursuit it may finally end in denial or a frank admission of the incapacity of pure reason to reach the Ultimate Reality. The essence of religion, on the other hand, is faith; and faith, like the bird, sees its 'trackless way' unattended by intellect which, in the words of the great mystic poet of Islam, 'only waylays the living heart of man and robs it of the invisible wealth of life that lies within'.[1] Yet it cannot be denied that faith is more than mere feeling. It has something like a cognitive content, and the existence of rival parties— scholastics and mystics— in the history of religion shows that idea is a vital element in religion. Apart from this, religion on its doctrinal side, as defined by Professor Whitehead, is 'a system of general truths which have the effect of transforming character when they are sincerely held and vividly apprehended'.[2] Now, since the transformation and guidance of man's inner and outer life is the essential aim of religion, it is obvious that the general truths which it embodies must not remain unsettled. No one would hazard action on the basis of a doubtful principle of conduct. Indeed, in view of its function, religion stands in greater need of a rational foundation of its ultimate principles than even the dogmas of science. Science may ignore a rational metaphysics; indeed, it has ignored it so far. Religion can hardly afford to ignore the search for a reconciliation of the oppositions of experience and a justification of the environment in which humanity finds itself. That is why Professor Whitehead has acutely remarked that 'the ages of faith are the ages of rationalism'.[3] But to rationalize faith is not to admit the superiority of philosophy over religion. Philosophy, no doubt, has jurisdiction to judge religion, but what is to be judged is of such a nature that it will not submit to the jurisdiction of philosophy except on its own terms. While sitting in judgement on religion, philosophy cannot give religion an inferior place among its data. Religion is not a departmental affair; it is neither mere thought, nor mere feeling, nor mere action; it is an expression of the whole man. Thus, in the evaluation of religion, philosophy must recognize the central position of religion and has no other alternative but to admit it as something focal in the process of reflective synthesis. Nor is there any reason to suppose that thought and intuition are essentially opposed to each other. They spring up from the same root and complement each other. The one grasps Reality piecemeal, the other grasps it in its wholeness. The one fixes its gaze on the eternal, the other on the temporal aspect of Reality. The one is present enjoyment of the whole of Reality; the other aims at traversing the whole by slowly specifying and closing up the various regions of the whole for exclusive observation. Both are in need of each other for mutual rejuvenation. Both seek visions of the same Reality which reveals itself to them in accordance with their function in life. In fact, intuition, as Bergson rightly says, is only a higher kind of intellect.[4]

The search for rational foundations in Islam may be regarded to have begun with the Prophet himself. His constant prayer was: 'God! grant me knowledge of the ultimate nature of things!'[5] The work of later mystics and non-mystic rationalists forms an exceedingly instructive chapter in the history of our culture, inasmuch as it reveals a longing for a coherent system of ideas, a spirit of whole-hearted devotion to truth, as well as the limitations of the age, which rendered the various theological movements in Islam less fruitful than they might have been in a different age. As we all know, Greek philosophy has been a great cultural force in the history of Islam. Yet a careful study of the Qur'«n and the various schools of scholastic theology that arose under the inspiration of Greek thought disclose the remarkable fact that while Greek philosophy very much broadened the outlook of Muslim thinkers, it, on the whole, obscured their vision of the Qur'«n. Socrates concentrated his attention on the human world alone. To him the proper study of man was man and not the world of plants, insects, and stars. How unlike the spirit of the Qur'«n, which sees in the humble bee a recipient of Divine inspiration[6] and constantly calls upon the reader to observe the perpetual change of the winds, the alternation of day and night, the clouds,[7] the starry heavens,[8] and the planets swimming through infinite space![9] As a true disciple of Socrates, Plato despised sense–perception which, in his view, yielded mere opinion and no real knowledge.[10] How unlike the Qur'«n, which regards 'hearing' and 'sight' as the most valuable Divine gifts[11] and declares them to be accountable to God for their activity in this world.[12] This is what the earlier Muslim students of the Qur'«n completely missed under the spell of classical speculation. They read the Qur'«n in the light of Greek thought. It took them over two hundred years to perceive - though not quite clearly - that the spirit of the Qur'«n was essentially anti-classical,[13] and the result of this perception was a kind of intellectual revolt, the full significance of which has not been realized even up to the present day. It was partly owing to this revolt and partly to his personal history that Ghaz«lâ based religion on philosophical scepticism - a rather unsafe basis for religion and not wholly justified by the spirit of the Qur'«n. Ghaz«lâ's chief opponent, Ibn Rushd, who defended Greek philosophy against the rebels, was led, through Aristotle, to what is known as the doctrine of Immortality of Active Intellect,[14] a doctrine which once wielded enormous influence on the intellectual life of France and Italy,[15] but which, to my mind, is entirely opposed to the view that the Qur'«n takes of the value and destiny of the human ego.[16] Thus Ibn Rushd lost sight of a great and fruitful idea in Islam and unwittingly helped the growth of that enervating philosophy of life which obscures man's vision of himself, his God, and his world. The more constructive among the Ash'arite thinkers were no doubt on the right path and anticipated some of the more modern forms of Idealism; yet, on the whole, the object of the Ash'arite movement was simply to defend orthodox opinion with the weapons of Greek dialectic. The Mu'tazilah, conceiving religion merely as a body of doctrines and ignoring it as a vital fact, took no notice of non-conceptual modes of approaching Reality and reduced religion to a mere system of logical concepts ending in a purely negative attitude. They failed to see that in the domain of knowledge - scientific or religious - complete independence of thought from concrete experience is not possible.

It cannot, however, be denied that Ghaz«lâ's mission was almost apostolic like that of Kant in Germany of the eighteenth century. In Germany rationalism appeared as an ally of religion, but she soon realized that the dogmatic side of religion was incapable of demonstration. The only course open to her was to eliminate dogma from the sacred record. With the elimination of dogma came the utilitarian view of morality, and thus rationalism completed the reign of unbelief. Such was the state of theological thought in Germany when Kant appeared. His *Critique of Pure Reason* revealed the limitations of human reason and reduced the whole work of the rationalists to a heap of ruins. And justly has he been described as God's greatest gift to his country. Ghaz«lâ's philosophical scepticism which, however, went a little too far, virtually did the same kind of work in the world of Islam in breaking the back of that proud but shallow rationalism which moved in the same direction as pre-Kantian rationalism in Germany. There is, however, one important difference between Ghaz«lâ's and Kant. Kant, consistently with his principles, could not affirm the possibility of a knowledge of God. Ghaz«lâ's, finding no hope in analytic thought, moved to mystic experience, and there found an independent content for religion. In this way he succeeded in securing for religion the right to exist independently of science and metaphysics. But the revelation of the total Infinite in mystic experience convinced him of the finitude and inconclusiveness of thought and drove him to draw a line of cleavage between thought and intuition. He failed to see that thought and intuition are organically related and that thought must necessarily simulate finitude and inconclusiveness because of its alliance with serial time. The idea that thought is essentially finite, and for this reason unable to capture the Infinite, is based on a mistaken notion of the movement of thought in knowledge. It is the inadequacy of the logical understanding which finds a multiplicity of mutually repellent individualities with no prospect of their ultimate reduction to a unity that makes us sceptical about the conclusiveness of thought. In fact, the logical understanding is incapable of seeing this multiplicity as a coherent universe. Its only method is generalization based on resemblances, but its generalizations are only fictitious unities which do not affect the reality of concrete things. In its deeper movement, however, thought is capable of reaching an immanent Infinite in whose self-unfolding movement the various finite concepts are merely moments. In its essential nature, then, thought is not static; it is dynamic and unfolds its internal infinitude in time like the seed which, from the very beginning, carries within itself the organic unity of the tree as a present fact. Thought is, therefore, the whole in its dynamic self-expression, appearing to the temporal vision as a series of definite specifications which cannot be understood except by a reciprocal reference. Their meaning lies not in their self-identity, but in the larger whole of which they are the specific aspects. This larger whole is to use a Qur'anic metaphor, a kind of 'Preserved Tablet',[17] which holds up the entire undetermined possibilities of knowledge as a present reality, revealing itself in serial time as a succession of finite concepts appearing to reach a unity which is already present in them. It is in fact the presence of the total Infinite in the movement of knowledge that makes finite thinking possible. Both Kant and Ghaz«lâ's failed to see that thought, in the very act of knowledge, passes beyond its own finitude. The finitudes of Nature are reciprocally exclusive. Not so the finitudes of thought which is, in its essential nature, incapable of limitation and cannot remain imprisoned in the narrow circuit of its own individuality. In the wide world beyond itself nothing is alien to it. It is in its progressive participation in the life of the apparently alien that thought demolishes the walls of its finitude and enjoys its potential infinitude. Its movement becomes possible only because of the implicit presence in its finite individuality of the infinite, which keeps alive within it the flame of aspiration and sustains it in its endless pursuit. It is a mistake to regard thought as inconclusive, for it too, in its own way, is a greeting of the finite with the infinite.

During the last five hundred years religious thought in Islam has been practically stationary. There was a time when European thought received inspiration from the world of Islam. The most remarkable phenomenon of modern history, however, is the enormous rapidity with which the world of Islam is spiritually moving towards the West. There is nothing wrong in this movement, for European culture, on its intellectual side, is only a further development of some of the most important phases of the culture of Islam. Our only fear is that the dazzling exterior of European culture may arrest our movement and we may fail to reach the true inwardness of that culture. During all the centuries of our intellectual stupor Europe has been seriously thinking on the great problems in which the philosophers and scientists of Islam were so keenly interested. Since the Middle Ages, when the schools of Muslim theology were completed, infinite advance has taken place in the domain of human thought and experience. The extension of man's power over Nature has given him a new faith and a fresh sense of superiority over the forces that constitute his environment. New points of view have been suggested, old problems have been re-stated in the light of fresh experience, and new problems have arisen. It seems as if the intellect of man is outgrowing its own most fundamental categories - time, space, and causality. With the advance of scientific thought even our concept of intelligibility is undergoing a change.[18] The theory of Einstein has brought a new vision of the universe and suggests new ways of looking at the problems common to both religion and philosophy. No wonder then that the younger generation of Islam in Asia and Africa demand a fresh orientation of their faith. With the reawakening of Islam, therefore, it is necessary to examine, in an independent spirit, what Europe has thought and how far the conclusions reached by her can help us in the revision and, if necessary, reconstruction, of theological thought in Islam. Besides this it is not possible to ignore generally anti-religious and especially anti-Islamic propaganda in Central Asia which has already crossed the Indian frontier. Some of the apostles of this movement are born Muslims, and one of them, Tewfâk Fikret, the Turkish poet, who died only a short time ago,[19] has gone to the extent of using our great poet-thinker, Mirz« 'Abd al-Q«dir Bedil of Akbar«b«d, for the purposes of this movement. Surely, it is high time to look to the essentials of Islam. In these lectures I propose to undertake a philosophical discussion of some of the basic of ideas of Islam, in the hope that this may, at least, be helpful towards a proper understanding of the meaning of Islam as a message to humanity. Also with a view to give a kind of ground-outline for further discussion, I propose, in this preliminary lecture, to consider the character of knowledge and religious experience.

The main purpose of the Qur'«n is to awaken in man the higher consciousness of his manifold relations with God and the universe. It is in view of this essential aspect of the Quranic teaching that Goethe, while making a general review of Islam as an educational force, said to Eckermann: 'You see this teaching never fails; with all our systems, we cannot go, and generally speaking no man can go, farther than that.'[20] The problem of Islam was really suggested by the mutual conflict, and at the same time mutual attraction, presented by the two forces of religion and civilization. The same problem confronted early Christianity. The great point in Christianity is the search for an independent content for spiritual life which, according to the insight of its founder, could be elevated, not by the forces of a world external to the soul of man, but by the revelation of a new world within his soul. Islam fully agrees with this insight and supplements it by the further insight that the illumination of the new world thus revealed is not something foreign to the world of matter but permeates it through and through.

Thus the affirmation of spirit sought by Christianity would come not by the renunciation of external forces which are already permeated by the illumination of spirit, but by a proper adjustment of man's relation to these forces in view of the light received from the world within. It is the mysterious touch of the ideal that animates and sustains the real, and through it alone we can discover and affirm the ideal. With Islam the ideal and the real are not two opposing forces which cannot be reconciled. The life of the ideal consists, not in a total breach with the real which would tend to shatter the organic wholeness of life into painful oppositions, but in the perpetual endeavour of the ideal to appropriate the real with a view eventually to absorb it, to convert it into itself and illuminate its whole being. It is the sharp opposition between the subject and the object, the mathematical without and the biological within, that impressed Christianity. Islam, however, faces the opposition with a view to overcome it. This essential difference in looking at a fundamental relation determines the respective attitudes of these great religions towards the problem of human life in its present surroundings. Both demand the affirmation of the spiritual self in man, with this difference only that Islam, recognizing the contact of the ideal with the real, says 'yes' to the world of matter[21] and points the way to master it with a view to discover a basis for a realistic regulation of life.

What, then, according to the Qur'«n, is the character of the universe which we inhabit? In the first place, it is not the result of a mere creative sport:

'We have not created the Heavens and the earth and whatever is between them in sport. We have not created them but for a serious end: but the greater part of them understand it not' (44:38-39).[22]

It is a reality to be reckoned with:

'Verily in the creation of the Heavens and of the earth, and in the succession of the night and of the day, are signs for men of understanding; who, standing and sitting and reclining, bear God in mind and reflect on the creation of the Heavens and of the earth, and say: "Oh, our Lord! Thou hast not created this in vain" (3:190-91).

Again the universe is so constituted that it is capable of extension:

'He (God) adds to His creation what He wills' (35:1).[23]

It is not a block universe, a finished product, immobile and incapable of change. Deep in its inner being lies, perhaps, the dream of a new birth:

'Say - go through the earth and see how God hath brought forth all creation; hereafter will He give it another birth' (29:20).

In fact, this mysterious swing and impulse of the universe, this noiseless swim of time which appears to us, human beings, as the movement of day and night, is regarded by the Qur'«n as one of the greatest signs of God:

'God causeth the day and the night to take their turn. Verily in this is teaching for men of insight' (24:44).

This is why the Prophet said: 'Do not vilify time, for time is God.'[24] And this immensity of time and space carries in it the promise of a complete subjugation by man whose duty is to reflect on the signs of God, and thus discover the means of realizing his conquest of Nature as an actual fact:

'See ye not how God hath put under you all that is in the Heavens, and all that is on the earth, and hath been bounteous to you of His favours both in relation to the seen and the unseen?' (31:20).

'And He hath subjected to you the night and the day, the sun and the moon, and the stars too are subject to you by His behest; verily in this are signs for those who understand' (16:12).

Such being the nature and promise of the universe, what is the nature of man whom it confronts on all sides? Endowed with a most suitable mutual adjustment of faculties he discovers himself down below in the scale of life, surrounded on all sides by the forces of obstruction:

'That of goodliest fabric We created man, then brought him down to the lowest of the low' (95:4-5).

And how do we find him in this environment? A 'restless'[25] being engrossed in his ideals to the point of forgetting everything else, capable of inflicting pain on himself in his ceaseless quest after fresh scopes for self-expression. With all his failings he is superior to Nature, inasmuch as he carries within him a great trust which, in the words of the Qur'«n, the heavens and the earth and the mountains refused to carry:

'Verily We proposed to the Heavens and to the earth and to the mountains to receive the trust (of personality), but they refused the burden and they feared to receive it. Man alone undertook to bear it, but hath proved unjust, senseless!' (33:72).

His career, no doubt, has a beginning, but he is destined, perhaps, to become a permanent element in the constitution of being.

'Thinketh man that he shall be thrown away as an object of no use? Was he not a mere embryo? Then he became thick blood of which God formed him and fashioned him, and made him twain, male and female. Is not He powerful enough to quicken the dead?' (75:36-40).

When attracted by the forces around him, man has the power to shape and direct them; when thwarted by them, he has the capacity to build a much vaster world in the depths of his own inner being, wherein he discovers sources of infinite joy and inspiration. Hard his lot and frail his being, like a rose-leaf, yet no form of reality is so powerful, so inspiring, and so beautiful as the spirit of man! Thus in his inmost being man, as conceived by the Qur'«n, is a creative activity, an ascending spirit who, in his onward march, rises from one state of being to another:

'But Nay! I swear by the sunset's redness and by the night and its gatherings and by the moon when at her full, that from state to state shall ye be surely carried onward' (84:16-19).

It is the lot of man to share in the deeper aspirations of the universe around him and to shape his own destiny as well as that of the universe, now by adjusting himself to its forces, now by putting the whole of his energy to mould its forces to his own ends and purposes. And in this process of progressive change God becomes a co-worker with him, provided man takes the initiative:

'Verily God will not change the condition of men, till they change what is in themselves' (13:11).

If he does not take the initiative, if he does not evolve the inner richness of his being, if he ceases to feel the inward push of advancing life, then the spirit within him hardens into stone and he is reduced to the level of dead matter. But his life and the onward march of his spirit depend on the establishment of connexions with the reality that confronts him.[26] It is knowledge that establishes these connexions, and knowledge is sense-perception elaborated by understanding.

'When thy Lord said to the Angels, "Verily I am about to place one in my stead on earth," they said, "Wilt Thou place there one who will do ill and shed blood, when we celebrate Thy praise and extol Thy holiness?" God said, "Verily I know what ye know not!" And He taught

Adam the names of all things, and then set them before the Angels, and said, "Tell me the names of these if ye are endowed with wisdom." They said, "Praise be to Thee! We have no knowledge but what Thou hast given us to know. Thou art the Knowing, the Wise". He said, "O Adam, inform them of the names." And when he had informed them of the names, God said, "Did I not say to you that I know the hidden things of the Heavens and of the earth, and that I know what ye bring to light and what ye hide?" (2:30-33).

The point of these verses is that man is endowed with the faculty of naming things, that is to say, forming concepts of them, and forming concepts of them is capturing them. Thus the character of man's knowledge is conceptual, and it is with the weapon of this conceptual knowledge that man approaches the observable aspect of Reality. The one noteworthy feature of the Qur'«n is the emphasis that it lays on this observable aspect of Reality. Let me quote here a few verses:

'Assuredly, in the creation of the Heavens and of the earth; and in the alternation of night and day; and in the ships which pass through the sea with what is useful to man; and in the rain which God sendeth down from Heaven, giving life to the earth after its death, and scattering over it all kinds of cattle; and in the change of the winds, and in the clouds that are made to do service between the Heavens and the earth - are signs for those who understand' (2:164).

'And it is He Who hath ordained for you that ye may be guided thereby in the darkness of the land and of the sea! Clear have We made Our signs to men of knowledge. And it is He Who hath created you of one breath, and hath provided you an abode and resting place (in the womb). Clear have We made Our signs for men of insight! And it is He Who sendeth down rain from Heaven: and We bring forth by it the buds of all the plants and from them bring We forth the green foliage, and the close-growing grain, and palm trees with sheaths of clustering dates, and gardens of grapes, and the olive, and the pomegranate, like and unlike. Look you on their fruits when they ripen. Truly herein are signs unto people who believe' (6:97-99).

'Hast thou not seen how thy Lord lengthens out the shadow? Had He pleased He had made it motionless. But We made the sun to be its guide; then draw it in unto Us with easy in drawing' (25:45-46).

'Can they not look up to the clouds, how they are created; and to the Heaven how it is upraised; and to the mountains how they are rooted, and to the earth how it is outspread?' (88:17-20).

'And among His signs are the creation of the Heavens and of the earth, and your variety of tongues and colours. Herein truly are signs for all men' (30:22).

No doubt, the immediate purpose of the Qur'«n in this reflective observation of Nature is to awaken in man the consciousness of that of which Nature is regarded a symbol. But the point to note is the general empirical attitude of the Qur'«n which engendered in its followers a feeling of reverence for the actual and ultimately made them the founders of modern science. It was a great point to awaken the empirical spirit in an age which renounced the visible as of no value in men's search after God. According to the Qur'«n, as we have seen before, the universe has a serious end. Its shifting actualities force our being into fresh formations. The intellectual effort to overcome the obstruction offered by it, besides enriching and amplifying our life, sharpens our insight, and thus prepares us for a more masterful insertion into subtler aspects of human experience. It is our reflective contact with the temporal flux of things which trains us for an intellectual vision of the non-temporal. Reality lives in its own appearances; and such a being as man, who has to maintain his life in an obstructing environment, cannot afford to ignore the visible. The Qur'«n opens our eyes to the great fact of change, through the appreciation and control of which alone it is possible to build a durable civilization. The cultures of Asia and, in fact, of the whole ancient world failed, because they approached Reality exclusively from within and moved from within outwards. This procedure gave them theory without power, and on mere theory no durable civilization can be based.

There is no doubt that the treatment of religious experience, as a source of Divine knowledge, is historically prior to the treatment of other regions of human experience for the same purpose. The Qur'«n, recognizing that the empirical attitude is an indispensable stage in the spiritual life of humanity, attaches equal importance to all the regions of human experience as yielding knowledge of the Ultimate Reality which reveals its symbols both within and without.[27] One indirect way of establishing connexions with the reality that confronts us is reflective observation and control of its symbols as they reveal themselves to sense-perception; the other way is direct association with that reality as it reveals itself within. The naturalism of the Qur'«n is only a recognition of the fact that man is related to nature, and this relation, in view of its possibility as a means of controlling her forces, must be exploited not in the interest of unrighteous desire for domination, but in the nobler interest of a free upward movement of spiritual life. In the interests of securing a complete vision of Reality, therefore, sense-perception must be supplemented by the perception of what the Qur'«n describes as *Fu'«d* or *Qalb*, i.e. heart:

'God hath made everything which He hath created most good; and began the creation of man with clay; then ordained his progeny from germs of life, from sorry water; then shaped him, and breathed of His spirit unto him, and gave you hearing and seeing and heart: what little thanks do ye return?' (32:7-9).

The 'heart' is a kind of inner intuition or insight which, in the beautiful words of Rëmâ, feeds on the rays of the sun and brings us into contact with aspects of Reality other than those open to sense-perception.[28] It is, according to the Qur'«n, something which 'sees', and its reports, if properly interpreted, are never false.[29] We must not, however, regard it as a mysterious special faculty; it is rather a mode of dealing with Reality in which sensation, in the physiological sense of the word, does not play any part.[30] Yet the vista of experience thus opened to us is as real and concrete as any other experience. To describe it as psychic, mystical, or super-natural does not detract from its value as experience. To the primitive man all experience was super-natural. Prompted by the immediate necessities of life he was driven to interpret his experience, and out of this interpretation gradually emerged 'Nature' in our sense of the word. The total-Reality, which enters our awareness and appears on interpretation as an empirical fact, has other ways of invading our consciousness and offers further opportunities of interpretation. The revealed and mystic literature of mankind bears ample testimony to the fact that religious experience has been too enduring and dominant in the history of mankind to be rejected as mere illusion. There seems to be no reason, then, to accept the normal level of human experience as fact and reject its other levels as mystical and emotional. The fact of religious experience are facts among other facts of human experience and, in the capacity of yielding knowledge by interpretation, one fact is as good as another. Nor is there anything irreverent in critically examining this region of human experience. The Prophet of Islam was the first critical observer of psychic phenomena. Bukha`ri` and other traditionists have given us a full account of his observation of the psychic Jewish youth, Ibn Sayy«d, whose ecstatic moods attracted the Prophet's notice.[31] He tested him, questioned him, and examined him in his various moods. Once he hid himself behind the stem of a tree to listen to his mutterings. The boy's mother, however, warned him of the approach of the Prophet. Thereupon the boy immediately shook off his mood and the Prophet remarked: 'If she had let him alone the thing would have been cleared up.'[32] The Prophet's companions, some of whom were present during the course of this first psychological observation in the history of Islam, and even later traditionists, who took good care to record this important fact, entirely misunderstood the significance of his attitude and interpreted it in their own innocent manner. Professor Macdonald, who seems to have no idea of the fundamental psychological difference between the mystic and the prophetic consciousness, finds 'humour enough in this picture of one prophet trying to investigate another after the method of the Society for Psychical Research.[33] A better appreciation of the spirit of the Qur'«n which, as I will show in a subsequent lecture,[34] initiated the cultural movement terminating in the birth of the modern empirical attitude, would have led the Professor to see something remarkably suggestive in the Prophet's observation of the psychic Jew. However, the first Muslim to see the meaning and value of the Prophet's attitude was Ibn Khaldën, who approached the contents of mystic consciousness in a more critical spirit and very nearly reached the modern hypothesis of subliminal selves.[35] As Professor Macdonald says, Ibn Khaldën 'had some most interesting psychological ideas, and that he would probably have been in close sympathy with Mr. William James's *Varieties of Religious Experience*'.[36] Modern psychology has only recently begun to realize the importance of a careful study of the contents of mystic consciousness, and we are not yet in possession of a really effective scientific method to analyse the contents of non-rational modes of consciousness. With the time at my disposal it is not possible to undertake an extensive inquiry into the history and the various degrees of mystic consciousness in point of richness and vividness. All that I can do is to offer a few general observations only on the main characteristics of mystic experience.

1. The first point to note is the immediacy of this experience. In this respect it does not differ from other levels of human experience which supply data for knowledge. All experience is immediate. As regions of normal experience are subject to interpretation of sense-data for our knowledge of the external world, so the region of mystic experience is subject to interpretation for our knowledge of God. The immediacy of mystic experience simply means that we know God just as we know other objects. God is not a mathematical entity or a system of concepts mutually related to one another and having no reference to experience.[37]

2. The second point is the unanalysable wholeness of mystic experience. When I experience the table before me, innumerable data of experience merge into the single experience of the table. Out of this wealth of data I select those that fall into a certain order of space and time and round them off in reference to the table. In the mystic state, however, vivid and rich it may be, thought is reduced to a minimum and such an analysis is not possible. But this difference of the mystic state from the ordinary rational consciousness does not mean discontinuance with the normal consciousness, as Professor William James erroneously thought. In either case it is the same Reality which is operating on us. The ordinary rational consciousness, in view of our practical need of adaptation to our environment, takes that Reality piecemeal, selecting successively isolated sets of stimuli for response. The mystic state brings us into contact with the total passage of Reality in which all the diverse stimuli merge into one another and form a single unanalysable unity in which the ordinary distinction of subject and object does not exist.

3. The third point to note is that to the mystic the mystic state is a moment of intimate association with a Unique Other Self, transcending, encompassing, and momentarily

suppressing the private personality of the subject of experience. Considering its content the mystic state is highly objective and cannot be regarded as a mere retirement into the mists of pure subjectivity. But you will ask me how immediate experience of God, as an Independent Other Self, is at all possible. The mere fact that the mystic state is passive does not finally prove the veritable 'otherness' of the Self experienced. This question arises in the mind because we assume, without criticism, that our knowledge of the external world through sense-perception is the type of all knowledge. If this were so, we could never be sure of the reality of our own self. However, in reply to it I suggest the analogy of our daily social experience. How do we know other minds in our social intercourse? It is obvious that we know our own self and Nature by inner reflection and sense-perception respectively. We possess no sense for the experience of other minds. The only ground of my knowledge of a conscious being before me is the physical movements similar to my own from which I infer the presence of another conscious being. Or we may say, after Professor Royce, that our fellows are known to be real because they respond to our signals and thus constantly supply the necessary supplement to our own fragmentary meanings. Response, no doubt, is the test of the presence of a conscious self, and the Qur'«n also takes the same view:

'And your Lord saith, call Me and I respond to your call' (40:60).

'And when My servants ask thee concerning Me, then I am nigh unto them and answer the cry of him that crieth unto Me' (2:186).

It is clear that whether we apply the physical criterion or the non-physical and more adequate criterion of Royce, in either case our knowledge of other minds remains something like inferential only. Yet we feel that our experience of other minds is immediate and never entertain any doubt as to the reality of our social experience. I do not, however, mean, at the present stage of our inquiry, to build on the implications of our knowledge of other minds, an idealistic argument in favour of the reality of a Comprehensive Self. All that I mean to suggest is that the immediacy of our experience in the mystic state is not without a parallel. It has some sort of resemblance to our normal experience and probably belongs to the same category.

4. Since the quality of mystic experience is to be directly experienced, it is obvious that it cannot be communicated.[38] Mystic states are more like feeling than thought. The interpretation which the mystic or the prophet puts on the content of his religious consciousness can be conveyed to others in the form of propositions, but the content itself cannot be so transmitted. Thus in the following verses of the Qur'«n it is the psychology and not the content of the experience that is given:

'It is not for man that God should speak to him, but by vision or from behind a veil; or He sendeth a messenger to reveal by His permission what He will: for He is Exalted, Wise' (42:51).

'By the star when it setteth,

Your compatriot erreth not, nor is he led astray.

Neither speaketh he from mere impulse.

The Qur'«n is no other than the revelation revealed to him:

One strong in power taught it him,

Endowed with wisdom with even balance stood he

In the highest part of the horizon:

Then came he nearer and approached,

And was at the distance of two bows or even closer -

And he revealed to the servant of God what he revealed:

His heart falsified not what he saw:

What! will ye then dispute with him as to what he saw?

He had seen him also another time

Near the *Sidrah* tree which marks the boundary:

Near which is the garden of repose:

When the *Sidrah* tree was covered with what covered it:

His eye turned not aside, nor did it wander:

For he saw the greatest of the signs of the Lord' (53:1-18).

The incommunicability of mystic experience is due to the fact that it is essentially a matter of inarticulate feeling, untouched by discursive intellect. It must, however, be noted that mystic feeling, like all feeling, has a cognitive element also; and it is, I believe, because of this cognitive element that it lends itself to the form of idea. In fact, it is the nature of feeling to seek expression in thought. It would seem that the two - feeling and idea - are the non-temporal and temporal aspects of the same unit of inner experience. But on this point I cannot do better than quote Professor Hocking who has made a remarkably keen study of feeling in justification of an intellectual view of the content of religious consciousness:

'What is that other-than-feeling in which feeling may end? I answer, consciousness of an object. Feeling is instability of an entire conscious self: and that which will restore the stability of this self lies not within its own border but beyond it. Feeling is outward-pushing, as idea is outward-reporting: and no feeling is so blind as to have no idea of its own object. As a feeling possesses the mind, there also possesses the mind, as an integral part of that feeling, some idea of the kind of thing which will bring it to rest. A feeling without a direction is as impossible as an activity without a direction: and a direction implies some objective. There are vague states of consciousness in which we seem to be wholly without direction; but in such cases it is remarkable that feeling is likewise in abeyance. For example, I may be dazed by a blow, neither realizing what has happened nor suffering any pain, and yet quite conscious that something has occurred: the experience waits an instant in the vestibule of consciousness, not as feeling but purely as fact, until idea has touched it and defined a course of response. At that same moment, it is felt as painful. If we are right, feeling is quite as much an objective consciousness as is idea: it refers always to something beyond the present self and has no existence save in directing the self toward that object in whose presence its own career must end!'[39]

Thus you will see that it is because of this essential nature of feeling that while religion starts with feeling, it has never, in its history, taken itself as a matter of feeling alone and has constantly striven after metaphysics. The mystic's condemnation of intellect as an organ of knowledge does not really find any justification in the history of religion. But Professor Hocking's passage just quoted has a wider scope than mere justification of idea in religion. The organic relation of feeling and idea throws light on the old theological controversy about verbal revelation which once gave so much trouble to Muslim religious thinkers.[40] Inarticulate feeling seeks to fulfil its destiny in idea which, in its turn, tends to develop out of itself its own visible garment. It is no mere metaphor to say that idea and word both simultaneously emerge out of the womb of feeling, though logical understanding cannot but take them in a temporal order and thus create its own difficulty by regarding them as mutually isolated. There is a sense in which the word is also revealed.

5. The mystic's intimate association with the eternal which gives him a sense of the unreality of serial time does not mean a complete break with serial time. The mystic state in respect of its uniqueness remains in some way related to common experience. This is clear from the fact that the mystic state soon fades away, though it leaves a deep sense of authority after it has passed away. Both the mystic and the prophet return to the normal levels of experience, but with this difference that the return of the prophet, as I will show later, may be fraught with infinite meaning for mankind.

For the purposes of knowledge, then, the region of mystic experience is as real as any other region of human experience and cannot be ignored merely because it cannot be traced back to sense-perception. Nor is it possible to undo the spiritual value of the mystic state by specifying the organic conditions which appear to determine it. Even if the postulate of modern psychology as to the interrelation of body and mind is assumed to be true, it is illogical to discredit the value of the mystic state as a revelation of truth. Psychologically speaking, all states, whether their content is religious or non-religious, are organically determined.[41] The scientific form of mind is as much organically determined as the religious. Our judgement as to the creations of genius is not at all determined or even remotely affected by what our psychologists may say regarding its organic conditions. A certain kind of temperament may be a necessary condition for a certain kind of receptivity; but the antecedent condition cannot be regarded as the whole truth about the character of what is received. The truth is that the organic causation of our mental states has nothing to do with the criteria by which we judge them to be superior or inferior in point of value. 'Among the visions and messages', says Professor William James,

'some have always been too patently silly, among the trances and convulsive seizures some have been too fruitless for conduct and character, to pass themselves off as significant, still less as divine. In the history of Christian mysticism the problem how to discriminate between such messages and experiences as were really divine miracles, and such others as the demon in his malice was able to counterfeit, thus making the religious person twofold more the child of hell he was before, has always been a difficult one to solve, needing all the sagacity and experience of the best directors of conscience. In the end it had come to our empiricist criterion: By their fruits ye shall know them, not by their roots'.[42]

The problem of Christian mysticism alluded to by Professor James has been in fact the problem of all mysticism. The demon in his malice does counterfeit experiences which creep into the circuit of the mystic state. As we read in the Qur'«n:

'We have not sent any Apostle or Prophet[43] before thee among whose desires Satan injected not some wrong desire, but God shall bring to nought that which Satan had suggested. Thus shall God affirm His revelations, for God is Knowing and Wise' (22:52).

And it is in the elimination of the satanic from the Divine that the followers of Freud have done inestimable service to religion; though I cannot help saying that the main theory of this newer psychology does not appear to me to be supported by any adequate evidence. If our vagrant impulses assert themselves in our dreams, or at other times we are not strictly ourselves, it does not follow that they remain imprisoned in a kind of lumber room behind the normal self. The occasional invasion of these suppressed impulses on the region of our normal self tends more to show the temporary disruption of our habitual system of responses rather than their perpetual presence in some dark corner of the mind. However, the theory is briefly this. During the process of our adjustment to our environment we are exposed to all sorts of stimuli. Our habitual responses to these stimuli gradually fall into a relatively fixed system, constantly growing in complexity by absorbing some and rejecting other impulses which do not fit in with our permanent system of responses. The rejected impulses recede into what is called the 'unconscious region' of the mind, and there wait for a suitable opportunity to assert themselves and take their revenge on the focal self. They may disturb our plans of action, distort our thought, build our dreams and phantasies, or carry us back to forms of primitive behaviour which the evolutionary process has left far behind. Religion, it is said, is a pure fiction created by these repudiated impulses of mankind with a view to find a kind of fairyland for free unobstructed movement. Religious *beliefs* and dogmas, according to the theory, are no more than merely primitive theories of Nature, whereby mankind has tried to redeem Reality from its elemental ugliness and to show it off as something nearer to the heart's desire than the facts of life would warrant. That there are religions and forms of art, which provide a kind of cowardly escape from the facts of life, I do not deny. All that I contend is that this is not true of all religions. No doubt, religious beliefs and dogmas have a metaphysical significance; but it is obvious that they are not interpretations of those data of experience which are the subject of the science of Nature. Religion is not physics or chemistry seeking an explanation of Nature in terms of causation; it really aims at interpreting a totally different region of human experience - religious experience - the data of which cannot be reduced to the data of any other science. In fact, it must be said in justice to religion that it insisted on the necessity of concrete experience in religious life long before science learnt to do so.[44] The conflict between the two is due not to the fact that the one is, and the other is not, based on concrete experience. Both seek concrete experience as a point of departure. Their conflict is due to the misapprehension that both interpret the same data of experience. We forget that religion aims at reaching the real significance of a special variety of human experience.

Nor is it possible to explain away the content of religious consciousness by attributing the whole thing to the working of the sex-impulse. The two forms of consciousness - sexual and religious - are often hostile or, at any rate, completely different to each other in point of their character, their aim, and the kind of conduct they generate. The truth is that in a state of religious passion we know a factual reality in some sense outside the narrow circuit of our personality. To the psychologist religious passion necessarily appears as the work of the subconscious because of the intensity with which it shakes up the depths of our being. In all knowledge there is an element of passion, and the object of knowledge gains or loses in objectivity with the rise and fall in the intensity of passion. That is most real to us which stirs up the entire fabric of our personality. As Professor Hocking pointedly puts it:

'If ever upon the stupid day-length time-span of any self or saint either, some vision breaks to roll his life and ours into new channels, it can only be because that vision admits into his soul some trooping invasion of the concrete fullness of eternity. Such vision doubtless means subconscious readiness and subconscious resonance too, - but the expansion of the unused air-cells does not argue that we have ceased to breathe the outer air: - the very opposite!'[45]

A purely psychological method, therefore, cannot explain religious passion as a form of knowledge. It is bound to fail in the case of our newer psychologists as it did fail in the case of Locke and Hume.

The foregoing discussion, however, is sure to raise an important question in your mind. Religious experience, I have tried to maintain, is essentially a state of feeling with a cognitive aspect, the content of which cannot be communicated to others, except in the form of a judgement. Now when a judgement which claims to be the interpretation of a certain region of human experience, not accessible to me, is placed before me for my assent, I am entitled to ask, what is the guarantee of its truth? Are we in possession of a test which would reveal its validity? If personal experience had been the only ground for acceptance of a judgement of this kind, religion would have been the possession of a few individuals only Happily we are in possession of tests which do not differ from those applicable to other forms of knowledge. These I call the intellectual test and the pragmatic test. By the intellectual test I mean critical interpretation, without any presuppositions of human experience, generally with a view to discover whether our interpretation leads us ultimately to a reality of the same character as is revealed by religious experience. The pragmatic test judges it by its fruits. The former is applied by the philosopher, the latter by the prophet. In the lecture that follows, I will apply the intellectual test.

Lecture I Notes:

1. Reference here is to the following verse from the mystical allegorical work: *ManÇiq al-ñair* (p. 243, v. 5), generally considered the magnum opus, of one of the greatest sufi poets and thinkers Farâd al-Dân 'AÇÇ«r' (d.c. 618/1220):

2. A. N. Whitehead, Religion in the Making, p. 5.

3. Ibid., p. 73.

4. Cf. H. L. Bergson, Creative Evolution, pp. 187-88; on this intuition-intellect relation see also Allama Iqbal's essay: *Bedil in the light of Bergson*, ed. Dr Tehsin Firaqi, pp. 22-23.

5. *Allahumm«arin« haq« 'iq al-ashy«kam«hâya*, a tradition, in one form or other, to be found in well-known Sufistic works, for example, 'Alâb. 'Uthm«n al-Hujwayrâ, *Kashf al-MaÁjëb*, p. 166; Mawl«n« Jal«l al-Dân Rëmâ, *Mathnawâ-i Ma'nawâ*, ii, 466-67; iv, 3567-68; v, 1765; MaÁmëd Shabistarâ (d. 720/1320), *Gulshan-i R«z*, verse 200, and 'Abd al-RaÁm«n J«mâ (d. 898/1492), *Law« 'ih*, p. 3.

6. Qur'«n, 16:68-69.

7. Ibid., 2:164; 24:43-44; 30:48; 35:9; 45:5.

8. Ibid., 15:16; 25:6; 37:6; 41:12; 50:6; 67:5; 85:1.

9. Ibid., 21:33; 36:40.

10. Cf. F. M. Cornford: *Plato's Theory of Knowledge*, pp. 29;109; also Bertrand Russell: *History of Western Philosophy*, chapter: 'Knowledge and Perception in Plato'.

11. Qur'«n, 16:78; 23:78; 32:9; 67:23.

12. Ibid., 17:36. References here, as also at other places in the *Lectures*, to a dozen Quranic verses in two sentences bespeak of what is uppermost in Allama Iqbal's mind, i.e. Quranic empiricism which by its very nature gives rise to a *Weltanschauung* of the highest religious order. He tells us, for example, that the general empirical attitude of the Qur'a'n engenders a feeling of reverence for the actual and that one way of entering into relation with Reality is through reflective observation and control of its perceptually revealed symbols (cf. below, pp. 11-12, italics mine; also Lecture V, p. 102, not 9).

13. For anti-classicism of the Qur'«n cf. Mazheruddân Âiddiqâ, *Concept of Muslim Culture in Iqbal*, pp. 13-25; also Lecture V, note 21.

14. See R. A. Tsanoff, *The Problem of Immortality* (a work listed at S. No. 37 in the *Descriptive Catalogue of Allama Iqbal's Personal Library*), pp. 75-77; cf. also B. H. Zedler, 'Averroes and Immortality', *New Scholasticism* (1954), pp. 436-53. It is to be noted that Tsanoff marshals the views of S. Munk (*Mé langes de philosophie*, pp. 454 ff.), E. Renan (*Averroes et l'averroisme*, pp. 152, 158), A Stockl (*Geschichte der Philosophie des Mittelalters*, 11, 117, 119), de Boer (*Geschichte der Philosophie*, p. 173) and M. Horten (*Die Hauptlehren des Averroes*, pp. 244 ff.) as against those of Carra de Vaux as presented by him in his work Avicenne, pp. 233 ff., as well as in the article: 'Averroes' in *Encyclopaedia of Religion and Ethics*, II, 264-65, and clinches the matter thus: 'certainly - and this is more significant for our purpose - it was as a denier of personal immortality that scholasticism received and criticised Averroes' (p. 77, II, 16-19). For a recent and more balanced view of 'Ibn Rushd's doctrine of immortality, cf. Roger Arnaldez and A. Z. Iskander, 'Ibn Rushd', *Dictionary of Scientific Biography*, XII, 7a-7b. It is to be noted, however, that M. E. Marmura in his article on 'Soul: Islamic Concepts' in *The Encyclopedia of Religion*, XIII, 465 clearly avers that Ibn Rushd's commentaries on Aristotle leave no room for a doctrine of individual immortality.

15. Cf. Tsanoff, op. cit., pp. 77-84, and M. Yěnus Farangi Mahallâ, *Ibn Rushd* (Urdu; partly based on Renan's *Averroes et l'averroisme*), pp. 347-59.

16. See Lecture IV, pp. 93-98, and Lecture VII, pp. 156-57.

17. Reference is to the expression lawÁ-in mahfĕzin used in the Quranic verse 85:22. For the interpretation this unique expression of the Qur'«n see M. Asad, *The Message of the Qur'«n*, p. 943, note; and Fazlur Rahman, Major Themes of the Qur'a'n, p. 98 - the latter seems to come quite close to Allama Iqbal's generally very keen perception of the meanings of the Qur'«n.

18. This comes quite close to the contemporary French philosopher Louis Rougier's statement in his *Philosophy and the New Physics* p. 146, II, 17-21. This work, listed at S. No. 15 in the *Descriptive Catalogue of Allama Iqbal's Personal Library*, is cited in Lecture III, p. 59.

19. Reference here is to Tevfåk Fikret, pseudonym of Mehmed Tevfik, also known as Tevfik Nazmâ, and not to Tawfik Fitrat as it got printed in the previous editions of the present work. Fikret, widely considered the founder of the modern school of Turkish poetry and remembered among other works for his collection of poems: Rub«b-i Shikeste ('The Broken Lute'), died in Istanbul on 18 August 1915 at the age of forty-eight. For an account of Fikret's literary career and his anti-religious views, cf. Niyazi Berkes, *The Development of Secularism in Turkey*, pp. 300-02 and 338-39; also Haydar Ali Dirioz's brief paper in Turkish on Fikret's birth-centenary translated by Dr M. H. Notqi in *Journal of the Regional Cultural Institute*, 1/4 (Autumn 1968), 12-15.

It is for Turkish-Persian scholars to determine the extent to which Fikret made use of the great poet-thinker Bedil (d. 1133/1721) for 'the anti-religious and especially anti-Islamic propaganda in Central Asia'. Among very many works on both Bedil and Fikret that have appeared since Allama's days and are likely to receive the scholars' attention, mention must be made of Allama's own short perceptive study: 'Bedil in the Light of Bergson', and unpublished essay in Allama's hand (20 folios) preserved in the Allama Iqbal Museum (Lahore); cf. Dr Ahmad Nabi Khan, *Relics of Allama Iqbal (Catalogue)*, 1, 25, with photographic reproduction of the first sheet.

20. Cf. John Oxenford (tr.), *Conversations of Goethe with Eckermann and Sorret*, p. 41.

21. The Qur'«n condemns monkery; see 57:27; 2:201; and 28:77. Cf. also *Speeches, Writings and Statements of Iqbal*, ed. A. L. Sherwani, p. 7, for Allama Iqbal's observations on the respective attitudes of Christianity and Islam towards the problems of life, leading to his keenly profound pronouncement: 'The religious ideal of Islam, therefore, is organically related to the social order which it has created'.

22. There are many verses of the Qur'«n wherein it has been maintained that the universe has not been created in sport (*l« 'ibân*) or in vain (*b«Çil-an*) but for a serious end or with truth (*bi'l-Áhaqq*). These are respectively: (a) 21:16; 44:38; (b) 3:191; 38:27; (c) 6:73; 10:5; 14:19; 15:85; 16:3; 29:44; 30:8; 39:5; 44:39; 45:22; 46:3; and 64:3.

23. See also the Quranic verse 51:47 wherein the phrase *inna la-mu`si'u`n* has been interpreted to clearly foreshadow the modern notion of the 'expanding universe' (cf. M. Asad, *The Message of the Qur'a`n*, p. 805, note 31).

24. Reference here is in particular to the Prophetic tradition worded as: *l«tasubbëal-dahra fa inn All«h huwa'l-dahru*, (AÁmad Àanbal, *Musnad*, V, 299 and 311). Cf. also Bukh«râ, *Tafsâr*: 45; *TauÁâd*: 35; *Adab`*: 101; and *Muslim*, Alf«z 2-4; for other variants of the *Áadâth SaÁâfa Hamm«m-Bin-Munabbih* (ed. Dr. M. Hamidullah) *Áadâth* 117, gives one of its earliest recorded texts.

In an exceedingly important section captioned *Al-Waqtu Saif-un* (Time is Sword) of his celebrated *Asr«r-i-Khudâ*, Allama Iqbal has referred to the above hadit`h thus:

Life is of Time and Time is of Life;

Do not abuse Time!' was the command of the Prophet. (trans. Nicholson)

25. Reference is to the Quranic verse 70:19 which says: 'Man has been created restless (*ha«ë'an*).'

26. This is very close to the language of the Qur'«n which speaks of the hardening of the hearts, so that they were like rocks: see 2:74; 5:13; 6:43; 39:22; and 57:16.

This shows that Allama Iqbal, through his keenly perceptive study of the Qur'«n, had psychically assimilated both its meanings and its diction so much so that many of his visions, very largely found in his poetical works, may be said to be born of this rare assimilation; cf. Dr Ghul«m Mustaf« Kh«n's voluminous *Iqb«l aur Qur'«n* (in Urdu).

27. Qur'«n, 41:35; also 51:20-21.

28. Reference here is to the *Mathnawâ*, ii, 52:

The bodily sense is eating the food of darkness

The spiritual sense is feeding from a sun (trans. Nicholson).

29. Qur'«n, 53:11-12.

30. Ibid., 22:46.

31. Cf. *Bukh«râ*, Jan«`iz, 79; Shah«dah 3; Jih«d: 160, 178; and *Muslim*, Fitan: 95-96. D. J. Halperin's article: 'The Ibn Âayy«d Traditions and the Legend of al-Dajj«l', *Journal of the American Oriental Society*, XCII/ii (1976), 213-25, gives an atomistic analytic account of the ah«dâth listed by him.

32. In Arabic: *lau tarakathu bayyana*, an invariable part of the text of a number of *ah«dâth* about Ibn Âayy«d; cf. D. B. Macdonald, *The Religious Attitude and Life in Islam*, pp. 35 ff.; this book, which represents Macdonald's reputed Haskell Lectures on Comparative Religion at Chicago University in 1906, seems to have received Allama's close attention in the present discussion.

33. *Ibid.*, p. 36.

34. Cf. Lecture V, pp. 100 ff.

35. The term 'subliminal self' was coined by F. W. H. Myers in the 1890's which soon became popular in 'religious psychology' to designate what was believed to be the larger portion of the self lying beyond the level of consciousness, yet constantly influencing thought and behaviour as in parapsychic phenomena. With William James the concept of subliminal self came to stand for the area of human experience in which contact with the Divine Life may occur (cf. *The Varieties of Religious Experience*, pp. 511-15).

36. Macdonald, *op. cit.*, p. 42.

37. Cf. MuÁyuddân Ibn al-'Arabâ's observation that 'God is a precept, the world is a concept', referred to in Lecture VII, p. 144, note 4.

38. *Ibid.*, p. 145, where it is observed: 'Indeed the incommunicability of religious experience gives us a clue to the ultimate nature of the human ego'.

39. W. E. Hocking, *The Meaning of God in Human Experience*, p. 66. It is important to note here that according to Richard C. Gilman this concept of the inextricable union of idea and feeling is the source of strong strain of mysticism is Hocking's philosophy, but it is a mysticism which does not abandon the role of intellect in clarifying and correcting intuition; cf. his article: 'Hocking, William Ernest', *Encyclopedia of Philosophy*, IV, 47 (italics mine).

40. Reference here perhaps is to the hot and long-drawn controversy between the Mu'tazilites (early Muslim rationalists) and the Ash'arties (the orthodox scholastics) on the issue of Khalq al-Qur'«n, i.e. the createdness or the eternity of the Qur'«n; for which see Lecture VI, note 9. The context of the passage, however, strongly suggests that Allama Iqbal means to refer here to the common orthodox belief that the text of the Qur'«n is verbally revealed, i.e. the 'word' is as much revealed as the 'meaning'. This has perhaps never been controverted and rarely if ever discussed in the history of Muslim theology - one notable instance of its discussion is that by Sh«h Walâ All«h in Sata'«t and *Fuyëz al-Àaramain*. Nevertheless, it is significant to note that there is some analogical empirical evidence in Allama's personal life in support of the orthodox belief in verbal revelation. Once asked by Professor Lucas, Principal of a local college, in a private discourse, whether, despite his vast learning, he too subscribed to belief in verbal revelation, Allama immediately replied that it was not a matter of belief with him but a veritable personal experience for it was thus, he added, he composed his poems under the spells of poetic inspiration - surely, Prophetic revelations are far more exalted. Cf. 'Abdul Majâd S«lik, *Dhikr-i Iqb«l*, pp. 244-45 and Faqir Sayyid WaÁâd-ud-Dân, *Rëzg«r-i Faqâr*, pp. 38-39. After Allama's epoch-making *mathnawi*: *Asr«r-i Khudâ* was published in 1915 and it had given rise to some bitter controversy because of his critique of '*ajami tasawwuf*, and of the great À«fiz, he in a letter dated 14 April 1916 addressed to Mah«r«ja Kishen Parsh«d confided strictly in a personal way: 'I did not compose the mathnawâ myself; I was made to (guided to), to do so'; cf. M. 'Abdull«h Quraishâ' *Naw«dir-i Iqb«l (Ghair MaÇbu'ah Khutët)*', *Sahâfah*, Lahore, 'Iqb«l Nambar' (October 1973), Letter No. 41, p. 168.

41. Cf. William James, op. cit., p. 15.

42. *Ibid.*, p. 21.

43. The designation 'apostle' (*rasël*) is applied to bearers of divine revelations which embody a new doctrinal system or dispensation; a 'prophet' (*nabâ*), on the other hand, is said to be one whom God has entrusted with enunciation of ethical principles on the basis of an already existing dispensation, or of principles common to all dispensations. Hence, every apostle is a prophet as well, but every prophet is not an apostle.

44. Cf. Lecture VII, pp. 143-144, where this point is reiterated.

45. E. W. Hocking, *op. cit.*, pp.106-107.

The Philosophical Test of the Revelations of Religious Experience

by Dr. Muhammad Iqbal

Scholastic philosophy has put forward three arguments for the existence of God. These arguments, known as the Cosmological, the Teleological, and the Ontological, embody a real movement of thought in its quest after the Absolute. But regarded as logical proofs, I am afraid, they are open to serious criticism and further betray a rather superficial interpretation of experience.

The cosmological argument views the world as a finite effect, and passing through a series of dependent sequences, related as causes and effects, stops at an uncaused first cause, because of the unthinkability of an infinite regress. It is, however, obvious that a finite effect can give only a finite cause, or at most an infinite series of such causes. To finish the series at a certain point, and to elevate one member of the series to the dignity of an uncaused first cause, is to set at naught the very law of causation on which the whole argument proceeds. Further, the first cause reached by the argument necessarily excludes its effect. And this means that the effect, constituting a limit to its own cause, reduces it to something finite. Again, the cause reached by the argument cannot be regarded as a necessary being for the obvious reason that in the relation of cause and effect the two terms of the relation are equally necessary to each other. Nor is the necessity of existence identical with the conceptual necessity of causation which is the utmost that this argument can prove. The argument really tries to reach the infinite by merely negating the finite. But the infinite reached by contradicting the finite is a false infinite, which neither explains itself nor the finite which is thus made to stand in opposition to the infinite. The true infinite does not exclude the finite; it embraces the finite without effacing its finitude, and explains and justifies its being. Logically speaking, then, the movement from the finite to the infinite as embodied in the cosmological argument is quite illegitimate; and the argument fails in toto. The teleological argument is no better. It scrutinizes the effect with a view to discover the character of its cause. From the traces of foresight, purpose, and adaptation in nature, it infers the existence of a self-conscious being of infinite intelligence and power. At best, it gives us a skilful external contriver working on a pre-existing dead and intractable material the elements of which are, by their own nature, incapable of orderly structures and combinations. The argument gives us a contriver only and not a creator; and even if we suppose him to be also the creator of his material, it does no credit to his wisdom to create his own difficulties by first creating intractable material, and then overcoming its resistance by the application of methods alien to its original nature. The designer regarded as external to his material must always remain limited by his material, and hence a finite designer whose limited resources compel him to overcome his difficulties after the fashion of a human mechanician. The truth is that the analogy on which the argument proceeds is of no value at all. There is really no analogy between the work of the human artificer and the phenomena of Nature. The human artificer cannot work out his plan except by selecting and isolating his materials from their natural relations and situations. Nature, however, constitutes a system of wholly interdependent members; her processes present no analogy to the architect's work which, depending on a progressive isolation and integration of its material, can offer no resemblance to the evolution of organic wholes in Nature. The ontological argument which has been presented in various forms by various thinkers has always appealed most to the speculative mind. The Cartesian form of the argument runs thus:

'To say that an attribute is contained in the nature or in the concept of a thing is the same as to say that the attribute is true of this thing and that it may be affirmed to be in it. But necessary existence is contained in the nature or the concept of God. Hence it may be with truth affirmed that necessary existence is in God, or that God exists.'[1]

Descartes supplements this argument by another. We have the idea of a perfect being in our mind. What is the source of the idea? It cannot come from Nature, for Nature exhibits nothing but change. It cannot create the idea of a perfect being. Therefore corresponding to the idea in our mind there must be an objective counterpart which is the cause of the idea of a perfect being in our mind. This argument is somewhat of the nature of the cosmological argument which I have already criticized. But whatever may be the form of the argument, it is clear that the conception of existence is no proof of objective existence. As in Kant's criticism of this argument the notion of three hundred dollars in my mind cannot prove that I have them in my pocket.[2] All that the argument proves is that the idea of a perfect being includes the idea of his existence. Between the idea of a perfect being in my mind and the objective reality of that being there is a gulf which cannot be bridged over by a transcendental act of thought. The argument, as stated, is in fact a petitio principii:[3] for it takes for granted the very point in question, i.e. the transition from the logical to the real. I hope I have made it clear to you that the ontological and the teleological arguments, as ordinarily stated, carry us nowhere. And the reason of their failure is that they look upon 'thought' as an agency working on things from without. This view of thought gives us a mere mechanician in the one case, and creates an unbridgeable gulf between the ideal and the real in the other. It is, however, possible to take thought not as a principle which organizes and integrates its material from the outside, but as a potency which is formative of the very being of its material. Thus regarded thought or idea is not alien to the original nature of things; it is their ultimate ground and constitutes the very essence of their being, infusing itself in them from the very beginning of their career and inspiring their onward march to a self-determined end. But our present situation necessitates the dualism of thought and being. Every act of human knowledge bifurcates what might on proper inquiry turn out to be a unity into a self that knows and a confronting 'other' that is known. That is why we are forced to regard the object that confronts the self as something existing in its own right, external to and independent of the self whose act of knowledge makes no difference to the object known. The true significance of the ontological and the teleological arguments will appear only if we are able to show that the human situation is not final and that thought and being are ultimately one. This is possible only if we carefully examine and interpret experience, following the clue furnished by the Qur'«n which regards experience within and without as symbolic of a reality described by it,[4] as 'the First and the Last, the Visible and the Invisible'.[5] This I propose to do in the present lecture.

Now experience, as unfolding itself in time, presents three main levels - the level of matter, the level of life, and the level of mind and consciousness - the subject-matter of physics, biology, and psychology, respectively. Let us first turn our attention to matter. In order exactly to appreciate the position of modern physics it is necessary to understand clearly what we mean by matter. Physics, as an empirical science, deals with the facts of experience, i.e. sense-experience. The physicist begins and ends with sensible phenomena, without which it is impossible for him to verify his theories. He may postulate imperceptible entities, such as atoms; but he does so because he cannot otherwise explain his sense-experience. Thus physics studies the material world, that is to say, the world revealed by the senses. The mental processes involved in this study, and similarly religious and aesthetic experience, though part of the total range of experience, are excluded from the scope of physics for the obvious reason that physics is restricted to the study of the material world, by which we mean the world of things we perceive. But when I ask you what are the things you perceive in the material world, you will, of course, mention the familiar things around you, e.g. earth, sky, mountains, chairs, tables, etc. When I further ask you what exactly you perceive of these things, you will answer - their qualities. It is clear that in answering such a question we are really putting an interpretation on the evidence of our senses. The interpretation consists in making a distinction between the thing and its qualities. This really amounts to a theory of matter, i.e. of the nature of sense-data, their relation to the perceiving mind and their ultimate causes. The substance of this theory is as follows:

'The sense objects (colours, sounds, etc.) are states of the perceiver's mind, and as such excluded from nature regarded as something objective. For this reason they cannot be in any proper sense qualities of physical things. When I say "The sky is blue," it can only mean that the sky produces a blue sensation in my mind, and not that the colour blue is a quality found in the sky. As mental states they are impressions, that is to say, they are effects produced in us. The cause of these effects is matter, or material things acting through our sense organs, nerves, and brain on our mind. This physical cause acts by contact or impact; hence it must possess the qualities of shape, size, solidity and resistance.'[6]

It was the philosopher Berkeley who first undertook to refute the theory of matter as the unknown cause of our sensations.[7] In our own times Professor Whitehead - an eminent mathematician and scientist - has conclusively shown that the traditional theory of materialism is wholly untenable. It is obvious that, on the theory, colours, sounds, etc., are subjective states only, and form no part of Nature. What enters the eye and the ear is not colour or sound, but invisible ether waves and inaudible air waves. Nature is not what we know her to be; our perceptions are illusions and cannot be regarded as genuine disclosures of Nature, which, according to the theory, is bifurcated into mental impressions, on the one hand, and the unverifiable, imperceptible entities producing these impressions, on the other. If physics constitutes a really coherent and genuine knowledge of perceptively known objects, the traditional theory of matter must be rejected for the obvious reason that it reduces the evidence of our senses, on which alone the physicist, as observer and experimenter, must rely, to the mere impressions of the observer's mind. Between Nature and the observer of Nature, the theory creates a gulf which he is compelled to bridge over by resorting to the doubtful hypothesis of an imperceptible something, occupying an absolute space like a thing in a receptacle and causing our sensation by some kind of impact. In the words of Professor Whitehead, the theory reduces one-half of Nature to a 'dream' and the other half to a 'conjecture'.[8] Thus physics, finding it necessary to criticize its own foundations, has eventually found reason to break its own idol, and the empirical attitude which appeared to necessitate scientific materialism has finally ended in a revolt against matter. Since objects, then, are not subjective states caused by something imperceptible called matter, they are genuine phenomena which constitute the very substance of Nature and which we know as they are in Nature. But the concept of matter has received the greatest blow from the hand of Einstein - another eminent physicist, whose discoveries have laid the foundation of a far-reaching revolution in the entire domain of human thought. 'The theory of Relativity by merging time into spacetime', says Mr. Russell,

'has damaged the traditional notion of substance more than all the arguments of the philosophers. Matter, for common sense, is something which persists in time and moves in space. But for modern relativity-physics this view is no longer tenable. A piece of matter has become not a persistent thing with varying states, but a system of inter-related events. The old solidity is gone, and with it the characteristics that to the materialist made matter seem more real than fleeting thoughts.'

According to Professor Whitehead, therefore, Nature is not a static fact situated in an a-dynamic void, but a structure of events possessing the character of a continuous creative flow which thought cuts up into isolated immobilities out of whose mutual relations arise the concepts of space and time. Thus we see how modern science utters its agreement with Berkeley's criticism which it once regarded as an attack on its very foundation. The scientific view of Nature as pure materiality is associated with the Newtonian view of space as an absolute void in which things are situated. This attitude of science has, no doubt, ensured its speedy progress; but the bifurcation of a total experience into two opposite domains of mind and matter has today forced it, in view of its own domestic difficulties, to consider the problems which, in the beginning of its career, it completely ignored. The criticism of the foundations of the mathematical sciences has fully disclosed that the hypothesis of a pure materiality, an enduring stuff situated in an absolute space, is unworkable. Is space an independent void in which things are situated and which would remain intact if all things were withdrawn? The ancient Greek philosopher Zeno approached the problem of space through the question of movement in space. His arguments for the unreality of movement are well known to the students of philosophy, and ever since his days the problem has persisted in the history of thought and received the keenest attention from successive generations of thinkers. Two of these arguments may be noted here.[9] Zeno, who took space to be infinitely divisible, argued that movement in space is impossible. Before the moving body can reach the point of its destination it must pass through half the space intervening between the point of start and the point of destination; and before it can pass through that half it must travel through the half of the half, and so on to infinity. We cannot move from one point of space to another without passing through an infinite number of points in the intervening space. But it is impossible to pass through an infinity of points in a finite time. He further argued that the flying arrow does not move, because at any time during the course of its flight it is at rest in some point of space. Thus Zeno held that movement is only a deceptive appearance and that Reality is one and immutable. The unreality of movement means the unreality of an independent space. Muslim thinkers of the school of al-Ash'arâdid not believe in the infinite divisibility of space and time. With them space, time, and motion are made up of points and instants which cannot be further subdivided. Thus they proved the possibility of movement on the assumption that infinitesimals do exist; for if there is a limit to the divisibility of space and time, movement from one point of space to another point is possible in a finite time.[10] Ibn Àazm, however, rejected the Ash'arite notion of infinitesimals,[11] and modern mathematics has confirmed his view. The Ash'arite argument, therefore, cannot logically resolve the paradox of Zeno. Of modern thinkers the French philosopher Bergson and the British mathematician Bertrand Russell have tried to refute Zeno's arguments from their respective standpoints. To Bergson movement, as true change, is the fundamental Reality. The paradox of Zeno is due to a wrong apprehension of space and time which are regarded by Bergson only as intellectual views of movement. It is not possible to develop here the argument of Bergson without a fuller treatment of the metaphysical concept of life on which the whole argument is based.[12] Bertrand Russell's argument proceeds on Cantor's theory of mathematical continuity[13] which he looks upon as one of the most important discoveries of modern mathematics.[14] Zeno's argument is obviously based on the assumption that space and time consist of infinite number of points and instants. On this assumption it is easy to argue that since between two points the moving body will be out of place, motion is impossible, for there is no place for it to take place. Cantor's discovery shows that space and time are continuous. Between any two points in space there is an infinite number of points, and in an infinite series no two points are next to each other. The infinite divisibility of space and time means the compactness of the points in the series; it does not mean that points are mutually isolated in the sense of having a gap between one another. Russell's answer to Zeno, then, is as follows:

'Zeno asks how can you go from one position at one moment to the next position at the next moment without in the transition being at no position at no moment? The answer is that there is no next position to any position, no next moment to any moment because between any two there is always another. If there were infinitesimals movement would be impossible, but there are none. Zeno therefore is right in saying that the arrow is at rest at every moment of its flight, wrong in inferring that therefore it does not move, for there is a one-one correspondence in a movement between the infinite series of positions and the infinite series of instants. According to this doctrine, then it is possible to affirm the reality of space, time, and movement, and yet avoid the paradox in Zeno's arguments.'[15]

Thus Bertrand Russell proves the reality of movement on the basis of Cantor's theory of continuity. The reality of movement means the independent reality of space and the objectivity of Nature. But the identity of continuity and the infinite divisibility of space is no solution of the difficulty. Assuming that there is a one-one correspondence between the infinite multiplicity of instants in a finite interval of time and an infinite multiplicity of points in a finite portion of space, the difficulty arising from the divisibility remains the same. The mathematical conception of continuity as infinite series applies not to movement regarded as an act, but rather to the picture of movement as viewed from the outside. The act of movement, i.e. movement as lived and not as thought, does not admit of any divisibility. The flight of the arrow observed as a passage in space is divisible, but its flight regarded as an act, apart from its realization in space, is one and incapable of partition into a multiplicity. In partition lies its destruction.

With Einstein space is real, but relative to the observer. He rejects the Newtonian concept of an absolute space. The object observed is variable; it is relative to the observer; its mass, shape, and size change as the observer's position and speed change. Movement and rest, too, are relative to the observer. There is, therefore, no such thing as a self-subsistent materiality of classical physics. It is, however, necessary here to guard against a misunderstanding. The use of the word 'observer' in this connexion has misled Wildon Carr into the view that the theory of Relativity inevitably leads to Monadistic Idealism. It is true that according to the theory the shapes, sizes, and durations of phenomena are not absolute. But as Professor Nunn points out, the space-time frame does not depend on the observer's mind; it depends on the point of the material universe to which his body is attached. In fact, the 'observer' can be easily replaced by a recording apparatus.[16] Personally, I believe that the ultimate character of Reality is spiritual: but in order to avoid a widespread misunderstanding it is necessary to point out that Einstein's theory, which, as a scientific theory, deals only with the structure of things, throws no light on the ultimate nature of things which possess that structure. The philosophical value of the theory is twofold. First, it destroys, not the objectivity of Nature, but the view of substance as simple location in space - a view which led to materialism in Classical Physics. 'Substance' for modern Relativity-Physics is not a persistent thing with variable states, but a system of interrelated events. In Whitehead's presentation of the theory the notion of 'matter' is entirely replaced by the notion of 'organism'. Secondly, the theory makes space dependent on matter. The universe, according to Einstein, is not a kind of island in an infinite space; it is finite but boundless; beyond it there is no empty space. In the absence of matter the universe would shrink to a point. Looking, however, at the theory from the standpoint that I have taken in these lectures, Einstein's Relativity presents one great difficulty, i.e. the unreality of time. A theory which takes time to be a kind of fourth dimension of space must, it seems, regard the future as something already given, as indubitably fixed as the past.[17] Time as a free creative movement has no meaning for the theory. It does not pass. Events do not happen; we simply meet them. It must not, however, be forgotten that the theory neglects certain characteristics of time as experienced by us; and it is not possible to say that the nature of time is exhausted by the characteristics which the theory does note in the interests of a systematic account of those aspects of Nature which can be mathematically treated. Nor is it possible for us laymen to understand what the real nature of Einstein's time is. It is obvious that Einstein's time is not Bergson's pure duration. Nor can we regard it as serial time. Serial time is the essence of causality as defined by Kant. The cause and its effect are mutually so related that the former is chronologically prior to the latter, so that if the former is not, the latter cannot be. If mathematical time is serial time, then on the basis of the theory it is possible, by a careful choice of the velocities of the observer and the system in which a given set of events is happening, to make the effect precede its cause.[18] It appears to me that time regarded as a fourth dimension of space really ceases to be time. A modern Russian writer, Ouspensky, in his book called Tertium Organum, conceives the fourth dimension to be the movement of a three-dimensional figure in a direction not contained in itself.[19] Just as the movement of the point, the line and the surface in a direction not contained in them gives us the ordinary three dimensions of space, in the same way the movement of the three-dimensional figure in a direction not contained in itself must give us the fourth dimension of space. And since time is the distance separating events in order of succession and binding them in different wholes, it is obviously a distance lying in a direction not contained in the three-dimensional space. As a new dimension this distance, separating events in the order of succession, is incommensurable with the dimensions of three-dimensional space, as a year is incommensurable with St. Petersburg. It is perpendicular to all directions of three-dimensional space, and is not parallel to any of them. Elsewhere in the same book Ouspensky describes our time-sense as a misty space-sense and argues, on the basis of our psychic constitution, that to one-, two- or three-dimensional beings the higher dimension must always appear as succession in time. This obviously means that what appears to us three-dimensional beings as time is in reality an imperfectly sensed space-dimension which in its own nature does not differ from the perfectly sensed dimensions of Euclidean space. In other words, time is not a genuine creative movement; and that what we call future events are not fresh happenings, but things already given and located in an unknown space. Yet in his search for a fresh direction, other than the three Euclidean dimensions, Ouspensky needs a real serial time, i.e. a distance separating events in the order of succession. Thus time which was needed and consequently viewed as succession for the purposes of one stage of the argument is quietly divested, at a later stage, of its serial character and reduced to what does not differ in anything from the other lines and dimensions of space. It is because of the serial character of time that Ouspensky was able to regard it as a genuinely new direction in space. If this characteristic is in reality an illusion, how can it fulfil Ouspensky's requirements of an original dimension?

Passing now to other levels of experience - life and consciousness. Consciousness may be imagined as a deflection from life. Its function is to provide a luminous point in order to enlighten the forward rush of life.[20] It is a case of tension, a state of self-concentration, by means of which life manages to shut out all memories and associations which have no bearing on a present action. It has no well-defined fringes; it shrinks and expands as the occasion demands. To describe it as an epiphenomenon of the processes of matter is to deny it as an independent activity, and to deny it as an independent activity is to deny the validity of all knowledge which is only a systematized expression of consciousness. Thus consciousness is a variety of the purely spiritual principle of life which is not a substance, but an organizing principle, a specific mode of behaviour essentially different to the behaviour of an externally worked machine. Since, however, we cannot conceive of a purely spiritual energy, except in association with a definite combination of sensible elements through which it reveals itself, we are apt to take this combination as the ultimate ground of spiritual energy. The discoveries of Newton in the sphere of matter and those of Darwin in the sphere of Natural History reveal a mechanism. All problems, it was believed, were really the problems of physics. Energy and atoms, with the properties self-existing in them, could explain everything including life, thought, will, and feeling. The concept of mechanism - a purely physical concept - claimed to be the all-embracing explanation of Nature. And the battle for and against mechanism is still being fiercely fought in the domain of Biology. The question, then, is whether the passage to Reality through the revelations of sense-perception necessarily leads to a view of Reality essentially opposed to the view that religion takes of its ultimate character. Is Natural Science finally committed to materialism? There is no doubt that the theories of science constitute trustworthy knowledge, because they are verifiable and enable us to predict and control the events of Nature. But we must not forget that what is called science is not a single systematic view of Reality. It is a mass of sectional views of Reality - fragments of a total experience which do not seem to fit together. Natural Science deals with matter, with life, and with mind; but the moment you ask the question how matter, life, and mind are mutually related, you begin to see the sectional character of the various sciences that deal with them and the inability of these sciences, taken singly, to furnish a complete answer to your question. In fact, the various natural sciences are like so many vultures falling on the dead body of Nature, and each running away with a piece of its flesh. Nature as the subject of science is a highly artificial affair, and this artificiality is the result of that selective process to which science must subject her in the interests of precision. The moment you put the subject of science in the total of human experience it begins to disclose a different character. Thus religion, which demands the whole of Reality and for this reason must occupy a central place in any synthesis of all the data of human experience, has no reason to be afraid of any sectional views of Reality. Natural Science is by nature sectional; it cannot, if it is true to its own nature and function, set up its theory as a complete view of Reality. The concepts we use in the organization of knowledge are, therefore, sectional in character, and their application is relative to the level of experience to which they are applied. The concept of 'cause', for instance, the essential feature of which is priority to the effect, is relative to the subject-matter of physical science which studies one special kind of activity to the exclusion of other forms of activity observed by others. When we rise to the level of life and mind the concept of cause fails us, and we stand in need of concepts of a different order of thought. The action of living organisms, initiated and planned in view of an end, is totally different to causal action. The subject-matter of our inquiry, therefore, demands the concepts of 'end' and 'purpose', which act from within unlike the concept of cause which is external to the effect and acts from without. No doubt, there are aspects of the activity of a living organism which it shares with other objects of Nature. In the observation of these aspects the concepts of physics and chemistry would be needed; but the behaviour of the organism is essentially a matter of inheritance and incapable of sufficient explanation in terms of molecular physics. However, the concept of mechanism has been applied to life and we have to see how far the attempt has succeeded. Unfortunately, I am not a biologist and must turn to biologists themselves for support. After telling us that the main difference between a living organism and a machine is that the former is self-maintaining and self-reproducing, J.S. Haldane says:

'It is thus evident that although we find within the living body many phenomena which, so long as we do not look closely, can be interpreted satisfactorily as physical and chemical mechanism, there are side by side other phenomena [i.e. self-maintenance and reproduction] for which the possibility of such interpretation seems to be absent. The mechanists assume that the bodily mechanisms are so constructed as to maintain, repair, and reproduce themselves. In the long process of natural selection, mechanisms of this sort have, they suggest, been evolved gradually.

'Let us examine this hypothesis. When we state an event in mechanical terms we state it as a necessary result of certain simple properties of separate parts which interact in the event. . . . The essence of the explanation or re-statement of the event is that after due investigation we have assumed that the parts interacting in the event have certain simple and definite properties, so that they always react in the same way under the same conditions. For a mechanical explanation the reacting parts must first be given. Unless an arrangement of parts with definite properties is given, it is meaningless to speak of mechanical explanation.

'To postulate the existence of a self-producing or self-maintaining mechanism is, thus, to postulate something to which no meaning can be attached. Meaningless terms are sometimes used by physiologists; but there is none so absolutely meaningless as the expression "mechanism of reproduction". Any mechanism there may be in the parent organism is absent in the process of reproduction, and must reconstitute itself at each generation, since the parent organism is reproduced from a mere tiny speck of its own body. There can be no mechanism of reproduction. The idea of a mechanism which is constantly maintaining or reproducing its own structure is self-contradictory. A mechanism which reproduced itself would be a mechanism without parts, and, therefore, not a mechanism.'[21]

Life is, then, a unique phenomenon and the concept of mechanism is inadequate for its analysis. Its 'factual wholeness', to use an expression of Driesch - another notable biologist - is a kind of unity which, looked at from another point of view, is also a plurality. In all the purposive processes of growth and adaptation to its environment, whether this adaptation is secured by the formation of fresh or the modification of old habits, it possesses a career which is unthinkable in the case of a machine. And the possession of a career means that the sources of its activity cannot be explained except in reference to a remote past, the origin of which, therefore, must be sought in a spiritual reality revealable in, but non-discoverable by, any analysis of spatial experience. It would, therefore, seem that life is foundational and anterior to the routine of physical and chemical processes which must be regarded as a kind of fixed behaviour formed during a long course of evolution. Further, the application of the mechanistic concepts to life, necessitating the view that the intellect itself is a product of evolution, brings science into conflict with its own objective principle of investigation. On this point I will quote a passage from Wildon Carr, who has given a very pointed expression to this conflict:

'If intellect is a product of evolution the whole mechanistic concept of the nature and origin of life is absurd, and the principle which science has adopted must clearly be revised. We have only to state it to see the self-contradiction. How can the intellect, a mode of apprehending reality, be itself an evolution of something which only exists as an abstraction of that mode of apprehending, which is the intellect? If intellect is an evolution of life, then the concept of the life which can evolve intellect as a particular mode of apprehending reality must be the concept of a more concrete activity than that of any abstract mechanical movement which the intellect can present to itself by analysing its apprehended content. And yet further, if the intellect be a product of the evolution of life, it is not absolute but relative to the activity of the life which has evolved it; how then, in such case, can science exclude the subjective aspect of the knowing and build on the objective presentation as an absolute? Clearly the biological sciences necessitate a reconsideration of the scientific principle.'[22]

I will now try to reach the primacy of life and thought by another route, and carry you a step farther in our examination of experience. This will throw some further light on the primacy of life and will also give us an insight into the nature of life as a psychic activity. We have seen that Professor Whitehead describes the universe, not as something static, but as a structure of events possessing the character of a continuous creative flow. This quality of Nature's passage in time is perhaps the most significant aspect of experience which the Qur'«n especially emphasizes and which, as I hope to be able to show in the sequel, offers the best clue to the ultimate nature of Reality. To some of the verses (3:190-91; 2:164; 24:44)[23] bearing on the point I have already drawn your attention. In view of the great importance of the subject I will add here a few more:

'Verily, in the alternations of night and of day and in all that God hath created in the Heavens and in the earth are signs to those who fear Him' (10:6).

'And it is He Who hath ordained the night and the day to succeed one another for those who desire to think on God or desire to be thankful' (25:62).

'Seest though not that God causeth the night to come in upon the day, and the day to come in upon the night; and that He hath subjected the sun and the moon to laws by which each speedeth along to an appointed goal?' (31:29).

'It is of Him that the night returneth on the day, and that the day returneth on the night' (39:5).

'And of Him is the change of the night and of the day' (23:80).

There is another set of verses which, indicating the relativity of our reckoning of time, suggests the possibility of unknown levels of consciousness;[24] but I will content myself with a discussion of the familiar, yet deeply significant, aspect of experience alluded to in the verses quoted above. Among the representatives of contemporary thought Bergson is the only thinker who has made a keen study of the phenomenon of duration in time. I will first briefly explain to you his view of duration and then point out the inadequacy of his analysis in order fully to bring out the implications of a completer view of the temporal aspect of existence. The ontological problem before us is how to define the ultimate nature of existence. That the universe persists in time is not open to doubt. Yet, since it is external to us, it is possible to be sceptical about its existence. In order completely to grasp the meaning of this persistence in time we must be in a position to study some privileged case of existence which is absolutely unquestionable and gives us the further assurance of a direct vision of duration. Now my perception of things that confront me is superficial and external; but my perception of my own self is internal, intimate, and profound. It follows, therefore, that conscious experience is that privileged case of existence in which we are in absolute contact with Reality, and an analysis of this privileged case is likely to throw a flood of light on the ultimate meaning of existence. What do I find when I fix my gaze on my own conscious experience? In the words of Bergson:

'I pass from state to state. I am warm or cold. I am merry or sad, I work or I do nothing, I look at what is around me or I think of something else. Sensations, feelings, volitions, ideas - such are the changes into which my existence is divided and which colour it in turns. I change then, without ceasing.'[25]

Thus, there is nothing static in my inner life; all is a constant mobility, an unceasing flux of states, a perpetual flow in which there is no halt or resting place. Constant change, however, is unthinkable without time. On the analogy of our inner experience, then, conscious existence means life in time. A keener insight into the nature of conscious experience, however, reveals that the self in its inner life moves from the centre outwards. It has, so to speak, two sides which may be described as appreciative and efficient. On its efficient side it enters into relation with what we call the world of space. The efficient self is the subject of associationist psychology - the practical self of daily life in its dealing with the external order of things which determine our passing states of consciousness and stamp on these states their own spatial feature of mutual isolation. The self here lives outside itself as it were, and, while retaining its unity as a totality, discloses itself as nothing more than a series of specific and consequently numberable states. The time in which the efficient self lives is, therefore, the time of which we predicate long and short. It is hardly distinguishable from space. We can conceive it only as a straight line composed of spatial points which are external to one another like so many stages in a journey. But time thus regarded is not true time, according to Bergson. Existence in spatialized time is spurious existence. A deeper analysis of conscious experience reveals to us what I have called the appreciative side of the self. With our absorption in the external order of things, necessitated by our present situation, it is extremely difficult to catch a glimpse of the appreciative self. In our constant pursuit after external things we weave a kind of veil round the appreciative self which thus becomes completely alien to us. It is only in the moments of profound meditation, when the efficient self is in abeyance, that we sink into our deeper self and reach the inner centre of experience. In the life-process of this deeper ego the states of consciousness melt into each other. The unity of the appreciative ego is like the unity of the germ in which the experiences of its individual ancestors exist, not as a plurality, but as a unity in which every experience permeates the whole. There is no numerical distinctness of states in the totality of the ego, the multiplicity of whose elements is, unlike that of the efficient self, wholly qualitative. There is change and movement, but change and movement are indivisible; their elements interpenetrate and are wholly non-serial in character. It appears that the time of the appreciative-self is a single 'now' which the efficient self, in its traffic with the world of space, pulverizes into a series of 'nows' like pearl beads in a thread. Here is, then, pure duration unadulterated by space. The Qur'«n with its characteristic simplicity alludes to the serial and non-serial aspects of duration in the following verses:

'And put thou thy trust in Him that liveth and dieth not, and celebrate His praise Who in six days created the Heavens and the earth, and what is between them, then mounted His Throne; the God of mercy' (25:58-59).

'All things We have created with a fixed destiny: Our command was but one, swift as the twinkling of an eye' (54:49-50).

If we look at the movement embodied in creation from the outside, that is to say, if we apprehend it intellectually, it is a process lasting through thousands of years; for one Divine day, in the terminology of the Qur'«n, as of the Old Testament, is equal to one thousand years.[26] From another point of view, the process of creation, lasting through thousands of years, is a single indivisible act, 'swift as the twinkling of an eye'. It is, however, impossible to express this inner experience of pure duration in words, for language is shaped on the serial time of our daily efficient self. Perhaps an illustration will further elucidate the point. According to physical science, the cause of your sensation of red is the rapidity of wave motion the frequency of which is 400 billions per second. If you could observe this tremendous frequency from the outside, and count it at the rate of 2,000 per second, which is supposed to be the limit of the perceptibility of light, it will take you more than six thousand years to finish the enumeration.[27] Yet in the single momentary mental act of perception you hold together a frequency of wave motion which is practically incalculable. That is how the mental act transforms succession into duration. The appreciative self, then, is more or less corrective of the efficient self, inasmuch as it synthesizes all the 'heres' and 'nows' - the small changes of space and time, indispensable to the efficient self - into the coherent wholeness of personality. Pure time, then, as revealed by a deeper analysis of our conscious experience, is not a string of separate, reversible instants; it is an organic whole in which the past is not left behind, but is moving along with, and operating in, the present. And the future is given to it not as lying before, yet to be traversed; it is given only in the sense that it is present in its nature as an open possibility.[28] It is time regarded as an organic whole that the Qur'«n describes as *Taqdâr* or the destiny - a word which has been so much misunderstood both in and outside the world of Islam. Destiny is time regarded as prior to the disclosure of its possibilities. It is time freed from the net of causal sequence - the diagrammatic character which the logical understanding imposes on it. In one word, it is time as felt and not as thought and calculated. If you ask me why the Emperor Huma«yën and Sh«h Tahm«sp of Persia were contemporaries, I can give you no causal explanation. The only answer that can possibly be given is that the nature of Reality is such that among its infinite possibilities of becoming, the two possibilities known as the lives of Hum«yën and Sh«h Tahm«sp should realize themselves together. Time regarded as destiny forms the very essence of things. As the Qur'«n says: 'God created all things and assigned to each its destiny.'[29] The destiny of a thing then is not an unrelenting fate working from without like a task master; it is the inward reach of a thing, its realizable possibilities which lie within the depths of its nature, and serially actualize themselves without any feeling of external compulsion. Thus the organic wholeness of duration does not mean that full-fledged events are lying, as it were, in the womb of Reality, and drop one by one like the grains of sand from the hour-glass. If time is real, and not a mere repetition of homogeneous moments which make conscious experience a delusion, then every moment in the life of Reality is original, giving birth to what is absolutely novel and unforeseeable. 'Everyday doth some new work employ Him',[30] says the Qur'«n. To exist in real time is not to be bound by the fetters of serial time, but to create it from moment to moment and to be absolutely free and original in creation. In fact, all creative activity is free activity. Creation is opposed to repetition which is a characteristic of mechanical action. That is why it is impossible to explain the creative activity of life in terms of mechanism. Science seeks to establish uniformities of experience, i.e. the laws of mechanical repetition. Life with its intense feeling of spontaneity constitutes a centre of indetermination, and thus falls outside the domain of necessity. Hence science cannot comprehend life. The biologist who seeks a mechanical explanation of life is led to do so because he confines his study to the lower forms of life whose behaviour discloses resemblances to mechanical action. If he studies life as manifested in himself, i.e. his own mind freely choosing, rejecting, reflecting, surveying the past and the present, and dynamically imagining the future, he is sure to be convinced of the inadequacy of his mechanical concepts.

On the analogy of our conscious experience, then, the universe is a free creative movement. But how can we conceive a movement independent of a concrete thing that moves? The answer is that the notion of 'things' is derivative. We can derive 'things' from movement; we cannot derive movement from immobile things. If, for instance, we suppose material atoms, such as the atoms of Democritus, to be the original Reality, we must import movement into them from the outside as something alien to their nature. Whereas if we take movement as original, static things may be derived from it. In fact, physical science has reduced all things to movement. The essential nature of the atom in modern science is electricity and not something electrified. Apart from this, things are not given in immediate experience as things already possessing definite contours, for immediate experience is a continuity without any distinctions in it. What we call things are events in the continuity of Nature which thought spatializes and thus regards as mutually isolated for purposes of action. The universe which seems to us to be a collection of things is not a solid stuff occupying a void. It is not a thing but an act. The nature of thought according to Bergson is serial; it cannot deal with movement, except by viewing it as a series of stationary points. It is, therefore, the operation of thought, working with static concepts, that gives the appearance of a series of immobilities to what is essentially dynamic in its nature. The co-existence and succession of these immobilities is the source of what we call space and time.

According to Bergson, then, Reality is a free unpredictable, creative, vital impetus of the nature of volition which thought spatializes and views as a plurality of 'things'. A full criticism of this view cannot be undertaken here. Suffice it to say that the vitalism of Bergson ends in an insurmountable dualism of will and thought. This is really due to the partial view of intelligence that he takes. Intelligence, according to him, is a spatializing activity; it is shaped on matter alone, and has only mechanical categories at its disposal. But, as I pointed out in my first lecture, thought has a deeper movement also.[31] While it appears to break up Reality into static fragments, its real function is to synthesize the elements of experience by employing categories suitable to the various levels which experience presents. It is as much organic as life. The movement of life, as an organic growth, involves a progressive synthesis of its various stages. Without this synthesis it will cease to be organic growth. It is determined by ends, and the presence of ends means that it is permeated by intelligence. Nor is the activity of intelligence possible without the presence of ends. In conscious experience life and thought permeate each other. They form a unity. Thought, therefore, in its true nature, is identical with life. Again, in Bergson's view the forward rush of the vital impulse in its creative freedom is unilluminated by the light of an immediate or a remote purpose. It is not aiming at a result; it is wholly arbitrary, undirected, chaotic, and unforeseeable in its behaviour. It is mainly here that Bergson's analysis of our conscious experience reveals its inadequacy. He regards conscious experience as the past moving along with and operating in the present. He ignores that the unity of consciousness has a forward looking aspect also. Life is only a series of acts of attention, and an act of attention is inexplicable without reference to a purpose, conscious or unconscious. Even our acts of perception are determined by our immediate interests and purposes. The Persian poet 'urfâ' has given a beautiful expression to this aspect of human perception. He says:[32]

'If your heart is not deceived by the mirage, be not proud of the sharpness of your understanding;
for your freedom from this optical illusion is due to your imperfect thirst.'

The poet means to say that if you had a vehement desire for drink, the sands of the desert would have given you the impression of a lake. Your freedom from the illusion is due to the absence of a keen desire for water. You have perceived the thing as it is because you were not interested in perceiving it as it is not. Thus ends and purposes, whether they exist as conscious or subconscious tendencies, form the warp and woof of our conscious experience. And the notion of purpose cannot be understood except in reference to the future. The past, no doubt, abides and operates in the present; but this operation of the past in the present is not the whole of consciousness. The element of purpose discloses a kind of forward look in consciousness. Purposes not only colour our present states of consciousness, but also reveal its future direction. In fact, they constitute the forward push of our life, and thus in a way anticipate and influence the states that are yet to be. To be determined by an end is to be determined by what ought to be. Thus past and future both operate in the present state of consciousness, and the future is not wholly undetermined as Bergson's analysis of our conscious experience shows. A state of attentive consciousness involves both memory and imagination as operating factors. On the analogy of our conscious experience, therefore, Reality is not a blind vital impulse wholly unilluminated by idea. Its nature is through and through teleological.

Bergson, however, denies the teleological character of Reality on the ground that teleology makes time unreal. According to him 'the portals of the future must remain wide open to Reality'. Otherwise, it will not be free and creative. No doubt, if teleology means the working out of a plan in view of a predetermined end or goal, it does make time unreal. It reduces the universe to a mere temporal reproduction of a pre-existing eternal scheme or structure in which individual events have already found their proper places, waiting, as it were, for their respective turns to enter into the temporal sweep of history. All is already given somewhere in eternity; the temporal order of events is nothing more than a mere imitation of the eternal mould. Such a view is hardly distinguishable from mechanism which we have already rejected.[33] In fact, it is a kind of veiled materialism in which fate or destiny takes the place of rigid determinism, leaving no scope for human or even Divine freedom. The world regarded as a process realizing a preordained goal is not a world of free, responsible moral agents; it is only a stage on which puppets are made to move by a kind of pull from behind. There is, however, another sense of teleology. From our conscious experience we have seen that to live is to shape and change ends and purposes and to be governed by them. Mental life is teleological in the sense that, while there is no far-off distant goal towards which we are moving, there is a progressive formation of fresh ends, purposes, and ideal scales of value as the process of life grows and expands. We become by ceasing to be what we are. Life is a passage through a series of deaths. But there is a system in the continuity of this passage. Its various stages, in spite of the apparently abrupt changes in our evaluation of things, are organically related to one another. The life-history of the individual is, on the whole, a unity and not a mere series of mutually ill-adapted events. The world-process, or the movement of the universe in time, is certainly devoid of purpose, if by purpose we mean a foreseen end - a far-off fixed destination to which the whole creation moves. To endow the world-process with purpose in this sense is to rob it of its originality and its creative character. Its ends are terminations of a career; they are ends to come and not necessarily premeditated. A time-process cannot be conceived as a line already drawn. It is a line in the drawing - an actualization of open possibilities. It is purposive only in this sense that it is selective in character, and brings itself to some sort of a present fulfilment by actively preserving and supplementing the past. To my mind nothing is more alien to the Quranic outlook than the idea that the universe is the temporal working out of a preconceived plan. As I have already pointed out, the universe, according to the Qur'«n, is liable to increase.[34] It is a growing universe and not an already completed product which left the hand of its maker ages ago, and is now lying stretched in space as a dead mass of matter to which time does nothing, and consequently is nothing.

We are now, I hope, in a position to see the meaning of the verse - 'And it is He Who hath ordained the night and the day to succeed one another for those who desire to think on God or desire to be thankful.'[35] A critical interpretation of the sequence of time as revealed in ourselves has led us to a notion of the Ultimate Reality as pure duration in which thought, life, and purpose interpenetrate to form an organic unity. We cannot conceive this unity except as the unity of a self - an all-embracing concrete self - the ultimate source of all individual life and thought. I venture to think that the error of Bergson consists in regarding pure time as prior to self, to which pure duration is predicable. Neither pure space nor pure time can hold together the multiplicity of objects and events. It is the appreciative act of an enduring self only which can seize the multiplicity of duration - broken up into an infinity of instants - and transform it to the organic wholeness of a synthesis. To exist in pure duration is to be a self, and to be a self is to be able to say 'I am'. Only that truly exists which can say 'I am'. It is the degree of the intuition of 'I-amness' that determines the place of a thing in the scale of being. We too say 'I am'. But our 'I-amness' is dependent and arises out of the distinction between the self and the not-self. The Ultimate Self, in the words of the Qur'«n, 'can afford to dispense with all the worlds'.[36] To Him the not-self does not present itself as a confronting 'other', or else it would have to be, like our finite self, in spatial relation with the confronting 'other'. What we call Nature or the not-self is only a fleeting moment in the life of God. His 'I-amness' is independent, elemental, absolute.[37] Of such a self it is impossible for us to form an adequate conception. As the Qur'«n says, 'Naught' is like Him; yet 'He hears and sees'.[38] Now a self is unthinkable without a character, i.e. a uniform mode of behaviour. Nature, as we have seen, is not a mass of pure materiality occupying a void. It is a structure of events, a systematic mode of behaviour, and as such organic to the Ultimate Self. Nature is to the Divine Self as character is to the human self. In the picturesque phrase of the Qur'«n it is the habit of Allah.[39] From the human point of view it is an interpretation which, in our present situation, we put on the creative activity of the Absolute Ego. At a particular moment in its forward movement it is finite; but since the self to which it is organic is creative, it is liable to increase, and is consequently boundless in the sense that no limit to its extension is final. Its boundlessness is potential, not actual. Nature, then, must be understood as a living, ever-growing organism whose growth has no final external limits. Its only limit is internal, i.e. the immanent self which animates and sustains the whole. As the Qur'«n says: 'And verily unto thy Lord is the limit' (53:42). Thus the view that we have taken gives a fresh spiritual meaning to physical science. The knowledge of Nature is the knowledge of God's behaviour. In our observation of Nature we are virtually seeking a kind of intimacy with the Absolute Ego; and this is only another form of worship.[40]

The above discussion takes time as an essential element in the Ultimate Reality. The next point before us, therefore, is to consider the late Doctor McTaggart's argument relating to the unreality of time.[41] Time, according to Doctor McTaggart, is unreal because every event is past, present, and future. Queen Anne's death, for instance, is past to us; it was present to her contemporaries and future to William III. Thus the event of Anne's death combines characteristics which are incompatible with each other. It is obvious that the argument proceeds on the assumption that the serial nature of time is final. If we regard past, present, and future as essential to time, then we picture time as a straight line, part of which we have travelled and left behind, and part lies yet untravelled before us. This is taking time, not as a living creative moment, but as a static absolute, holding the ordered multiplicity of fully-shaped cosmic events, revealed serially, like the pictures of a film, to the outside observer. We can indeed say that Queen Anne's death was future to William III, if this event is regarded as already fully shaped, and lying in the future, waiting for its happening. But a future event, as Broad justly points out, cannot be characterized as an event.[42] Before the death of Anne the event of her death did not exist at all. During Anne's life the event of her death existed only as an unrealized possibility in the nature of Reality which included it as an event only when, in the course of its becoming, it reached the point of the actual happening of that event. The answer to Doctor McTaggart's argument is that the future exists only as an open possibility, and not as a reality. Nor can it be said that an event combines incompatible characteristics when it is described both as past and present. When an event X does happen it enters into an unalterable relation with all the events that have happened before it. These relations are not at all affected by the relations of X with other events which happen after X by the further becoming of Reality. No true or false proposition about these relations will ever become false or true. Hence there is no logical difficulty in regarding an event as both past and present. It must be confessed, however, that the point is not free from difficulty and requires much further thinking. It is not easy to solve the mystery of time.[43] Augustine's profound words are as true today as they were when they were uttered: 'If no one questions me of time, I know it: if I would explain to a questioner I know it not.'[44] Personally, I am inclined to think that time is an essential element in Reality. But real time is not serial time to which the distinction of past, present, and future is essential; it is pure duration, i.e. change without succession, which McTaggart's argument does not touch. Serial time is pure duration pulverized by thought - a kind of device by which Reality exposes its ceaseless creative activity to quantitative measurement. It is in this sense that the Qur'«n says: 'And of Him is the change of the night and of the day.'[45]

But the question you are likely to ask is - 'Can change be predicated of the Ultimate Ego?' We, as human beings, are functionally related to an independent world-process. The conditions of our life are mainly external to us. The only kind of life known to us is desire, pursuit, failure, or attainment - a continuous change from one situation to another. From our point of view life is change, and change is essentially imperfection. At the same time, since our conscious experience is the only point of departure for all knowledge, we cannot avoid the limitation of interpreting facts in the light of our own inner experience. An anthropomorphic conception is especially unavoidable in the apprehension of life; for life can be apprehended from within only. As the poet N«sir 'Alâ of Sirhind imagines the idol saying to the Brahmin:

> 'Thou hast made me after Thine own image! After all what hast Thou seen beyond Thyself?'[46]

It was the fear of conceiving Divine life after the image of human life that the Spanish Muslim theologian Ibn Àazm hesitated to predicate life of God, and ingeniously suggested that God should be described as living, not because He is living in the sense of our experience of life, but only because He is so described in the Qur'«n.[47] Confining himself to the surface of our conscious experience and ignoring its deeper phases, Ibn Àazm must have taken life as a serial change, a succession of attitudes towards an obstructing environment. Serial change is obviously a mark of imperfection; and, if we confine ourselves to this view of change, the difficulty of reconciling Divine perfection with Divine life becomes insuperable. Ibn Àazm must have felt that the perfection of God can be retained only at the cost of His life. There is, however, a way out of the difficulty. The Absolute Ego, as we have seen, is the whole of Reality. He is not so situated as to take a perspective view of an alien universe; consequently, the phases of His life are wholly determined from within. Change, therefore, in the sense of a movement from an imperfect to a relatively perfect state, or vice versa, is obviously inapplicable to His life. But change in this sense is not the only possible form of life. A deeper insight into our conscious experience shows that beneath the appearance of serial duration there is true duration. The Ultimate Ego exists in pure duration wherein change ceases to be a succession of varying attitudes, and reveals its true character as continuous creation, 'untouched by weariness'[48] and unseizable 'by slumber or sleep'.[49] To conceive the Ultimate Ego as changeless in this sense of change is to conceive Him as utter inaction, a motiveless, stagnant neutrality, an absolute nothing. To the Creative Self change cannot mean imperfection. The perfection of the Creative Self consists, not in a mechanistically conceived immobility, as Aristotle might have led Ibn Àazm to think. It consists in the vaster basis of His creative activity and the infinite scope of His creative vision. God's life is self-revelation, not the pursuit of an ideal to be reached. The 'not-yet' of man does mean pursuit and may mean failure; the 'not-yet' of God means unfailing realization of the infinite creative possibilities of His being which retains its wholeness throughout the entire process.

In the Endless, self-repeating
flows for evermore The Same.
Myriad arches, springing, meeting,
hold at rest the mighty frame.
Streams from all things love of living,
grandest star and humblest clod.
All the straining, all the striving
is eternal peace in God.[50] (GOETHE)

Thus a comprehensive philosophical criticism of all the facts of experience on its efficient as well as appreciative side brings us to the conclusion that the Ultimate Reality is a rationally directed creative life. To interpret this life as an ego is not to fashion God after the image of man. It is only to accept the simple fact of experience that life is not a formless fluid, but an organizing principle of unity, a synthetic activity which holds together and focalizes the dispersing dispositions of the living organism for a constructive purpose. The operation of thought which is essentially symbolic in character veils the true nature of life, and can picture it only as a kind of universal current flowing through all things. The result of an intellectual view of life, therefore, is necessarily pantheistic. But we have a first-hand knowledge of the appreciative aspect of life from within. Intuition reveals life as a centralizing ego. This knowledge, however imperfect as giving us only a point of departure, is a direct revelation of the ultimate nature of Reality. Thus the facts of experience justify the inference that the ultimate nature of Reality is spiritual, and must be conceived as an ego. But the aspiration of religion soars higher than that of philosophy. Philosophy is an intellectual view of things; and, as such, does not care to go beyond a concept which can reduce all the rich variety of experience to a system. It sees Reality from a distance as it were. Religion seeks a closer contact with Reality. The one is theory; the other is living experience, association, intimacy. In order to achieve this intimacy thought must rise higher than itself, and find its fulfilment in an attitude of mind which religion describes as prayer - one of the last words on the lips of the Prophet of Islam.[51]

Lecture II Notes: THE PHILOSOPHICAL TEST OF THE REVELATIONS OF RELIGIOUS EXPERIENCE

1. Cf. E.S. Haldane and G.R.T. Ross (trs.), *The Philosophical Works of Descartes*, II, 57.

2. Cf. *The Critique of Pure Reason*, trans. N.'Kemp Smith, p. 505.

3. The logical fallacy of assuming in the premisses of that which is to be proved in the conclusion.

4. Qur'«n, 41:53, also 51:20-21.

5. *Ibid.*, 57:3.

6. Cf. R.F.A. Hoernle, *Matter, Life, Mind and God*, pp. 69-70.

7. Cf. H. Barker, article 'Berkeley' in *Encyclopaedia of Religion and Ethics*, especially the section; 'Metaphysics of Immaterialism'; see also Lecture IV, p. 83, for Allama Iqbal's acute observations in refutation of 'the hypothesis of matter as an independent existence'.

8. Cf. A.N. Whitehead, *The Concept of Nature*, p. 30. This is what Whitehead has called the 'theory of bifurcation of Nature' based on the dichotomy of 'simply located material bodies of Newtonian physics' and the 'pure sensations' of Hume. According to this theory, Nature is split up into two disparate or isolated parts; the one known to us through our immediate experiences of colours, sounds, scents, etc., and the other, the world of unperceived scientific entities of molecules, atoms, electrons, ether, etc. - colourless, soundless, unscented - which so act upon the mind through 'impact' as to produce in it the 'illusions' of sensory experiences in which it delights. The theory thus divides totality of being into a reality which does not appear and is thus a mere 'conjecture' and appearances which are not real and so are mere 'dream'. Whitehead outright rejects 'bifurcation'; and insists that the red glow of sunset is as much 'part of Nature' as the vibrations of molecules and that the scientist cannot dismiss the red glow as a 'psychic addition' if he is to have a coherent 'Concept of Nature'. This view of Whitehead, the eminent mathematician, expounded by him in 1920 (i.e. four years before his appointment to the chair of Philosophy at Harvard at the age of sixty-three) was widely accepted by the philosophers. Lord Richard Burdon Haldane, one of the leading neo-Hegelian British philosophers, said to be the first philosophical writer on the Theory of Relativity, gave full support to Whitehead's views on 'bifurcation' as well as on 'Relativity' in his widely-read *Reign of Relativity* to which Allama Iqbal refers in Lecture III, p. 57, and tacitly also perhaps in lecture V. The way Lord Haldane has stated in this work his defence of Whitehead's views of Relativity (enunciated by him especially in Concept of Nature) even as against those of Einstein, one is inclined to surmise that it was perhaps Reign of Relativity (incidentally also listed at S. No. 276 in the *Descriptive Catalogue of Allama's Personal Library*) more than any other work that led Allama Iqbal to make the observation: 'Whitehead's view of Relativity is likely to appeal to Muslim students more than that of Einstein in whose theory time loses its character of passage and mysteriously translates itself into utter space' (Lecture V, p. 106).

9. Allama Iqbal states here Zeno's first and third arguments; for all the four arguments of Zeno on the unreality of motion, see John Burnet, *Greek philosophy; Thales to Plato*, p. 84; they generally go by names; the 'dichotomy'; the 'Achilles'; the 'arrow'; and the 'stadium'. It may be added that our primary source for Zeno's famous and controversial arguments is Aristotle Physics (VI, 9, 239b) which is generally said to have been first translated into Arabic by IsÁ«q b. Àunain (c. 845-910/911), the son of the celebrated Àunain b. IsÁ«q. Aristotle's Physics is also said to have been commented on later by the Christian Abë'Alâa -Àasan b. al-Samh (c. 945-1027); cf. S.M. Stern, 'Ibn-al-Samh', *Journal of the Royal Asiatic Society* (1956), pp. 31-44. Even so it seems that Zeno's arguments as stated by Aristotle were known to the Muslim thinkers much earlier, maybe through Christian-Syriac sources, for one finds the brilliant Mu'tazilite Naïï«m (d. 231/845) meeting Zeno's first argument in terms of his ingenious idea of tafrah jump referred to by Allama Iqbal in Lecture III, pp. 63-64.

10. Cf. T.J. de Boer, article 'Atomic Theory (Muhammadan)', in *Encyclopaedia of Religion and Ethics*, II, 202-203; D.B. Macdonald, *Development of Muslim Theology*, pp. 201 ff. and Majid Fakhry, *Islamic Occasionalism*, pp. 33-43.

11. Cf. *Kit«b al-FiÄal*, V, 92-102.

12. For Bergson's criticism of Zeno's arguments cf. *Creative Evolution*, pp. 325-30, and also the earlier work Time and Free Will, pp.113-15.

13. Cf. A.E. Taylor, article 'Continuity' in *Encyclopaedia of Religion and Ethics*, IV, 97-98.

14. Cf. Bertrand Russell, *Our Knowledge of the External World*, pp. 169-88;

also *Mysticism and Logic*, pp. 84-91.

15. This is not Russell's own statement but that of H. Wildon Carr made during the course of his exposition of Russell's views on the subject; see Wildon Carr, *The General Principle of Relativity*, p. 36.

16. Views of H. Wildon Carr and especially of Sir T. Percy Nunn on relativity in the present context are to be found in their symposium papers on 'The Idealistic Interpretation of Einstein's Theory' published in the *Proceedings of the Aristotelian Society*, N.S. XXII (1921-22), 123-27 and 127-30. Wildon Carr's, *Doctrine of Monadistic Idealism*, however, is to be found much more fully expounded in his *General Principle of Relativity* (1920) and *A Theory of Monads: Outlines of the Philosophy of the Principle of Relativity* (1922); passages from both of these books have been quoted in the present lecture (cf. notes 15 and 22).

T. Percy Nunn, best known as an educationist, wrote little philosophy; but whatever little he wrote, it made him quite influential with the leading contemporary British philosophers: Whitehead, Samuel Alexander, Russell, Broad, and others. He is said to have first formulated the characteristic doctrines of neo-Realism, an important philosophical school of the century which had its zealot and able champions both in England and in the United States. His famous symposium paper: 'Are Secondary Qualities Independent of Perception?' read in a meeting of the Aristotelian Society in 1909 was widely studied and discussed and as J. Passmore puts it: 'it struck Bertrand Russell's roving fancy' (*A Hundred Years of Philosophy*, p. 258). It is significant to note that Nunn's correction put on Wildon Carr's idealistic interpretation of relativity in the present passage is to be found almost in the same philosophical diction in Russell's valuable article: 'Relativity; Philosophical Consequences', in *Encyclopaedia Britannica* (1953), XIX, 99d, Russell says: 'It is a mistake to suppose that relativity adopts any idealistic picture of the world . . . . The 'observer' who is often mentioned in expositions of relativity need not be a mind, but may be a photographic plate or any kind of recording instrument.'

17. On this rather debatable interpretation of Einstein's theory of relativity see Dr M. Razi-ud-dân Âiddâqâ, 'Iqbal's Conception of Time and Space' in *Iqbal As A Thinker*, pp. 29-31, and Philipp Frank, 'Philosophical Interpretations and Misinterpretations of the Theory of Relativity', in H. Feigel and Mary Broadbeck (eds.), *Readings in the Philosophy of Science*, pp. 222-26, reprinted from his valuable work. *Interpretations and Misinterpretations of Modern Physics* (1938).

18. Cf. Hans Reichenbach, 'The Philosophical Significance of the Theory of Relativity', in P.A. Schilpp (ed.), *Albert-Einstein: Philosopher-Scientist*, section iv.

19. Cf. *Tertium Organum*, pp. 33f.

20. Compare this with Bergson's view of consciousness in Creative Evolution, pp. 189f.

21. This is a passage from J.S. Haldane's Symposium Paper: 'Are Physical, Biological and Psychological Categories Irreducible?' read in July 1918 at the joint session of the Aristotelian Society, the British Psychological Society and the Mind Association; see *Proceedings of the Aristotelian Society*, XVII, (1917-1918), 423-24, reproduced in H. Wildon Carr (ed.), *Life and Finite Individuality*, pp. 15-16.

22. *A Theory of Monads*, pp. 5-6.

23. Cf. Lecture I, pp. 8-11.

24. Cf. the Quranic verses quoted on p. 39; to these may be added 22:47, 32:5, and 70:4 - according to this last verse a day is of the measure of fifty thousand years.

25. *Creative Evolution*, p. 1.

26. The Qur'«n says: 'And behold a day with thy sustainer is as a thousand years of your reckoning' (22:47). So also, according to the Old Testament: 'One day is with the Lord as a thousand years' (Psalms, xc.'4).

27. According to Bergson, this period may be as long as 25,000 years; cf. *Matter and Memory*, pp. 272-73.

28. For further elucidation of future as an open possibility' cf. Lecture III, p.'63.

29. See among others the Quranic verses 25:2; 54:49 and the earliest on this subject in the chronological order of the sërahs: 87:2-3.

These last two short verses speak of four Divine ways governing all creation and so also man, viz. God's creating a thing (*khalaqa*), making it complete (*fa sawwa*), assigning a destiny to it or determining its nature (*qaddara*) and guiding it to its fulfilment (*fa hada*).

Allama Iqbal's conception of destiny (*taqdâr*) as 'the inward reach of a thing, its realizable possibilities which lie within the depth of its nature, and serially actualize themselves without any feeling of external compulsion' [italics mine] understood in terms of the Divine ways embodied in the above two short verses, seems to be singularly close to the text and the unique thought-forms of the Qur'«n. There is no place in this conception of destiny for the doctrine of Fatalism as preached by some Muslim scholastic theologians whose interpretation of the verses of the Qur'«n for this purpose is more often a palpable misinterpretation (Lecture IV, p. 89); nor for the doctrine of determinism as expounded by the philosophers who, cut off from the inner life-impulse given by Islam, think of all things in terms of the inexorable law of cause and effect which governs the human ego as much as the 'environment' in which it is placed. They fail to realize that the origin of the law of 'cause and effect' lies in the depths of the transcendental ego which has devised it or caused it under divine guidance to realize its divinely assigned destiny of understanding and mastering all things (p. 86); also *Æsr«r-i Khudâ*, many verses especially those in the earlier sections.

30. Qur'«n, 55:29.

31. Cf. Lecture I, p. 5.

32. See Shiblâ Nu'm«nâ, Shi'r al-'Ajam, II, 114.

33. This is a reference to pp. 33-36.

34. Cf. Lecture I, p. 8 and note 23.

35. The Quranic verse 25:62 quoted on p. 37.

36. Reference is to the Quranic expression: *Ghanâyy-un 'ani'i-'«lamân* found in verses 3:97 and 29:6.

37. This is a reference to the Quranic verse 20:14: 'Verily, I - I alone - am God; there is no deity save Me. Hence, worship Me alone, and be constant in prayer, so as to remember Me.'

38. Qur'«n, 42:11.

39. The reference is to the Quranic expression sunnat Allah found in 33:62; 35:43; 40:84-85; 48:23, etc.

40. Cf. Lecture III, p. 83, where Allama Iqbal observes: 'The scientific observer of Nature is a kind of mystic seeker in the act of prayer.'

41. McTaggart's argument referred to here was advanced by him in his article; 'The Unreality of Time' in *Mind* (N.S.), XVII/68 (October 1908), 457-74, reproduced later in *Nature of Existence*, II, 9-31, as well as in the posthumous *Philosophical Studies*, pp. 110-31. McTaggart has been called 'an outstanding giant in the discussion of the reality or unreality of time' and his aforesaid article has been most discussed in recent philosophical literature on Time. Of articles in defence of McTaggart's position, mention may be made of Michael Dummett: 'A Defence of McTaggart's Proof of the Unreality of Time' in *Philosophical Review*, XIX (1960), 497-504. But he was criticised by C.D. Borad, the greatest expositor of his philosophy (cf. his commentary: *Examination of McTaggart's Philosophy*, Vol. I, 1933, and Vol. II in two parts, 1938), in *Scientific Thought*, to which Allama Iqbal has referred in the present discussion, as well as in his valuable article: 'Time' in *Encyclopaedia of Religion and Ethics*, XII, 339a; and earlier than Broad by Reyburn in his article 'Idealism and the Reality of Time' in *Mind* (Oct.1913), pp. 493-508 which has been briefly summarized by J. Alexander Gunn in *Problem of Time: A Historical and Critical Study*, pp. 345-47.

42. Cf. C.D. Broad, *Scientific Thought*, p. 79.

43. This is much like Broad's admitting at the conclusion of his examination of McTaggart's argument that time 'is the hardest knot in the whole of Philosophy', ibid., p. 84.

44. *The Confessions of St. Augustine*, xi, 17; cf. O. Spengler, *The Decline of the West*, I, 140, where Augustine's observation is quoted in connection with 'destiny'.

45. Reference is to the Quranic verse 23:80 quoted on p. 37 above.

46. Cf. M. Afdal Sarkhwush, Kalim«t al-Shu'ar«', p. 77, where this verse is given as under:

47. Cf. *Kit«b al-FiÄal*, II,158; also 1. Goldziher, *The Z«hirâs*, pp. 113 f.

48. Qur'«Än, 50:38.

49. Ibid., 2:255.

50. Goethe, *Alterswerke* (Hamburg edition), I, 367, quoted by Spengler, *op. cit.*, on fly-leaf with translation on p. 140. For locating this passage in Goethe's *Alterswerke*, I am greatly indebted to Professor Dr Annemarie Schimmel.

51. Reference here is to the Prophet's last words: '*al-sal«tu al-sal«tu wa m«malakat aim«nukum*' (meaning: be mindful of your prayers and be kind to persons subject to your authority) reported through three different chains of transmitters in AÄmad b. Àanbal's *Musnad*: VI, 290, 311 and 321.

The Conception of God and the Meaning of Prayer

by Dr. Muhammad Iqbal

We have seen that the judgement based upon religious experience fully satisfies the intellectual test. The more important regions of experience, examined with an eye on a synthetic view, reveal, as the ultimate ground of all experience, a rationally directed creative will which we have found reasons to describe as an ego. In order to emphasize the individuality of the Ultimate Ego the Qur'«n gives Him the proper name of Allah, and further defines Him as follows:

'Say: Allah is One:
All things depend on Him;
He begetteth not, and He is not begotten;
And there is none like unto Him' (112:1-4).

But it is hard to understand what exactly is an individual. As Bergson has taught us in his Creative Evolution, individuality is a matter of degrees and is not fully realized even in the case of the apparently closed off unity of the human being.[1] 'In particular, it may be said of individuality', says Bergson:

'that while the tendency to individuate is everywhere present in the organized world, it is everywhere opposed by the tendency towards reproduction. For the individuality to be perfect, it would be necessary that no detached part of the organism could live separately. But then reproduction would be impossible. For what is reproduction but the building up of a new organism with a detached fragment of the old? Individuality, therefore, harbours its own enemy at home.'[2]

In the light of this passage it is clear that the perfect individual, closed off as an ego, peerless and unique, cannot be conceived as harbouring its own enemy at home. It must be conceived as superior to the antagonistic tendency of reproduction. This characteristic of the perfect ego is one of the most essential elements in the Quranic conception of God; and the Qur'«n mentions it over and over again, not so much with a view to attack the current Christian conception as to accentuate its own view of a perfect individual.[3] It may, however, be said that the history of religious thought discloses various ways of escape from an individualistic conception of the Ultimate Reality which is conceived as some vague, vast, and pervasive cosmic element,[4] such as light. This is the view that Farnell has taken in his Gifford Lectures on the Attributes of God. I agree that the history of religion reveals modes of thought that tend towards pantheism; but I venture to think that in so far as the Quranic identification of God with light is concerned Farnell's view is incorrect. The full text of the verse of which he quotes a portion only is as follows:

'God is the light of the Heavens and of the earth. His light is like a niche in which is a lamp - the encased in a glass, - the glass, as it were, a star'[5] (24:35).

No doubt, the opening sentence of the verse gives the impression of an escape from an individualistic conception of God. But when we follow the metaphor of light in the rest of the verse, it gives just the opposite impression. The development of the metaphor is meant rather to exclude the suggestion of a formless cosmic element by centralizing the light in a flame which is further individualized by its encasement in a glass likened unto a well-defined star. Personally, I think the description of God as light, in the revealed literature of Judaism, Christianity, and Islam, must now be interpreted differently. The teaching of modern physics is that the velocity of light cannot be exceeded and is the same for all observers whatever their own system of movement. Thus, in the world of change, light is the nearest approach to the Absolute. The metaphor of light as applied to God, therefore, must, in view of modern knowledge, be taken to suggest the Absoluteness of God and not His Omnipresence which easily lends itself to a pantheistic interpretation.

There is, however, one question which will be raised in this connexion. Does not individuality imply finitude? If God is an ego and as such an individual, how can we conceive Him as infinite? The answer to this question is that God cannot be conceived as infinite in the sense of spatial infinity. In matters of spiritual valuation mere immensity counts for nothing. Moreover, as we have seen before, temporal and spatial infinities are not absolute. Modern science regards Nature not as something static, situated in an infinite void, but a structure of interrelated events out of whose mutual relations arise the concepts of space and time. And this is only another way of saying that space and time are interpretations which thought puts upon the creative activity of the Ultimate Ego. Space and time are possibilities of the Ego, only partially realized in the shape of our mathematical space and time. Beyond Him and apart from His creative activity, there is neither time nor space to close Him off in reference to other egos. The Ultimate Ego is, therefore, neither infinite in the sense of spatial infinity nor finite in the sense of the space-bound human ego whose body closes him off in reference to other egos. The infinity of the Ultimate Ego consists in the infinite inner possibilities of His creative activity of which the universe, as known to us, is only a partial expression. In one word God's infinity is intensive, not extensive.[6] It involves an infinite series, but is not that series.

The other important elements in the Quranic conception of God, from a purely intellectual point of view, are Creativeness, Knowledge, Omnipotence, and Eternity. I shall deal with them serially.

Finite minds regard nature as a confronting 'other' existing *per se*, which the mind knows but does not make. We are thus apt to regard the act of creation as a specific past event, and the universe appears to us as a manufactured article which has no organic relation to the life of its maker, and of which the maker is nothing more than a mere spectator. All the meaningless theological controversies about the idea of creation arise from this narrow vision of the finite mind.[7] Thus regarded the universe is a mere accident in the life of God and might not have been created. The real question which we are called upon to answer is this: Does the universe confront God as His 'other', with space intervening between Him and it? The answer is that, from the Divine point of view, there is no creation in the sense of a specific event having a 'before' and an 'after'. The universe cannot be regarded as an independent reality standing in opposition to Him. This view of the matter will reduce both God and the world to two separate entities confronting each other in the empty receptacle of an infinite space. We have seen before that space, time, and matter are interpretations which thought puts on the free creative energy of God.[8] They are not independent realities existing per se, but only intellectual modes of apprehending the life of God. The question of creation once arose among the disciples of the well-known saint B«Yazâd of Bist«m. One of the disciples very pointedly put the common-sense view saying: 'There was a moment of time when God existed and nothing else existed beside Him.' The saint's reply was equally pointed. 'It is just the same now', said he, 'as it was then.' The world of matter, therefore, is not a stuff co-eternal with God, operated upon by Him from a distance as it were. It is, in its real nature, one continuous act which thought breaks up into a plurality of mutually exclusive things. Professor Eddington has thrown further light on this important point, and I take the liberty to quote from his book, Space, Time and Gravitation:

'We have a world of point-events with their primary interval-relations. Out of these an unlimited number of more complicated relations and qualities can be built up mathematically, describing various features of the state of the world. These exist in nature in the same sense as an unlimited number of walks exist on an open moor. But the existence is, as it were, latent unless some one gives a significance to the walk by following it; and in the same way the existence of any one of these qualities of the world only acquires significance above its fellows if a mind singles it out for recognition. Mind filters out matter from the meaningless jumble of qualities, as the prism filters out the colours of the rainbow from the chaotic pulsations of white light. Mind exalts the permanent and ignores the transitory; and it appears from the mathematical study of relations that the only way in which mind can achieve her object is by picking out one particular quality as the permanent substance of the perceptual world, partitioning a perceptual time and space for it to be permanent in, and, as a necessary consequence of this Hobson's choice, the laws of gravitation and mechanics and geometry have to be obeyed. Is it too much to say that the mind's search for permanence has created the world of physics?'[9]

The last sentence in this passage is one of the deepest things in Professor Eddington's book. The physicist has yet to discover by his own methods that the passing show of the apparently permanent world of physics which the mind has created in its search for permanence is rooted in something more permanent, conceivable only as a self which alone combines the opposite attributes of change and permanence, and can thus be regarded as both constant and variable.

There is, however, one question which we must answer before we proceed further. In what manner does the creative activity of God proceed to the work of creation? The most orthodox and still popular school of Muslim theology, I mean the Ash'arite, hold that the creative method of Divine energy is atomic; and they appear to have based their doctrine on the following verse of the Qur'«n:

'And no one thing is here, but with Us are its store-houses; and We send it not down but in fixed quantities' (15:21).

The rise and growth of atomism in Islam - the first important indication of an intellectual revolt against the Aristotelian idea of a fixed universe - forms one of the most interesting chapters in the history of Muslim thought. The views of the school of BaÄrah were first shaped by AbëH«shim[10] (A.D. 933) and those of the school of Baghdad by that most exact and daring theological thinker, AbëBakr B«qil«nâ[11] (A.D.1013). Later in the beginning of the thirteenth century we find a thoroughly systematic description in a book called the Guide of the Perplexed by Moses Maimonides– a Jewish theologian who was educated in the Muslim universities of Spain.[12] A French translation of this book was made by Munk in 1866, and recently Professor Macdonald of America has given an excellent account of its contents in the *Isis* from which Dr. Zwemer has reprinted it in *The Moslem World* of January 1928.[13] Professor Macdonald, however, has made no attempt to discover the psychological forces that determined the growth of atomistic kal«m in Islam. He admits that there is nothing like the atomism of Islam in Greek thought, but, unwilling as he is to give any credit for original thought to Muslim thinkers,[14] and finding a surface resemblance between the Islamic theory and the views of a certain sect of Buddhism, he jumps to the conclusion that the origin of the theory is due to Buddhistic influences on the thought of Islam.[15] Unfortunately, a full discussion of the sources of this purely speculative theory is not possible in this lecture. I propose only to give you some of its more salient features, indicating at the same time the lines on which the work of reconstruction in the light of modern physics ought, in my opinion, to proceed.

According to the Ash'arite school of thinkers, then, the world is compounded of what they call *jaw«hir*– infinitely small parts or atoms which cannot be further divided. Since the creative activity of God is ceaseless the number of the atoms cannot be finite. Fresh atoms are coming into being every moment, and the universe is therefore constantly growing. As the Qur'«n says: 'God adds to His creation what He wills.'[16] The essence of the atom is independent of its existence. This means that existence is a quality imposed on the atom by God. Before receiving this quality the atom lies dormant, as it were, in the creative energy of God, and its existence means nothing more than Divine energy become visible. The atom in its essence, therefore, has no magnitude; it has its position which does not involve space. It is by their aggregation that atoms become extended and generate space.[17] Ibn Aazm, the critic of atomism, acutely remarks that the language of the Qur'«n makes no difference in the act of creation and the thing created. What we call a thing, then, is in its essential nature an aggregation of atomic acts. Of the concept of 'atomic act', however, it is difficult to form a mental picture. Modern physics too conceives as action the actual atom of a certain physical quantity. But, as Professor Eddington has pointed out, the precise formulation of the Theory of Quanta of action has not been possible so far; though it is vaguely believed that the atomicity of action is the general law and that the appearance of electrons is in some way dependent on it.[18]

Again we have seen that each atom occupies a position which does not involve space. That being so, what is the nature of motion which we cannot conceive except as the atom's passage through space? Since the Ashʻarite regarded space as generated by the aggregation of atoms, they could not explain movement as a body's passage through all the points of space intervening between the point of its start and destination. Such an explanation must necessarily assume the existence of void as an independent reality. In order, therefore, to get over the difficulty of empty space, Naïïᴀm resorted to the notion of *ñafrah* or jump; and imagined the moving body, not as passing through all the discrete positions in space, but as jumping over the void between one position and another. Thus, according to him, a quick motion and a slow motion possess the same speed; but the latter has more points of rest.[19] I confess I do not quite understand this solution of the difficulty. It may, however, be pointed out that modern atomism has found a similar difficulty and a similar solution has been suggested. In view of the experiments relating to Planck's Theory of Quanta, we cannot imagine the moving atom as continuously traversing its path in space. 'One of the most hopeful lines of explanation', says Professor Whitehead in his *Science and the Modern World*,

'is to assume that an electron does not continuously traverse its path in space. The alternative notion as to its mode of existence is that it appears at a series of discrete positions in space which it occupies for successive durations of time. It is as though an automobile, moving at the average rate of thirty miles an hour along a road, did not traverse the road continuously, but appeared successively at the successive milestones' remaining for two minutes at each milestone.'[20]

Another feature of this theory of creation is the doctrine of accident, on the perpetual creation of which depends the continuity of the atom as an existent. If God ceases to create the accidents, the atom ceases to exist as an atom.[21] The atom possesses inseparable positive or negative qualities. These exist in opposed couples, as life and death, motion and rest, and possess practically no duration. Two propositions follow from this: (i) Nothing has a stable nature. (ii) There is a single order of atoms, i.e. what we call the soul is either a finer kind of matter, or only an accident.

I am inclined to think that in view of the idea of continuous creation which the Ashʻarite intended to establish there is an element of truth in the first proposition. I have said before that in my opinion the spirit of the Qur'«n is on the whole anti-classical.[22] I regard the Ashʻarite thought on this point as a genuine effort to develop on the basis of an Ultimate Will or Energy a theory of creation which, with all its shortcomings, is far more true to the spirit of the Qur'«n than the Aristotelian idea of a fixed universe.[23] The duty of the future theologians of Islam is to reconstruct this purely speculative theory, and to bring it into closer contact with modern science which appears to be moving in the same direction.

The second proposition looks like pure materialism. It is my belief that the Ashʻarite view that the *Nafs* is an accident is opposed to the real trend of their own theory which makes the continuous existence of the atom dependent on the continuous creation of accidents in it. It is obvious that motion is inconceivable without time. And since time comes from psychic life, the latter is more fundamental than motion. No psychic life, no time: no time, no motion. Thus it is really what the Ashʻarites call the accident which is responsible for the continuity of the atom as such. The atom becomes or rather looks spatialized when it receives the quality of existence. Regarded as a phase of Divine energy, it is essentially spiritual. The *Nafs* is the pure act; the body is only the act become visible and hence measurable. In fact the Ashʻarite vaguely anticipated the modern notion of point-instant; but they failed rightly to see the nature of the mutual relation between the point and the instant. The instant is the more fundamental of the two; but the point is inseparable from the instant as being a necessary mode of its manifestation. The point is not a thing, it is only a sort of looking at the instant. Rūmī is far more true to the spirit of Islam than Ghazālā when he says:[24]

Reality is, therefore, essentially spirit. But, of course, there are degrees of spirit. In the history of Muslim thought the idea of degrees of Reality appears in the writings of Shihābuddīn Suhrawardī Maqtūl. In modern times we find it worked out on a much larger scale in Hegel and, more recently, in the late Lord Haldane's *Reign of Relativity*, which he published shortly before his death.[25] I have conceived the Ultimate Reality as an Ego; and I must add now that from the Ultimate Ego only egos proceed. The creative energy of the Ultimate Ego, in whom deed and thought are identical, functions as ego-unities. The world, in all its details, from the mechanical movement of what we call the atom of matter to the free movement of thought in the human ego, is the self-revelation of the 'Great I am'.[26] Every atom of Divine energy, however low in the scale of existence, is an ego. But there are degrees in the expression of egohood. Throughout the entire gamut of being runs the gradually rising note of egohood until it reaches its perfection in man. That is why the Qur'ān declares the Ultimate Ego to be nearer to man than his own neck-vein.[27] Like pearls do we live and move and have our being in the perpetual flow of Divine life.

Thus a criticism, inspired by the best traditions of Muslim thought, tends to turn the Ash'arite scheme of atomism into a spiritual pluralism, the details of which will have to be worked out by the future theologians of Islam. It may, however, be asked whether atomicity has a real seat in the creative energy of God, or presents itself to us as such only because of our finite mode of apprehension. From a purely scientific point of view I cannot say what the final answer to this question will be. From the psychological point of view one thing appears to me to be certain. Only that is, strictly speaking, real which is directly conscious of its own reality. The degree of reality varies with the degree of the feeling of egohood. The nature of the ego is such that, in spite of its capacity to respond to other egos, it is self-centred and possesses a private circuit of individuality excluding all egos other than itself.[28] In this alone consists its reality as an ego. Man, therefore, in whom egohood has reached its relative perfection, occupies a genuine place in the heart of Divine creative energy, and thus possesses a much higher degree of reality than things around him. Of all the creations of God he alone is capable of consciously participating in the creative life of his Maker.[29] Endowed with the power to imagine a better world, and to mould what is into what ought to be, the ego in him, aspires, in the interests of an increasingly unique and comprehensive individuality, to exploit all the various environments on which he may be called upon to operate during the course of an endless career. But I would ask you to wait for a fuller treatment of this point till my lecture on the Immortality and Freedom of the Ego. In the meantime, I want to say a few words about the doctrine of atomic time which I think is the weakest part of the Ash'arite theory of creation. It is necessary to do so for a reasonable view of the Divine attribute of Eternity.

The problem of time has always drawn the attention of Muslim thinkers and mystics. This seems to be due partly to the fact that, according to the Qur'ān, the alternation of day and night is one of the greatest signs of God, and partly to the Prophet's identification of God with *Dahr* (time) in a well-known tradition referred to before.[30] Indeed, some of the greatest Muslim Sufis believed in the mystic properties of the word *Dahr*. According to Muḥyuddīn Ibn al-'Arabī, *Dahr* is one of the beautiful names of God, and Rāzā tells us in his commentary on the Qur'ān that some of the Muslim saints had taught him to repeat the word

Dahr, Daihur, or *Daihar*. The Ash'arite theory of time is perhaps the first attempt in the history of Muslim thought to understand it philosophically. Time, according to the Ash'arite, is a succession of individual 'nows'. From this view it obviously follows that between every two individual 'nows' or moments of time, there is an unoccupied moment of time, that is to say, a void of time. The absurdity of this conclusion is due to the fact that they looked at the subject of their inquiry from a wholly objective point of view. They took no lesson from the history of Greek thought, which had adopted the same point of view and had reached no results. In our own time Newton described time as 'something which in itself and from its own nature flows equally.'[31] The metaphor of stream implied in this description suggests serious objections to Newton's equally objective view of time. We cannot understand how a thing is affected on its immersion in this stream, and how it differs from things that do not participate in its flow. Nor can we form any idea of the beginning, the end, and the boundaries of time if we try to understand it on the analogy of a stream. Moreover, if flow, movement, or 'passage' is the last word as to the nature of time, there must be another time to time the movement of the first time, and another which times the second time, and so on to infinity. Thus the notion of time as something wholly objective is beset with difficulties. It must, however, be admitted that the practical Arab mind could not regard time as something unreal like the Greeks. Nor can it be denied that, even though we possess no sense-organ to perceive time, it is a kind of flow and has, as such, a genuine objective, that is to say, atomic aspect. In fact, the verdict of modern science is exactly the same as that of the Ash'arite; for recent discoveries in physics regarding the nature of time assume the discontinuity of matter. The following passage from Professor Rougier's *Philosophy and New Physics* is noteworthy in this connexion:

'Contrary to the ancient adage, natura non facit saltus, it becomes apparent that the universe varies by sudden jumps and not by imperceptible degrees. A physical system is capable of only a finite number of distinct states . . . . Since between two different and immediately consecutive states the world remains motionless, time is suspended, so that time itself is discontinuous: there is an atom of time.'[32]

The point, however, is that the constructive endeavour of the Ash'arite, as of the moderns, was wholly lacking in psychological analysis, and the result of this shortcoming was that they altogether failed to perceive the subjective aspect of time. It is due to this failure that in their theory the systems of material atoms and time-atoms lie apart, with no organic relation between them. It is clear that if we look at time from a purely objective point of view serious difficulties arise; for we cannot apply atomic time to God and conceive Him as a life in the making, as Professor Alexander appears to have done in his Lectures on Space, Time, and Deity.[33] Later Muslim theologians fully realized these difficulties. Mull« Jal«luddân Daw«nâ in a passage of his *Zaur«'*, which reminds the modern student of Professor Royce's view of time, tells us that if we take time to be a kind of span which makes possible the appearance of events as a moving procession and conceive this span to be a unity, then we cannot but describe it as an original state of Divine activity, encompassing all the succeeding states of that activity. But the Mull« takes good care to add that a deeper insight into the nature of succession reveals its relativity, so that it disappears in the case of God to Whom all events are present in a single act of perception. The Sufi poet 'Ir«qâ[34] has a similar way of looking at the matter. He conceives infinite varieties of time, relative to the varying grades of being, intervening between materiality and pure spirituality. The time of gross bodies which arises from the revolution of the heavens is divisible into past, present, and future; and its nature is such that as long as one day does not pass away the succeeding day does not come. The time of immaterial beings is also serial in character, but its passage is such that a whole year in the time of gross bodies is not more than a day in the time of an immaterial being. Rising higher and higher in the scale of immaterial beings we reach Divine time - time which is absolutely free from the quality of passage, and consequently does not admit of divisibility, sequence, and change. It is above eternity; it has neither beginning nor end. The eye of God sees all the visibles, and His ear hears all the audibles in one indivisible act of perception. The priority of God is not due to the priority of time; on the other hand, the priority of time is due to God's priority.[35] Thus Divine time is what the Qur'«n describes as the 'Mother of Books'[36] in which the whole of history, freed from the net of causal sequence, is gathered up in a single supereternal 'now'. Of all the Muslim theologians, however, it is Fakhruddân R«zâ who appears to have given his most serious attention to the problem of time. In his "Eastern Discussions," R«zâ subjects to a searching examination all the contemporary theories of time. He too is, in the main, objective in his method and finds himself unable to reach any definite conclusions. 'Until now,' he says,

'I have not been able to discover anything really true with regard to the nature of time; and the main purpose of my book is to explain what can possibly be said for or against each theory without any spirit of partisanship, which I generally avoid, especially in connexion with the problem of time.'[37]

The above discussion makes it perfectly clear that a purely objective point of view is only partially helpful in our understanding of the nature of time. The right course is a careful psychological analysis of our conscious experience which alone reveals the true nature of time. I suppose you remember the distinction that I drew in the two aspects of the self, appreciative and efficient. The appreciative self lives in pure duration, i.e. change without succession. The life of the self consists in its movement from appreciation to efficiency, from intuition to intellect, and atomic time is born out of this movement. Thus the character of our conscious experience - our point of departure in all knowledge - gives us a clue to the concept which reconciles the opposition of permanence and change, of time regarded as an organic whole or eternity, and time regarded as atomic. If then we accept the guidance of our conscious experience, and conceive the life of the all-inclusive Ego on the analogy of the finite ego, the time of the Ultimate Ego is revealed as change without succession, i.e. an organic whole which appears atomic because of the creative movement of the ego. This is what Mâr D«m«d and Mull«B«qir mean when they say that time is born with the act of creation by which the Ultimate Ego realizes and measures, so to speak, the infinite wealth of His own undetermined creative possibilities. On the one hand, therefore, the ego lives in eternity, by which term I mean non-successional change; on the other, it lives in serial time, which I conceive as organically related to eternity in the sense that it is a measure of non-successional change. In this sense alone it is possible to understand the Quranic verse: 'To God belongs the alternation of day and night.'[38] But on this difficult side of the problem I have said enough in my preceding lecture. It is now time to pass on to the Divine attributes of Knowledge and Omnipotence.

The word 'knowledge', as applied to the finite ego, always means discursive knowledge - a temporal process which moves round a veritable 'other', supposed to exist *per se* and confronting the knowing ego. In this sense knowledge, even if we extend it to the point of omniscience, must always remain relative to its confronting 'other', and cannot, therefore, be predicated of the Ultimate Ego who, being all-inclusive, cannot be conceived as having a perspective like the finite ego. The universe, as we have seen before, is not an 'other' existing *per se* in opposition to God. It is only when we look at the act of creation as a specific event in the life-history of God that the universe appears as an independent 'other'. From the standpoint of the all-inclusive Ego there is no 'other'. In Him thought and deed, the act of knowing and the act of creating, are identical. It may be argued that the ego, whether finite or infinite, is inconceivable without a confronting non-ego, and if there is nothing outside the Ultimate Ego, the Ultimate Ego cannot be conceived as an ego. The answer to this argument is that logical negations are of no use in forming a positive concept which must be based on the character of Reality as revealed in experience. Our criticism of experience reveals the Ultimate Reality to be a rationally directed life which, in view of our experience of life, cannot be conceived except as an organic whole, a something closely knit together and possessing a central point of reference.[39] This being the character of life, the ultimate life can be conceived only as an ego. Knowledge, in the sense of discursive knowledge, however infinite, cannot, therefore, be predicated of an ego who knows, and, at the same time, forms the ground of the object known. Unfortunately, language does not help us here. We possess no word to express the kind of knowledge which is also creative of its object. The alternative concept of Divine knowledge is omniscience in the sense of a single indivisible act of perception which makes God immediately aware of the entire sweep of history, regarded as an order of specific events, in an eternal 'now'. This is how Jalāluddân Dawānâ, 'Irāqâ, and Professor Royce in our own times conceived God's knowledge.[40] There is an element of truth in this conception. But it suggests a closed universe, a fixed futurity, a predetermined, unalterable order of specific events which, like a superior fate, has once for all determined the directions of God's creative activity. In fact, Divine knowledge regarded as a kind of passive omniscience is nothing more than the inert void of pre-Einsteinian physics, which confers a semblance of unity on things by holding them together, a sort of mirror passively reflecting the details of an already finished structure of things which the finite consciousness reflects in fragments only. Divine knowledge must be conceived as a living creative activity to which the objects that appear to exist in their own right are organically related. By conceiving God's knowledge as a kind of reflecting mirror, we no doubt save His fore-knowledge of future events; but it is obvious that we do so at the expense of His freedom. The future certainly pre-exists in the organic whole of God's creative life, but it pre-exists as an open possibility, not as a fixed order of events with definite outlines. An illustration will perhaps help us in understanding what I mean. Suppose, as sometimes happens in the history of human thought, a fruitful idea with a great inner wealth of applications emerges into the light of your consciousness. You are immediately aware of the idea as a complex whole; but the intellectual working out of its numerous bearings is a matter of time. Intuitively all the possibilities of the idea are present in your mind. If a specific possibility, as such, is not intellectually known to you at a certain moment of time, it is not because your knowledge is defective, but because there is yet no possibility to become known. The idea reveals the possibilities of its application with advancing experience, and sometimes it takes more than one generation of thinkers before these possibilities are exhausted. Nor is it possible, on the view of Divine knowledge as a kind of passive omniscience, to reach the idea of a creator. If history is regarded merely as a gradually revealed photo of a predetermined order of events, then there is no room in it for novelty and initiation. Consequently, we can attach no meaning to the word 'creation', which has a meaning for us only in view of our own capacity for original action. The truth is that the whole theological controversy relating to predestination is due to pure speculation with no eye on the spontaneity of life, which is a fact of actual experience. No doubt, the emergence of egos endowed with the power of spontaneous and hence unforeseeable action is, in a sense, a limitation on the freedom of the all-inclusive Ego. But this limitation is not externally imposed. It is born out of His own creative freedom whereby He has chosen finite egos to be participators of His life, power, and freedom.

But how, it may be asked, is it possible to reconcile limitation with Omnipotence? The word 'limitation' need not frighten us. The Qur'«n has no liking for abstract universals. It always fixes its gaze on the concrete which the theory of Relativity has only recently taught modern philosophy to see. All activity, creational or otherwise, is a kind of limitation without which it is impossible to conceive God as a concrete operative Ego. Omnipotence, abstractly conceived, is merely a blind, capricious power without limits. The Qur'«n has a clear and definite conception of Nature as a cosmos of mutually related forces.[41] It, therefore, views Divine omnipotence as intimately related to Divine wisdom, and finds the infinite power of God revealed, not in the arbitrary and the capricious, but in the recurrent, the regular, and the orderly. At the same time, the Qur'«n conceives God as 'holding all goodness in His hands'.[42] If, then, the rationally directed Divine will is good, a very serious problem arises. The course of evolution, as revealed by modern science, involves almost universal suffering and wrongdoing. No doubt, wrongdoing is confined to man only. But the fact of pain is almost universal, thought it is equally true that men can suffer and have suffered the most excruciating pain for the sake of what they have believed to be good. Thus the two facts of moral and physical evil stand out prominent in the life of Nature. Nor can the relativity of evil and the presence of forces that tend to transmute it be a source of consolation to us; for, in spite of all this relativity and transmutation, there is something terribly positive about it. How is it, then, possible to reconcile the goodness and omnipotence of God with the immense volume of evil in His creation? This painful problem is really the crux of Theism. No modern writer has put it more accurately than Naumann in his *Briefe Ü ber Religion* 'We possess', he says:

'a knowledge of the world which teaches us a God of power and strength, who sends out life and death as simultaneously as shadow and light, and a revelation, a faith as to salvation which declares the same God to be father. The following of the world-God produces the morality of the struggle for existence, and the service of the Father of Jesus Christ produces the morality of compassion. And yet they are not two gods, but one God. Somehow or other, their arms intertwine. Only no mortal can say where and how this occurs.'[43]

To the optimist Browning all is well with the world;[44] to the pessimist Schopenhauer the world is one perpetual winter wherein a blind will expresses itself in an infinite variety of living things which bemoan their emergence for a moment and then disappear for ever.[45] The issue thus raised between optimism and pessimism cannot be finally decided at the present stage of our knowledge of the universe. Our intellectual constitution is such that we can take only a piecemeal view of things. We cannot understand the full import of the great cosmic forces which work havoc, and at the same time sustain and amplify life. The teaching of the Qur'«n, which believes in the possibility of improvement in the behaviour of man and his control over natural forces, is neither optimism nor pessimism. It is meliorism, which recognizes a growing universe and is animated by the hope of man's eventual victory over evil.

But the clue to a better understanding of our difficulty is given in the legend relating to what is called the Fall of Man. In this legend the Qur'«n partly retains the ancient symbols, but the legend is materially transformed with a view to put an entirely fresh meaning into it. The Quranic method of complete or partial transformation of legends in order to besoul them with new ideas, and thus to adapt them to the advancing spirit of time, is an important point which has nearly always been overlooked both by Muslim and non-Muslim students of Islam. The object of the Qur'«n in dealing with these legends is seldom historical; it nearly always aims at giving them a universal moral or philosophical import. And it achieves this object by omitting the names of persons and localities which tend to limit the meaning of a legend by giving it the colour of a specific historical event, and also by deleting details which appear to belong to a different order of feeling. This is not an uncommon method of dealing with legends. It is common in non-religious literature. An instance in point is the legend of *Faust*,[46] to which the touch of Goethe's genius has given a wholly new meaning.

Turning to the legend of the Fall we find it in a variety of forms in the literatures of the ancient world. It is, indeed, impossible to demarcate the stages of its growth, and to set out clearly the various human motives which must have worked in its slow transformation. But confining ourselves to the Semitic form of the myth, it is highly probable that it arose out of the primitive man's desire to explain to himself the infinite misery of his plight in an uncongenial environment, which abounded in disease and death and obstructed him on all sides in his endeavour to maintain himself. Having no control over the forces of Nature, a pessimistic view of life was perfectly natural to him. Thus, in an old Babylonian inscription, we find the serpent (phallic symbol), the tree, and the woman offering an apple (symbol of virginity) to the man. The meaning of the myth is clear - the fall of man from a supposed state of bliss was due to the original sexual act of the human pair. The way in which the Qur'«n handles this legend becomes clear when we compare it with the narration of the Book of Genesis.[47] The remarkable points of difference between the Quranic and the Biblical narrations suggest unmistakably the purpose of the Quranic narration.

1. The Qur'«n omits the serpent and the rib-story altogether. The former omission is obviously meant to free the story from its phallic setting and its original suggestion of a pessimistic view of life. The latter omission is meant to suggest that the purpose of the Quranic narration is not historical, as in the case of the Old Testament, which gives us an account of the origin of the first human pair by way of a prelude to the history of Israel. Indeed, in the verses which deal with the origin of man as a living being, the Qur'«n uses the words *Bashar* or *Ins«n*, not ÿdam, which it reserves for man in his capacity of God's vicegerent on earth.[48] The purpose of the Qur'«n is further secured by the omission of proper names mentioned in the Biblical narration - Adam and Eve.[49] The word Adam is retained and used more as a concept than as the name of a concrete human individual. This use of the word is not without authority in the Qur'«n itself. The following verse is clear on the point:

'We created you; then fashioned you; then said We to the angels, "prostrate yourself unto Adam" (7:11).

2. The Qur'«n splits up the legend into two distinct episodes– the one relating to what it describes simply as 'the tree'[50] and the other relating to the 'tree of eternity' and the 'kingdom that faileth not'.[51] The first episode is mentioned in the 7th and the second in the 20th Sërah of the Qur'«n. According to the Qur'«n, Adam and his wife, led astray by Satan whose function is to create doubts in the minds of men, tasted the fruit of both the trees, whereas according to the Old Testament man was driven out of the Garden of Eden immediately after his first act of disobedience, and God placed, at the eastern side of the garden, angels and a flaming sword, turning on all sides, to keep the way to the tree of life.[52]

3. The Old Testament curses the earth for Adam's act of disobedience;[53] the Qur'«n declares the earth to be the 'dwelling place' of man and a 'source of profit' to him[54] for the possession of which he ought to be grateful to God. 'And We have established you on the earth and given you therein the supports of life. How little do ye give thanks!' (7:10).[55] Nor is there any reason to suppose that the word *Jannat* (Garden) as used here means the supersensual

paradise from which man is supposed to have fallen on this earth. According to the Qur'«n, man is not a stranger on this earth. 'And We have caused you to grow from the earth', says the Qur'«n.[56] The *Jannat*, mentioned in the legend, cannot mean the eternal abode of the righteous. In the sense of the eternal abode of the righteous, *Jannat* is described by the Qur'«n to be the place 'wherein the righteous will pass to one another the cup which shall engender no light discourse, no motive to sin'.[57] It is further described to be the place 'wherein no weariness shall reach the righteous, nor forth from it shall they be cast'.[58] In the *Jannat* mentioned in the legend, however, the very first event that took place was man's sin of disobedience followed by his expulsion. In fact, the Qur'«n itself explains the meaning of the word as used in its own narration. In the second episode of the legend the garden is described as a place 'where there is neither hunger, nor thirst, neither heat nor nakedness'.[59] I am, therefore, inclined to think that the *Jannat* in the Quranic narration is the conception of a primitive state in which man is practically unrelated to his environment and consequently does not feel the sting of human wants the birth of which alone marks the beginning of human culture.

Thus we see that the Quranic legend of the Fall has nothing to do with the first appearance of man on this planet. Its purpose is rather to indicate man's rise from a primitive state of instinctive appetite to the conscious possession of a free self, capable of doubt and disobedience. The Fall does not mean any moral depravity; it is man's transition from simple consciousness to the first flash of self-consciousness, a kind of waking from the dream of nature with a throb of personal causality in one's own being. Nor does the Qur'«n regard the earth as a torture-hall where an elementally wicked humanity is imprisoned for an original act of sin. Man's first act of disobedience was also his first act of free choice; and that is why, according to the Quranic narration, Adam's first transgression was forgiven.[60] Now goodness is not a matter of compulsion; it is the self's free surrender to the moral ideal and arises out of a willing co-operation of free egos. A being whose movements are wholly determined like a machine cannot produce goodness. Freedom is thus a condition of goodness. But to permit the emergence of a finite ego who has the power to choose, after considering the relative values of several courses of action open to him, is really to take a great risk; for the freedom to choose good involves also the freedom to choose what is the opposite of good. That God has taken this risk shows His immense faith in man; it is for man now to justify this faith. Perhaps such a risk alone makes it possible to test and develop the potentialities of a being who was created of the 'goodliest fabric' and then 'brought down to be the lowest of the low'.[61] As the Qur'«n says: 'And for trial will We test you with evil and with good' (21:35).[62] Good and evil, therefore, though opposites, must fall within the same whole. There is no such thing as an isolated fact; for facts are systematic wholes the elements of which must be understood by mutual reference. Logical judgement separates the elements of a fact only to reveal their interdependence.

Further, it is the nature of the self to maintain itself as a self. For this purpose it seeks knowledge, self-multiplication, and power, or, in the words of the Qur'«n, 'the kingdom that never faileth'. The first episode in the Quranic legend relates to man's desire for knowledge, the second to his desire for self-multiplication and power. In connexion with the first episode it is necessary to point out two things. Firstly, the episode is mentioned immediately after the verses describing Adam's superiority over the angels in remembering and reproducing the names of things.[63] The purpose of these verses, as I have shown before, is to bring out the conceptual character of human knowledge.[64] Secondly, Madame Blavatsky[65] who possessed a remarkable knowledge of ancient symbolism, tells us in her book, called *Secret Doctrine*, that with the ancients the tree was a cryptic symbol for occult knowledge. Adam was forbidden to taste the fruit of this tree obviously because his finitude as a self, his sense-equipment, and his intellectual faculties were, on the whole, attuned to a different type of knowledge, i.e. the type of knowledge which necessitates the toil of patient observation and admits only of slow accumulation. Satan, however, persuaded him to eat the forbidden fruit of occult knowledge and Adam yielded, not because he was elementally wicked, but because being 'hasty' ('ajĕl)[66] by nature he sought a short cut to knowledge. The only way to correct this tendency was to place him in an environment which, however painful, was better suited to the unfolding of his intellectual faculties. Thus Adam's insertion into a painful physical environment was not meant as a punishment; it was meant rather to defeat the object of Satan who, as an enemy of man, diplomatically tried to keep him ignorant of the joy of perpetual growth and expansion. But the life of a finite ego in an obstructing environment depends on the perpetual expansion of knowledge based on actual experience. And the experience of a finite ego to whom several possibilities are open expands only by method of trial and error. Therefore, error which may be described as a kind of intellectual evil is an indispensable factor in the building up of experience.

The second episode of the Quranic legend is as follows:

'But Satan whispered him (Adam): said he, O Adam! shall I show thee the tree of Eternity and the Kingdom that faileth not? And they both ate thereof, and their nakedness appeared to them, and they began to sew of the leaves of the garden to cover them, and Adam disobeyed his Lord, and went astray. Afterwards his Lord chose him for Himself, and was turned towards him, and guided him.' (20:120-22).

The central idea here is to suggest life's irresistible desire for a lasting dominion, an infinite career as a concrete individual. As a temporal being, fearing the termination of its career by death, the only course open to it is to achieve a kind of collective immortality by self-multiplication. The eating of the forbidden fruit of the tree of eternity is life's resort to sex-differentiation by which it multiplies itself with a view to circumvent total extinction. It is as if life says to death: 'If you sweep away one generation of living things, I will produce another'. The Qur'«n rejects the phallic symbolism of ancient art, but suggests the original sexual act by the birth of the sense of shame disclosed in Adam's anxiety to cover the nakedness of his body. Now to live is to possess a definite outline, a concrete individuality. It is in the concrete individuality, manifested in the countless varieties of living forms that the Ultimate Ego reveals the infinite wealth of His Being. Yet the emergence and multiplication of individualities, each fixing its gaze on the revelation of its own possibilities and seeking its own dominion, inevitably brings in its wake the awful struggle of ages. 'Descend ye as enemies of one another', says the Qur'«n.[67] This mutual conflict of opposing individualities is the world-pain which both illuminates and darkens the temporal career of life. In the case of man in whom individuality deepens into personality, opening up possibilities of wrongdoing, the sense of the tragedy of life becomes much more acute. But the acceptance of selfhood as a form of life involves the acceptance of all the imperfections that flow from the finitude of selfhood. The Qur'«n represents man as having accepted at his peril the trust of personality which the heavens, the earth, and the mountains refused to bear:

'Verily We proposed to the heavens and to the earth and to the mountains to receive the "trust" but they refused the burden and they feared to receive it. Man undertook to bear it, but hath proved unjust, senseless!' (33:72).

Shall we, then, say no or yes to the trust of personality with all its attendant ills? True manhood, according to the Qur'«n, consists in 'patience under ills and hardships'.[68] At the present stage of the evolution of selfhood, however, we cannot understand the full import of the discipline which the driving power of pain brings. Perhaps it hardens the self against a possible dissolution. But in asking the above question we are passing the boundaries of pure thought. This is the point where faith in the eventual triumph of goodness emerges as a religious doctrine. 'God is equal to His purpose, but most men know it not' (12:21).

I have now explained to you how it is possible philosophically to justify the Islamic conception of God. But as I have said before, religious ambition soars higher than the ambition of philosophy.[69] Religion is not satisfied with mere conception; it seeks a more intimate knowledge of and association with the object of its pursuit. The agency through which this association is achieved is the act of worship or prayer ending in spiritual illumination. The act of worship, however, affects different varieties of consciousness differently. In the case of the prophetic consciousness it is in the main creative, i.e. it tends to create a fresh ethical world wherein the Prophet, so to speak, applies the pragmatic test to his revelations. I shall further develop this point in my lecture on the meaning of Muslim Culture.[70] In the case of the mystic consciousness it is in the main cognitive. It is from this cognitive point of view that I will try to discover the meaning of prayer. And this point of view is perfectly justifiable in view of the ultimate motive of prayer. I would draw your attention to the following passage from the great American psychologist, Professor William James:

'It seems to probable that in spite of all that "science" may do to the contrary, men will continue to pray to the end of time, unless their mental nature changes in a manner which nothing we know should lead us to expect. The impulse to pray is a necessary consequence of the fact that whilst the innermost of the empirical selves of a man is a Self of the social sort, it yet can find its only adequate Socius [its "great companion"] in an ideal world.

'. . . most men, either continually or occasionally, carry a reference to it in their breast. The humblest outcast on this earth can feel himself to be real and valid by means of this higher recognition. And, on the other hand, for most of us, a world with no such inner refuge when the outer social self failed and dropped from us would be the abyss of horror. I say "for most of us", because it is probable that individuals differ a good deal in the degree in which they are haunted by this sense of an ideal spectator. It is a much more essential part of the consciousness of some men than of others. Those who have the most of it are possibly the most religious men. But I am sure that even those who say they are altogether without it deceive themselves, and really have it in some degree.'[71]

Thus you will see that, psychologically speaking, prayer is instinctive in its origin. The act of prayer as aiming at knowledge resembles reflection. Yet prayer at its highest is much more than abstract reflection. Like reflection it too is a process of assimilation, but the assimilative process in the case of prayer draws itself closely together and thereby acquires a power unknown to pure thought. In thought the mind observes and follows the working of Reality; in the act of prayer it gives up its career as a seeker of slow-footed universality and rises higher than thought to capture Reality itself with a view to become a conscious participator in its life. There is nothing mystical about it. Prayer as a means of spiritual illumination is a normal vital act by which the little island of our personality suddenly discovers its situation in a larger whole of life. Do not think I am talking of auto-suggestion. Auto-suggestion has nothing to do with the opening up of the sources of life that lie in the depths of the human ego. Unlike spiritual illumination which brings fresh power by shaping human personality, it leaves no permanent life-effects behind. Nor am I speaking of some occult and special way of knowledge. All that I mean is to fix your attention on a real human experience which has a history behind it and a future before it. Mysticism has, no doubt, revealed fresh regions of the self by making a special study of this experience. Its literature is illuminating; yet its set phraseology shaped by the thought-forms of a worn-out metaphysics has rather a deadening effect on the modern mind. The quest after a nameless nothing, as disclosed in Neo-Platonic mysticism - be it Christian or Muslim - cannot satisfy the modern mind which, with its habits of concrete thinking, demands a concrete living experience of God. And the history of the race shows that the attitude of the mind embodied in the act of worship is a condition for such an experience. In fact, prayer must be regarded as a necessary complement to the intellectual activity of the observer of Nature. The scientific observation of Nature keeps us in close contact with the behaviour of Reality, and thus sharpens our inner perception for a deeper vision of it. I cannot help quoting here a beautiful passage from the mystic poet Rĕmâ in which he describes the mystic quest after Reality:[72]

The Sĕfi's book is not composed of ink and letters: it is not but a heart white as snow.
The scholar's possession is pen-marks. What is the Sĕfi's possession? - foot-marks.
The Sĕfi stalks the game like a hunter: he sees the musk-deer's track and follows the footprints.
For some while the track of the deer is the proper clue for him, but afterwards it is the musk-gland of the deer that is his guide.
To go one stage guided by the scent of the musk-gland is better than a hundred stages of following the track and roaming about.[73]

The truth is that all search for knowledge is essentially a form of prayer. The scientific observer of Nature is a kind of mystic seeker in the act of prayer. Although at present he follows only the footprints of the musk-deer, and thus modestly limits the method of his quest, his thirst for knowledge is eventually sure to lead him to the point where the scent of the musk-gland is a better guide than the footprints of the deer. This alone will add to his power over Nature and give him that vision of the total-infinite which philosophy seeks but cannot find. Vision without power does bring moral elevation but cannot give a lasting culture. Power without vision tends to become destructive and inhuman. Both must combine for the spiritual expansion of humanity.

The real object of prayer, however, is better achieved when the act of prayer becomes congregational. The spirit of all true prayer is social. Even the hermit abandons the society of men in the hope of finding, in a solitary abode, the fellowship of God. A congregation is an association of men who, animated by the same aspiration, concentrate themselves on a single object and open up their inner selves to the working of a single impulse. It is a psychological truth that association multiplies the normal man's power of perception, deepens his emotion, and dynamizes his will to a degree unknown to him in the privacy of his individuality. Indeed, regarded as a psychological phenomenon, prayer is still a mystery; for psychology has not yet discovered the laws relating to the enhancement of human sensibility in a state of association. With Islam, however, this socialization of spiritual illumination through associative prayer is a special point of interest. As we pass from the daily congregational prayer to the annual ceremony round the central mosque of Mecca, you can easily see how the Islamic institution of worship gradually enlarges the sphere of human association.

Prayer, then, whether individual or associative, is an expression of man's inner yearning for a response in the awful silence of the universe. It is a unique process of discovery whereby the searching ego affirms itself in the very moment of self-negation, and thus discovers its own worth and justification as a dynamic factor in the life of the universe. True to the psychology of mental attitude in prayer, the form of worship in Islam symbolizes both affirmation and negation. Yet, in view of the fact borne out by the experience of the race that prayer, as an inner act, has found expression in a variety of forms, the Qur'«n says:

'To every people have We appointed ways of worship which they observe. Therefore let them not dispute this matter with thee, but bid them to thy Lord for thou art on the right way: but if they debate with thee, then say: God best knoweth what ye do! He will judge between

you on the Day of Resurrection, as to the matters wherein ye differ' (22:67-69).

The form of prayer ought not to become a matter of dispute.[74] Which side you turn your face is certainly not essential to the spirit of prayer. The Qur'«n is perfectly clear on this point:

'The East and West is God's: therefore whichever way ye turn, there is the face of God' (2:115).

'There is no piety in turning your faces towards the East or the West, but he is pious who believeth in God, and the Last Day, and the angels, and the scriptures, and the prophets; who for the love of God disburseth his wealth to his kindred, and to the orphans, and the needy, and the wayfarer, and those who ask, and for ransoming; who observeth prayer, and payeth the legal alms, and who is of those who are faithful to their engagements when they have engaged in them; and patient under ills and hardships, in time of trouble: those are they who are just, and those are they who fear the Lord' (2:177).

Yet we cannot ignore the important consideration that the posture of the body is a real factor in determining the attitude of the mind. The choice of one particular direction in Islamic worship is meant to secure the unity of feeling in the congregation, and its form in general creates and fosters the sense of social equality inasmuch as it tends to destroy the feeling of rank or race superiority in the worshippers. What a tremendous spiritual revolution will take place, practically in no time, if the proud aristocratic Brahmin of South India is daily made to stand shoulder to shoulder with the untouchable! From the unity of the all-inclusive Ego who creates and sustains all egos follows the essential unity of all mankind.[75] The division of mankind into races, nations, and tribes, according to the Qur'«n, is for purposes of identification only.[76] The Islamic form of association in prayer, therefore, besides its cognitive value, is further indicative of the aspiration to realize this essential unity of mankind as a fact in life by demolishing all barriers which stand between man and man.

Lecture III Notes: THE CONCEPTION OF GOD AND THE MEANING OF PRAYER

1. Cf. *Creative Evolution*, p. 13; also pp. 45-46.

2. *Ibid.*, p. 14.

3. See Qur'«n, for example, 2:163, 4:171, 5:73, 6:19, 13:16, 14:48, 21:108, 39:4 and 40:16 on the Unity of Allah and 4:171, 6:101, 10:68, 17:111, 19:88-92 emphatically denying the Christian doctrine of His sonship.

4. Cf. L.R. *Farnell, The Attributes of God*, p. 56.

5. The full translation here is 'a glistening star', required by the nass of the Qur'«n, '*Kaukab-un îurrây-ën*'.

6. On this fine distinction of God's infinity being intensive and not extensive, see further Lecture IV, p. 94.

7. For the long-drawn controversy on the issue of the creation of the universe, see, for instance, Ghazz«lâ, Tah«fut al-Fal«sifah, English translation by S.A. Kam«lâ: *Incoherence of the Philosophers*, pp. 13-53, and Ibn Rushd, *Tah«fut al-Tah«fut, English translation* by Simon van den Bergh: *The Incoherence of the Incoherence*, pp. 1-69; cf. also G.F. Hourani, 'Alghaz«lâ and the Philosophers on the Origin of the World', *The Muslim World*, XLVII/2(1958), 183-91, 308-14 and M. Saeed Sheikh, 'Al-Ghaz«lâ: Metaphysics', *A History of Muslim Philosophy* ed. M.M. Sharif, I, 598-608.

8. Cf. *Lecture* II, 28, 49.

9. A.S. Eddington, *Space, Time and Gravitation*, pp. 197-98 (italics by Allama Iqbal).

10. For AbuHashim's theory of atomism cf. T.J. de Boer, 'Atomic Theory (Muhammadan)', *Encyclopaedia of Religion and Ethics*, II, 202-03. De Boer's account is based on Abë Rashâd Sa'âd's *Kit«b al-Mas« 'il Fi'l-Khil«f*, ed. and trans. into German by Arthur Biram (Leyden,1902).

11. Cf. Ibn Khaldën, *Muqaddimah*, English translation by F. Rosenthal, III, 50-51, where B«qill«nâ is said to have introduced the conceptions of atom(al-jawhar al-fard), vacuum and accidents into the Ash'artie Kal«m. R. J. McCarthy, who has edited and also translated some of B«qill«nâ's texts, however, considers this to be unwarranted; see his article 'al-B«kâll«nâ's' in the *Encyclopaedia of Islam* (New edition), I, 958-59. From the account of Muslim atomism given in al-Ash'arâ's *Maq«l«t al-Isl«miyân*, this much has, however, to be conceded that atomism was keenly discussed by the Muslim scholastic theologians long before B«qill«nâ.

12. For the life and works of Maimonides and his relationship with Muslim philosophy, cf. S. Pines, *The Guide of the Perpelexed* (New English translation, Chicago University Press, 1963), 'Introduction' by the translator and an 'Introductory Essay' by L. Strauss; cf. also Sarton, *Introduction to the History of Science*, II, 369-70 and 376-77.

13. D.B. Macdonald, 'Continuous Re-creation and Atomic Time in Moslem Scholastic Theology', *The Moslem World*, XVII/i (1928), 6-28; reprinted from *Isis*, IX (1927), 326-44. This article is focussed on Maimonides' well-known 'Twelve Propositions of the Katam'.

14. Macdonald, 'Continuous Re-creation and Atomic Time . . .' in *op. cit.*, p.'24.

15. *Ibid.*, pp. 25-28. See also *The Religious Attitude and Life in Islam*, p. 320, where Macdonald traces the pantheistic developments in later sufi schools to Buddhistic and Vedantic influences.

16. Qur'«n, 35:1.

17. Cf. de Boer, 'Atomic Theory (Muhammadan)', in op. cit., II, 203.

18. Cf. Eddington, *op. cit.*, p. 200.

19. For an account of Naïï«m's notion of *al-tafrah* or jump, see Ash'arâ, *Maq«l«t al-Isl«miyân*, II, 18; Ibn Àazm, *Kit«b al-FiÃal*, V, 64-65, and Shahrast«nâ, *Kit«b al-Milal wa'l-NiÃal*, pp. 38-39; cf. also Isr«'ânâ, *Al-Tabsâr*, p. 68, Majid Fakhry, *Islamic Occasionalism*, p. 39, and H.A. Wolfson: *The Philosophy of the Kal«m*, pp. 514-17.

20. A.N. Whitehead, *Science and the Modern World*, p. 49.

21. A view, among others held by B«qill«nâ who bases it on the Quranic verses 8:67 and 46:24 which speak of the transient nature of the things of this world. Cf. Kit«b al-Tamhâd, p. 18.

22. Lecture I, p. 3; see also Lecture V, p. 102, note 21.

23. For Ash'arites' theory of the perpetual re-creation of the universe basing it on the Absolute Power and Will of God, cf. Majid Fakhry, *Islamic Occasionalism*, pp. 15, 117 ff. and M. Saeed Sheikh, 'Al-Ghaz«lâ; Metaphysics', in *op. cit.*, I, 603-08.

24. In R.A. Nicholson's edition of the *Mathnawâ* this verse (i.1812) reads as under:

Wine became intoxicated with us, not we with it;

The body came into being from us, not we from it.

25. Viscount Richard Burdon Haldane, the elder brother of John Scott Haldane, from whose Symposium Paper Allama Iqbal has quoted at length in Lecture II, p. 35, was a leading neo-Hegelian British philosopher and a distinguished statesman who died on 19 August 1928. Allama's using the expression 'the late Lord Haldane' is indicative of the possible time of his writing the present Lecture which together with the first two Lectures was delivered in Madras (5-8 Jan. 1929). The 'idea of degrees of reality and knowledge', is very vigorously expounded by Haldane in *The Reign of Relativity* (1921) as also in his earlier two-volume Gifford Lectures: *The Pathway to Reality* (1903-04) in which he also expounded the Principle of Relativity on purely philosophical grounds even before the publication of Einstein's theory; cf. Rudolf Metz, *A Hundred Years of British Philosophy*, p. 315.

26. This is a reference to the Qur'an, 20:14.

27. *Ibid.*, 50:16.

28. For further elucidation of the privacy of the ego, see Lecture IV, pp. 79-80.

29. Cf. p. 64 where Iqbal says that God 'out of His own creative freedom . . . . has chosen finite egos to be participators of His life, power, and freedom'.

30. The tradition: 'Do not vilify time, for time is God' referred to in Lecture I, p. 8.

31. Cf. *The Mathematical Principles of Natural Philosophy*, Vol. I, Definition viii, Scholium i.

32. Cf. Louis Rougier, *Philosophy and the New Physics* (An Essay on the Relativity Theory and the Theory of Quanta), p. 143. The work belongs to the earlier phase of Rougier's philosophical output, a phase in which he was seized by the new discoveries of physicists and mathematicians such as Henry Poincare (celestial mechanics and new geometry), Max Planck (quantium theory) Nicolas L. Carnot (thermodynamics), Madame Curie (radium and its compounds) and Einstein (principle of relativity). This was followed by his critical study of theories of knowledge: rationalism and scholasticism, ending in his thesis of the diversity of 'metaphysical temperaments' and the 'infinite plasticity' of the human mind whereby it takes delight in 'quite varied forms of intelligibility'. To the final phase of Rougier's philosophical productivity belongs *La Metaphysique et le langage* (1960) in which he elaborated the conception of plurality of language in philosophical discourse. Rougier also wrote on history of ideas (scientific, philosophical, religious) and on contemporary political and economical problems - his *Les Mystiques politiques et leurs incidences internationales* (1935) and *Les Mystiques économiques* (1949) are noteworthy.

It is to be noted that both the name 'Louis Rougier' and the title of his book *Philosophy and the New Physics* cited in the passage quoted by Allama Iqbal are given puzzlingly incorrectly in the previous editions of *Reconstruction* including the one by Oxford University Press (London, 1934); and these were not noticed even by Madame Eva Meyerovitch in her French translation: *Reconstruire la pensee religieuse de l'Islam* (Paris, 1955, p. 83). It would have been well-nigh impossible for me to find out the author's name and title of the book correctly had I not received the very kindly help of the Dutch scholar the Reverend Dr. Jan Slomp and Mlle Mauricette Levasseur of Bibliothé que Nationale, Paris, who also supplied me with many useful particulars about the life and works of Rougier. The last thing that I heard was that this French philosopher who taught in various universities including the ones in Cairo and New York and who participated in various Congresses and was the President of the Paris International Congress of Scientific Philosophy in 1935, passed away on 14 October 1982 at the age of ninety-three.

33. Cf. Space, *Time and Deity*, II, 396-98; also Allama Iqbal's letter dated 24 January 1921 addressed to R.A. Nicholson (*Letters of Iqbal*, ed. B.A. Dar, pp. 141-42) where, while disagreeing with Alexander's view of God, he observes: 'I believe there is a Divine tendency in the universe, but this tendency will eventually find its complete expression in a higher man, not in a God subject to Time, as Alexander implies in his discussion of the subject.'

34. The Sufi poet named here as well as in Lectures V and VII as (Fakhr al-Dân) 'Ir«qâ, we are told, is really 'Ain al-Quî«t Abu'l-Mu'«lâ 'Abdullah b. Muhammad b. 'Alâ b. al-Àasan b. 'Alâ al-Miy«njâ al-Hamad«nâ whose tractate on space and time: *Gh«yat al-Imk«n fi Dir«yat al-Mak«n* (54 pp.) has been edited by Rahim Farmanish (Tehran, 1338 S/1959); cf. English translation of the tractate by A.H. Kamali, section captioned: 'Observations', pp. i-v; also B.A. Dar, 'Iqbal aur Mas'alah-i Zam«n-o-Mak«n' in *Fikr-i Iqbal ke Munawwar Goshay*, ed. Salim Akhtar, pp. 149-51. Nadhr S«birâ, however, strongly pleads that the real author of the tractate was Shaikh T«j al-Dân Mahmëd b. Khud«-d«d Ashnawâ, as also hinted by Allama Iqbal in his Presidential Address delivered at the Fifth Indian Oriental Conference (1928) (Speeches, Writings and Statements of Iqbal,'p. 137). Cf. Shaikh Mahmëd Ashnawâ's tractate: *Gh«yat al Imk«n fi Ma'rifat al-Zam«n wa'l-Mak«n* (42 pp.) edited by Nadhr S«birâ, 'Introduction' embodying the editor's research about the MSS of the tractate and the available data of its author; also H«jâKhalâfah, *Kashf al-Zunën*, II, 1190, and A. Monzavi, *A Catalogue of Persian Manuscripts*, vol. II, Part I, MSS 7556-72.

Cf. also Maul«n«Imti«z 'AlâKh«n 'Arshâ, 'Zam«n-o-Mak«n kâ Bahth ke Muta'allaq 'All«mah Iqb«l k« aik Ma'«khidh: 'Ir«qâya Ashnawâ', *Maq«l«t: Iqb«l 'ÿlamâ K«ngras* (Iqbal Centenary Papers Presented at the International Congress on Allama Mohammad Iqbal: 2-8 December 1977), IV, 1-10 wherein Maul«n«' Arshâ traces a new MS of the tractate in the Raza Library, Rampur, and suggests the possibility of its being the one used by Allama Iqbal in these Lectures as well as in his Address: 'A Plea for Deeper Study of Muslim Scientists'.

It may be added that there remains now no doubt as to the particular MS of this unique Sufi tractate on 'Space and Time' used by Allama Iqbal, for fortunately it is well preserved in the Allama Iqbal Museum, Lahore (inaugurated by the President of Pakistan on 26 September 1984). The MS, according to a note in Allama's own hand dated 21 October 1935, was transcribed for him by the celebrated religious scholar Sayyid Anwar Sh«h K«shmârâ Cf. Dr Ahmad Nabi Khan, *Relics of Allama Iqbal* (Catalogue), p. 12.

For purposes of present annotation we have referred to Rahi`m Farmanish's edition of Hamad«nâ's *Gh«yat al-Imk«n fi Dir«yat al-Mak«n* (Tehran, 1338/1959) and to A.H. Kamali's English translation of it (Karachi, 1971) where needed. This translation, however, is to be used with caution.

35. Cf. 'Ain al-Quz«t Hamad«nâ, *op. cit.*, p. 51; English translation, p. 36.

36. The Quranic expression umm *al-kit«b* occurs in 3:7, 13:39 and 43:4.

37. Cf. *al-Mab«hith al-Mashriqâgah*, I, 647; the Arabic text of the passage quoted in English is as under:

38. Reference here is in particular to the Qur'«n 23:80 quoted in Lecture II, p.'37.

39. Cf. Lecture II, p. 49, where, summing up his philosophical 'criticism' of experience, Allama Iqbal says: 'facts of experience justify the inference that the ultimate nature of Reality is spiritual and must be conceived as an ego.'

40. Cf. 'Ain al-Quz«t Hamad«nâ, *op. cit.*, p. 50; English translation, p. 36. For Royce's view of knowledge of all things as a whole at once (*totum simul*), see his World and the Individual, II, 141.

41. About the cosmic harmony and unity of Nature the Qur'«n says: 'Thou seest no incongruity in the creation of the Beneficent. Then look again. Canst thou see any disorder? Then turn thy eye again and again - thy look will return to thee concused while it is fatigued' (67:3-4).

42. Qur'«n, 3:26 and 73: see also 57:29.

43. Cf. Joseph Friedrich Naumann, *Briefe ü ber Religion*, p. 68; also Lecture VI, note 38. The German text of the passage quoted in English is as under:

"Wir haben eine Welterkenntnis, die uns einen Gott der Macht und Starke lehrt, der Tod und Leben wie Schatten und Licht gleichzeitig versendet, und eine Offenbarung, einen Heilsglauben, der von demselben Gott sagt, dass er Vater sei. Die Nachfolge des Weltgottes ergibt die Sittlichkeit des Kampfes ums Dasein, und der Dienst des Vaters Jesu Christi ergibt die Sittlichkeit der Barmherzigkeit. Es sind aber nicht zwei Gotter, sondern einer. Irgendwie greifen ihre Arme ineinander. Nur kann kein Sterblicher sagen, wo und wie das geschieht."

44. Reference is to Browning's famous lines in 'Pippa Passes':

God is in the heaven -
All is right with the world.'

45. Cf. Schopenhauer, *World as Will and Idea*, trans. R.B. Haldane and J. Kemp, Book iv, section 57.

46. For the origin and historical growth of the legend of *Faust* before Goethe's masterly work on it, cf. Mary Beare's article 'Faust' in Cassell's *Encyclopaedia of Literature*, 1, 217-19.

47. Cf. Genesis, chapter iii.

48. Strictly speaking, the word Adam for man in his capacity of God's vicegerent on earth has been used in the Qur'«n only in 2:30-31.

49. Cf. Genesis, iii, 20.

50. Qur'«n, 7:19.

51. *Ibid.*, 20:120.

52. Cf. Genesis, iii, 24.

53. *Ibid.*, iii,17.

54. Qur'«n, 2:36 and 7:24.

55. Cf. also verses 15:19-20.

56. *Ibid.*, 71:17.

57. *Ibid.*, 52:23.

58. *Ibid.*, 15:48.

59. *Ibid.*, 20:118-119.

60. *Ibid.*, 2:35-37; also 20:120-122.

61. *Ibid.*, 95:4-5.

62. Cf. also verses 2:155 and 90:4.

63. *Ibid.*, 2:31-34.

64. Lecture I, pp. 10-11.

65. Madame Helena Petrovna Blavatsky (1831-1891) is a noted spiritualist and theosophist of Russian birth, who in collaboration with Col. H.S. Olcott and W.A. Judge founded Theosophical Society in New York in November 1873. Later she transferred her activities to India where in 1879 she established the office of the Society in Bombay and in 1883 in Adyar near Madras with the following three objects: (i) to form a nucleus of the universal brotherhood of humanity; (ii) to promote the study of comparative religion, philosophy and science, and (iii) to investigate the unexplained laws of nature and powers latent in man. *The Secret Doctrine* (1888) deals, broadly speaking, with 'Cosmogenesis' and 'Anthropogenesis' in a ponderous way; though largely based on Vedantic thought the 'secret doctrine' is claimed to carry in it the essence of all religions.

For the mention of tree as 'a cryptic symbol for occult knowledge' in *The Secret Doctrine*, cf. I, 187: 'The Symbol for Sacred and Secret knowledge in antiquity was universally a Tree, by which a scripture or a Record was also meant'; III, 384: 'Ormzad . . . is also the creator of the Tree' (of Occult and Spiritual Knowledge and Wisdom) from which the mystic and the mysterious Baresma is taken', and IV, 159: 'To the Eastern Occultist the Tree of Knowledge (leads) to the light of the eternal present Reality'.

It may be added that Allama Iqbal seems to have a little more than a mere passing interest in the Theosophical Society and its activities for, as reported by Dr M. 'Abdull«h Chaghat«'â, he, during his quite busy stay in Madras (5-8 Jan. 1929) in connection with the present Lectures, found time to pay a visit to the head office of the Society at Adyar. One may also note in *Development of Metaphysics in Persia* (p. 10, note 2) reference to a small work *Reincarnation* by the famous Annie Besant (President of the Theosophical Society, 1907-1933, and the first and the only English woman who served as President of the Indian National Congress in 1917) and added to this are the two books published by the Theosophical Society in Allama's personal library (cf. *Descriptive Catalogue of Allama Iqbal's Personal Library*, No. 81 and *Relics of Allama Iqbal; Catalogue* IV, 11). All this, however, does not enable one to determine the nature of Allama Iqbal's interest in the Theosophical Society.

66. Qur'«n, 17; 11; also 21:37. The tree which Adam was forbidden to approach (2:35 and 7:19), according to Allama Iqbal's remarkably profound and rare understanding of the Qur'«n, is the tree of 'occult knowledge', to which man in all ages has been tempted to resort in unfruitful haste. This, in Allama's view, is opposed to the inductive knowledge 'which is most characteristic of Islamic teachings'. He indeed, tells us in Lecture V (p. 101) that 'the birth of Islam is the birth of inductive intellect.' True, this second kind of knowledge is so toilsome and painfully slow: yet this knowledge alone unfolds man's creative intellectual faculties and makes him the master of his environment and thus God's true vicegerent on earth. If this is the true approach to knowledge, there is little place in it for Mme Blavatsky's occult spiritualism or theosophism. Allama Iqbal was in fact opposed to all kinds of occultism. In one of his dialogues, he is reported to have said that 'the forbidden tree' (*shajr-i mamnë'ah*) of the Qur'«n is no other than the occultistic *taÄawwuf* which prompts the patient to seek some charm or spell rather than take the advice of a physician. The *taÄawwuf*, he added, which urges us to close our eyes and ears and instead to concentrate on the inner vision and which teaches us to leave the arduous ways of conquering Nature and instead take to some easier spiritual ways, has done the greatest harm to science. [Cf. Dr Abu'l-Laith Siddâqâ, *Malfëz«t-i Iqb«l*, pp. 138-39]. It must, however, be added that Allama Iqbal does speak of a genuine or higher kind of *taÄawwuf* which soars higher than all sciences and all philosophies. In it the human ego so to say discovers himself as an individual deeper than his conceptually describable habitual selfhood. This happens in the ego's contact with the Most Real which brings about in it a kind of 'biological transformation' the description of which surpasses all ordinary language and all usual categories of thought. 'This experience can embody itself only in a world-making or world-shaking act, and in this form alone', we are told, 'can this timeless experience . . . make itself visible to the eye of history' (Lecture VII, p. 145).

67. Qur'«n, 2:36; 7:24; 20:123.

68. *Ibid.*, 2:177; 3:200.

69. Lecture II, p. 58.

70. Lecture V, pp. 119ff.

71. *The Principles of Psychology*, I, 316.

72. Cf. R.A. Nicholson (ed. and tr.), *The Mathnawi of Jalalëddân Rëmâ*, Vol. IV (Books i and ii - text), ii, w. 159-162 and 164.

73. Cf. ibid., Vol. IV, 2 (Books i and ii - translation), p. 230. It is to be noted that quite a few minor changes made by Allama Iqbal in Nicholson's English translation of the verses quoted here from the *Mathnawâ* are due to his dropping Nicholson's parentheses used by him for keeping his translation literally as close to the text as it was possible. Happily, Allama's personal copies of Volumes 2-5 and 7 of Nicholson's edition of the Mathnawi are preserved in Allama Iqbal Museum (Lahore) and it would be rewarding to study his usual marginal marks and jottings on these volumes.

74. Cf. the Quranic verse 3:191 where so far as private prayers are concerned the faithful ones are spoken of remembering God standing and sitting and lying on their sides.

75. The Qur'«n speaks of all mankind as 'one community'; see verses 2:213, 10:19.

76. Ibid., 49:13.

The Human Ego – His Freedom and Immortality

by Dr. Muhammad Iqbal

THE Qur'«n in its simple, forceful manner emphasizes the individuality and uniqueness of man, and has, I think, a definite view of his destiny as a unity of life.[1] It is in consequence of this view of man as a unique individuality which makes it impossible for one individual to bear the burden of another,[2] and entitles him only to what is due to his own personal effort,[3] that the Qur'«n is led to reject the idea of redemption. Three things are perfectly clear from the Qur'«n:

(i) That man is the chosen of God:

'Afterwards his Lord chose him [Adam] for himself and turned towards, him, and guided him, (20:122).

(ii) That man, with all his faults, is meant to be the representative of God on earth:

'When thy Lord said to the angels, "Verily I am about to place one in my stead on Earth", they said, 'Wilt Thou place there one who will do ill therein and shed blood when we celebrate Thy praise and extol Thy holiness?' God said, "Verily I know what you know not", (2:30).

'And it is He Who hath made you His representatives on the Earth, and hath raised some of you above others by various grades, that He may prove you by His gifts' (6:165).

(iii) That man is the trustee of a free personality which he accepted at his peril:

'Verily We proposed to the Heavens, and to the Earth, and to the mountains to receive the "trust", but they refused the burden and they feared to receive it. Man undertook to bear it, but hath proved unjust, senseless!' (33:72).

Yet it is surprising to see that the unity of human consciousness which constitutes the centre of human personality never really became a point of interest in the history of Muslim thought. The *Mutakallimën* regarded the soul as a finer kind of matter or a mere accident which dies with the body and is re-created on the Day of Judgement. The philosophers of Islam received inspiration from Greek thought. In the case of other schools, it must be remembered that the expansion of Islam brought within its fold peoples belonging to different creed-communities, such as Nestorians, Jews, Zoroastrians, whose intellectual outlook had been formed by the concepts of a culture which had long dominated the whole of middle and western Asia. This culture, on the whole Magian in its origin and development, has a structurally dualistic soul-picture which we find more or less reflected in the theological thought of Islam.[4] Devotional Sufism alone tried to understand the meaning of the unity of inner experience which the Qur'«n declares to be one of the three sources of knowledge,[5] the other two being History and Nature. The development of this experience in the religious life of Islam reached its culmination in the well-known words of Hall«j - 'I am the creative truth.' The contemporaries of Hall«j, as well as his successors, interpreted these words pantheistically; but the fragments of Hall«j, collected and published by the French Orientalist, L. Massignon, leave no doubt that the martyr-saint could not have meant to deny the transcendence of God.[6] The true interpretation of his experience, therefore, is not the drop slipping into the sea, but the realization and bold affirmation in an undying phrase of the reality and permanence of the human ego in a profounder personality. The phrase of Hall«j seems almost a challenge flung against the *Mutakallimën*. The difficulty of modern students of religion, however, is that this type of experience, though perhaps perfectly normal in its beginnings, points, in its maturity, to unknown levels of consciousness. Ibn Khaldën, long ago, felt the necessity of an effective scientific method to investigate these levels.[7] Modern psychology has only recently realized the necessity of such a method, but has not yet been able to go beyond the discovery of the characteristic features of the mystic levels of consciousness.[8] Not being yet in possession of a scientific method to deal with the type of experience on which such judgements as that of Hall«j are based, we cannot avail ourselves of its possible capacity as a knowledge-yielding experience. Nor can the concepts of theological systems, draped in the terminology of a practically dead metaphysics, be of any help to those who happen to possess a different intellectual background. The task before the modern Muslim is, therefore, immense. He has to rethink the whole system of Islam without completely breaking with the past. Perhaps the first Muslim who felt the urge of a new spirit in him was Sh«h Walâall«h of Delhi. The man, however, who fully realized the importance and immensity of the task, and whose deep insight into the inner meaning of the history of Muslim thought and life, combined with a broad vision engendered by his wide experience of men and manners, would have made him a living link between the past and the future, was Jam«luddân Afgh«nâ. If his indefatigable but divided energy could have devoted itself entirely to Islam as a system of human belief and conduct, the world of Islam, intellectually speaking, would have been on a much more solid ground today. The only course open to us is to approach modern knowledge with a respectful but independent attitude and to appreciate the teachings of Islam in the light of that knowledge, even though we may be led to differ from those who have gone before us. This I propose to do in regard to the subject of the present lecture.

In the history of modern thought it is Bradley who furnishes the best evidence for the impossibility of denying reality to the ego. In his *Ethical Studies*[9] he assumes the reality of the self; in his Logic[10] he takes it only as a working hypothesis. It is in his *Appearance and Reality* that he subjects the ego to a searching examination.[11] Indeed, his two chapters on the meaning and reality of the self may be regarded as a kind of modern Upanishad on the unreality of the *Jâv«tm«*.[12] According to him, the test of reality is freedom from contradiction and since his criticism discovers the finite centre of experience to be infected with irreconcilable oppositions of change and permanence, unity and diversity, the ego is a mere illusion. Whatever may be our view of the self - feeling, self-identity, soul, will - it can be examined only by the canons of thought which in its nature is relational, and all 'relations involve contradictions'. Yet, in spite of the fact that his ruthless logic has shown the ego to be a mass of confusion, Bradley has to admit that the self must be 'in some sense real', 'in some sense an indubitable fact'.[13] We may easily grant that the ego, in its finitude, is imperfect as a unity of life. Indeed, its nature is wholly aspiration after a unity more inclusive, more effective, more balanced, and unique. Who knows how many different kinds of environment it needs for its organization as a perfect unity? At the present stage of its organization it is unable to maintain the continuity of its tension without constant relaxation of sleep. An insignificant stimulus may sometimes disrupt its unity and nullify it as a controlling energy. Yet, however thought may dissect and analyse, our feeling of egohood is ultimate and is powerful enough to extract from Professor Bradley the reluctant admission of its reality.

The finite centre of experience, therefore, is real, even though its reality is too profound to be intellectualized. What then is the characteristic feature of the ego? The ego reveals itself as a unity of what we call mental states. Mental states do not exist in mutual isolation. They mean and involve one another. They exist as phases of a complex whole, called mind. The organic unity, however, of these interrelated states or, let us say, events is a special kind of unity. It fundamentally differs from the unity of a material thing; for the parts of a material thing can exist in mutual isolation. Mental unity is absolutely unique. We cannot say that one of my beliefs is situated on the right or left of my other belief. Nor is it possible to say that my appreciation of the beauty of the T«j varies with my distance from ẙgra. My thought of space is not spatially related to space. Indeed, the ego can think of more than one space-order. The space of waking consciousness and dream-space have no mutual relation. They do not interfere with or overlap each other. For the body there can be but a single space. The ego, therefore, is not space-bound in the sense in which the body is space-bound. Again, mental and physical events are both in time, but the time-span of the ego is fundamentally different to the time-span of the physical event. The duration of the physical event is stretched out in space as a present fact; the ego's duration is concentrated within it and linked with its present and future in a unique manner. The formation of a physical event discloses certain present marks which show that it has passed through a time-duration; but these marks are merely emblematic of its time duration; not time-duration itself. True time–duration belongs to the ego alone.

Another important characteristic of the unity of the ego is its essential privacy which reveals the uniqueness of every ego. In order to reach a certain conclusion all the premises of a syllogism must be believed in by one and the same mind. If I believe in the proposition 'all men are mortal', and another mind believes in the proposition 'Socrates is a man', no inference is possible. It is possible only if both the propositions are believed in by me. Again, my desire for a certain thing is essentially mine. Its satisfaction means my private enjoyment. If all mankind happen to desire the same thing, the satisfaction of their desire will not mean the satisfaction of my desire when I do not get the thing desired. The dentist may sympathize with my toothache, but cannot experience the feeling of my toothache. My pleasures, pains, and desires are exclusively mine, forming a part and parcel of my private ego alone. My feelings, hates and loves, judgements and resolutions, are exclusively mine. God Himself cannot feel, judge, and choose for me when more than one course of action are open to me. Similarly, in order to recognize you, I must have known you in the past. My recognition of a place or person means reference to my past experience, and not the past experience of another ego. It is this unique interrelation of our mental states[14] that we express by the word 'I', and it is here that the great problem of psychology begins to appear. What is the nature of this 'I'?

To the Muslim school of theology of which Ghazzâlâ is the chief exponent,[15] the ego is a simple, indivisible, and immutable soul-substance, entirely different from the group of our mental states and unaffected by the passage of time. Our conscious experience is a unity, because our mental states are related as so many qualities to this simple substance which persists unchanged during the flux of its qualities. My recognition of you is possible only if I persist unchanged between the original perception and the present act of memory. The interest of this school, however, was not so much psychological as metaphysical. But whether we take the soul-entity as an explanation of the facts of our conscious experience, or as a basis for immortality, I am afraid it serves neither psychological nor metaphysical interest. Kant's fallacies of pure reason are well known to the student of modern philosophy.[16] The 'I think', which accompanies every thought is, according to Kant, a purely formal condition of thought, and the transition from a purely formal condition of thought to ontological substance is logically illegitimate.[17] Even apart from Kant's way of looking at the subject of experience, the indivisibility of a substance does not prove its indestructibility; for the indivisible substance, as Kant himself remarks, may gradually disappear into nothingness like an intensive quality or cease to exist all of a sudden.[18] Nor can this static view of substance serve any psychological interest. In the first place, it is difficult to regard the elements of our conscious experience as qualities of a soul-substance in the sense in which, for instance, the weight of a physical body is the quality of that body. Observation reveals experience to be particular acts of reference, and as such they possess a specific being of their own. They constitute, as Laird acutely remarks, 'a new world and not merely new features in an old world'. Secondly, even if we regard experiences as qualities, we cannot discover how they inhere in the soul-substance. Thus we see that our conscious experience can give us no clue to the ego regarded as a soul-substance; for by hypothesis the soul-substance does not reveal itself in experience. And it may further be pointed out that in view of the improbability of different soul-substances controlling the same body at different times, the theory can offer no adequate explanation of phenomena such as alternating personality, formerly explained by the temporary possession of the body by evil spirits.

Yet the interpretation of our conscious experience is the only road by which we can reach the ego, if at all. Let us, therefore, turn to modern psychology and see what light it throws on the nature of the ego. William James conceives consciousness as 'a stream of thought' - a conscious flow of changes with a felt continuity.[19] He finds a kind of gregarious principle working in our experiences which have, as it were, 'hooks' on them, and thereby catch up one another in the flow of mental life.[20] The ego consists of the feelings of personal life, and is, as such, part of the system of thought. Every pulse of thought, present or perishing, is an indivisible unity which knows and recollects. The appropriation of the passing pulse by the present pulse of thought, and that of the present by its successor, is the ego.[21] This description of our mental life is extremely ingenious; but not, I venture to think, true to consciousness as we find it in ourselves. Consciousness is something single, presupposed in all mental life, and not bits of consciousness, mutually reporting to one another. This view of consciousness, far from giving us any clue to the ego, entirely ignores the relatively permanent element in experience. There is no continuity of being between the passing thoughts. When one of these is present, the other has totally disappeared; and how can the passing thought, which is irrevocably lost, be known and appropriated by the present thought? I do not mean to say that the ego is over and above the mutually penetrating multiplicity we call experience. Inner experience is the ego at work. We appreciate the ego itself in the act of perceiving, judging, and willing. The life of the ego is a kind of tension caused by the ego invading the environment and the environment invading the ego. The ego does not stand outside this arena of mutual invasion. It is present in it as a directive energy and is formed and disciplined by its own experience. The Qur'«n is clear on this directive function of the ego:

'And they ask thee of the soul. Say: the soul proceedeth from my Lord's *Amr* [Command]: but of knowledge, only a little to you is given' (17:85).

In order to understand the meaning of the word Amr, we must remember the distinction which the Qur'«n draws between *Amr* and *Khalq*. Pringle-Pattison deplores that the English language possesses only one word - 'creation' - to express the relation of God and the universe of extension on the one hand, and the relation of God and the human ego on the other. The Arabic language is, however, more fortunate in this respect. It has two words: *Khalq* and *Amr* to express the two ways in which the creative activity of God reveals itself to us. *Khalq* is creation; *Amr* is direction. As the Qur'«n says: 'To Him belong creation and direction.'[22] The verse quoted above means that the essential nature of the soul is directive, as it proceeds from the directive energy of God, though we do not know how Divine *Amr* functions as ego-unities. The personal pronoun used in the expression *Rabbâ* ('my Lord') throws further light on the nature and behaviour of the ego. It is meant to suggest that the soul must be taken as something individual and specific, with all the variations in the range, balance, and effectiveness of its unity. 'Every man acteth after his own manner: but your Lord well knoweth who is best guided in his path' (17:84). Thus my real personality is not a thing; it is an act. My experience is only a series of acts, mutually referring to one another, and held together by the unity of a directive purpose. My whole reality lies in my directive attitude. You cannot perceive me like a thing in space, or a set of experiences in temporal order; you must interpret, understand, and appreciate me in my judgements, in my will-attitudes, aims, and aspirations.

The next question is: how does the ego emerge within the spatio-temporal order?[23] The teaching of the Qur'«n is perfectly clear on this point:

'Now of fine clay We have created man: Then We placed him, a moist germ, in a safe abode; then made We the moist germ a clot of blood: then made the clotted blood into a piece of flesh; then made the piece of flesh into bones: and We clothed the bones with flesh; then brought forth man of yet another make.

'Blessed, therefore, be God - the most excellent of makers' (23:12-14).

The 'yet another make' of man develops on the basis of physical organism - that colony of sub-egos through which a profounder Ego constantly acts on me, and thus permits me to build up a systematic unity of experience. Are then the soul and its organism two things in the sense of Descartes, independent of each other, though somehow mysteriously united? I am inclined to think that the hypothesis of matter as an independent existence is perfectly gratuitous. It can be justified only on the ground of our sensation of which matter is supposed to be at least a part cause, other than myself. This something other than myself is supposed to possess certain qualities, called primary which correspond to certain sensations in me; and I justify my belief in those qualities on the ground that the cause must have some resemblance with the effect. But there need be no resemblance between cause and effect. If my success in life causes misery to another man, my success and his misery have no resemblance with each other. Yet everyday experience and physical science proceed on the assumption of an independent existence of matter. Let us, therefore, provisionally assume that body and soul are two mutually independent, yet in some mysterious way united, things. It was Descartes who first stated the problem, and I believe his statement and final view of the problem were largely influenced by the Manichaean inheritance of early Christianity. However, if they are mutually independent and do not affect each other, then the changes of both run on exactly parallel lines, owing to some kind of pre-established harmony, as Leibniz thought. This reduces the soul to a merely passive spectator of the happenings of the body. If, on the other hand, we suppose them to affect each other, then we cannot find any observable facts to show how and where exactly their interaction takes place, and which of the two takes the initiative. The soul is an organ of the body which exploits it for physiological purposes, or the body is an instrument of the soul, are equally true propositions on the theory of interaction. Lange's theory of emotion tends to show that the body takes the initiative in the act of interaction.[24] There are, however, facts to contradict this theory, and it is not possible to detail these facts here. Suffice it to indicate that even if the body takes the initiative, the mind does enter as a consenting factor at a definite stage in the development of emotion, and this is equally true of other external stimuli which are constantly working on the mind. Whether an emotion will grow further, or that a stimulus will continue to work, depends on my attending to it. It is the mind's consent which eventually decides the fate of an emotion or a stimulus.

Thus parallelism and interaction are both unsatisfactory. Yet mind and body become one in action. When I take up a book from my table, my act is single and indivisible. It is impossible to draw a line of cleavage between the share of the body and that of the mind in this act. Somehow they must belong to the same system, and according to the Qur'«n they do belong to the same system.[25] 'To Him belong *Khalq* (creation) and *Amr* (direction),[26] how is such a thing conceivable? We have seen that the body is not a thing situated in an absolute void; it is a system of events or acts.[27] The system of experiences we call soul or ego is also a system of acts. This does not obliterate the distinction of soul and body; it only brings them closer to each other. The characteristic of the ego is spontaneity; the acts composing the body repeat themselves. The body is accumulated action or habit of the soul; and as such undetachable from it. It is a permanent element of consciousness which, in view of this permanent element, appears from the outside as something stable. What then is matter? A colony of egos of a low order out of which emerges the ego of a higher order, when their association and interaction reach a certain degree of coordination. It is the world reaching the point of self-guidance wherein the Ultimate Reality, perhaps, reveals its secret, and furnishes a clue to its ultimate nature. The fact that the higher emerges out of the lower does not rob the higher of its worth and dignity. It is not the origin of a thing that matters, it is the capacity, the significance, and the final reach of the emergent that matter. Even if we regard the basis of soul-life as purely physical, it by no means follows that the emergent can be resolved into what has conditioned its birth and growth. The emergent, as the advocates of the Emergent Evolution teach us, is an unforeseeable and novel fact on its own plane of being, and cannot be explained mechanistically. Indeed the evolution of life shows that, though in the beginning the mental is dominated by the physical, the mental, as it grows in power, tends to dominate the physical and may eventually rise to a position of complete independence. Nor is there such a thing as a purely physical level in the sense of possessing a materiality, elementally incapable of evolving the creative synthesis we call life and mind, and needing a transcendental Deity to impregnate it with the sentient and the mental. The Ultimate Ego that makes the emergent emerge is immanent in Nature, and is described by the Qur'«n, as 'the First and the Last, the Visible and the Invisible.'[28]

This view of the matter raises a very important question. We have seen that the ego is not something rigid. It organizes itself in time, and is formed and disciplined by its own experience. It is further clear that streams of causality flow into it from Nature and from it to

Nature. Does the ego then determine its own activity? If so, how is the self-determination of the ego related to the determinism of the spatio-temporal order? Is personal causality a special kind of causality, or only a disguised form of the mechanism of Nature? It is claimed that the two kinds of determinism are not mutually exclusive and that the scientific method is equally applicable to human action. The human act of deliberation is understood to be a conflict of motives which are conceived, not as the ego's own present or inherited tendencies of action or inaction, but as so many external forces fighting one another, gladiator-like, on the arena of the mind. Yet the final choice is regarded as a fact determined by the strongest force, and not by the resultant of contending motives, like a purely physical effect.[29] I am, however, firmly of the opinion that the controversy between the advocates of Mechanism and Freedom arises from a wrong view of intelligent action which modern psychology, unmindful of its own independence as a science, possessing a special set of facts to observe, was bound to take on account of its slavish imitation of physical sciences. The view that ego-activity is a succession of thoughts and ideas, ultimately resolvable to units of sensations, is only another form of atomic materialism which forms the basis of modern science. Such a view could not but raise a strong presumption in favour of a mechanistic interpretation of consciousness. There is, however, some relief in thinking that the new German psychology, known as Configuration Psychology,[30] may succeed in securing the independence of Psychology as a science, just as the theory of Emergent Evolution may eventually bring about the independence of Biology. This newer German psychology teaches us that a careful study of intelligent behaviour discloses the fact of 'insight' over and above the mere succession of sensations.[31] This 'insight' is the ego's appreciation of temporal, spatial, and causal relation of things - the choice, that is to say of data, in a complex whole, in view of the goal or purpose which the ego has set before itself for the time being. It is this sense of striving in the experience of purposive action and the success which I actually achieve in reaching my 'ends' that convince me of my efficiency as a personal cause. The essential feature of a purposive act is its vision of a future situation which does not appear to admit any explanation in terms of Physiology. The truth is that the causal chain wherein we try to find a place for the ego is itself an artificial construction of the ego for its own purposes. The ego is called upon to live in a complex environment, and he cannot maintain his life in it without reducing it to a system which would give him some kind of assurance as to the behaviour of things around him. The view of his environment as a system of cause and effect is thus an indispensable instrument of the ego, and not a final expression of the nature of Reality. Indeed in interpreting Nature in this way the ego understands and masters its environment, and thereby acquires and amplifies its freedom.[32]

Thus the element of guidance and directive control in the ego's activity clearly shows that the ego is a free personal causality. He shares in the life and freedom of the Ultimate Ego who, by permitting the emergence of a finite ego, capable of private initiative, has limited this freedom of His own free will. This freedom of conscious behaviour follows from the view of ego-activity which the Qur'«n takes. There are verses which are unmistakably clear on this point:

'And say: The truth is from your Lord: Let him, then, who will, believe: and let him who will, be an unbeliever' (18:29).

'If ye do well to your own behoof will ye do well: and if ye do evil against yourselves will ye do it' (17:7).

Indeed Islam recognizes a very important fact of human psychology, i.e. the rise and fall of the power to act freely, and is anxious to retain the power to act freely as a constant and undiminished factor in the life of the ego. The timing of the daily prayer which, according to the Qur'«n, restores 'self-possession' to the ego by bringing it into closer touch with the ultimate source of life and freedom, is intended to save the ego from the mechanizing effects of sleep and business. Prayer in Islam is the ego's escape from mechanism to freedom.

It cannot, however, be denied that the idea of destiny runs throughout the Qur'«n. This point is worth considering, more especially because Spengler in his *Decline of the West* seems to think that Islam amounts to a complete negation of the ego.[33] I have already explained to you my view of *Taqdâr* (destiny) as we find it in the Qur'«n.[34] As Spengler himself points out, there are two ways of making the world our own. The one is intellectual; the other, for want of a better expression, we may call vital. The intellectual way consists in understanding the world as a rigid system of cause and effect. The vital is the absolute acceptance of the inevitable necessity of life, regarded as a whole which in evolving its inner richness creates serial time. This vital way of appropriating the universe is what the Qur'«n describes as Im«n. Im«n is not merely a passive belief in one or more propositions of a certain kind; it is living assurance begotten of a rare experience. Strong personalities alone are capable of rising to this experience and the higher 'Fatalism' implied in it. Napoleon is reported to have said: 'I am a thing, not a person'. This is one way in which unitive experience expresses itself. In the history of religious experience in Islam which, according to the Prophet, consists in the 'creation of Divine attributes in man', this experience has found expression in such phrases as 'I am the creative truth' (Àall«j), 'I am Time' (Muhammad), 'I am the speaking Qur'«n' ('Alâ), 'Glory to me' (B«Yazâd). In the higher Sufism of Islam unitive experience is not the finite ego effacing its own identity by some sort of absorption into the infinite Ego; it is rather the Infinite passing into the loving embrace of the finite.[35] As Rëmâ says:

'Divine knowledge is lost in the knowledge of the saint! And how is it possible for people to believe in such a thing?'

The fatalism implied in this attitude is not negation of the ego as Spengler seems to think; it is life and boundless power which recognizes no obstruction, and can make a man calmly offer his prayers when bullets are showering around him.

But is it not true, you will say, that a most degrading type of Fatalism has prevailed in the world of Islam for many centuries? This is true, and has a history behind it which requires separate treatment. It is sufficient here to indicate that the kind of Fatalism which the European critics of Islam sum up in the word *Qismat* was due partly to philosophical thought, partly to political expediency, and partly to the gradually diminishing force of the life-impulse, which Islam originally imparted to its followers. Philosophy, searching for the meaning of cause as applied to God, and taking time as the essence of the relation between cause and effect, could not but reach the notion of a transcendent God, prior to the universe, and operating upon it from without. God was thus conceived as the last link in the chain of causation, and, consequently, the real author of all that happens in the universe. Now the practical materialism of the opportunist Umayyad rulers of Damascus needed a peg on which to hang their misdeeds at Karbal«, and to secure the fruits of Amâr Mu'«wâyy«h's revolt against the possibilities of a popular rebellion. Ma'bad is reported to have said to Àasan of BaÄra that the Umayyads killed Muslims, and attributed their acts to the decrees of God. 'These enemies of God', replied Àasan, 'are liars.'[36] Thus arose, in spite of open protests by Muslim divines, a morally degrading Fatalism, and the constitutional theory known as the 'accomplished fact'[37] in order to support vested interests. This is not at all surprising. In our own times philosophers have furnished a kind of intellectual justification for the finality of the present capitalistic structure of society. Hegel's view of Reality as an infinitude of reason from which follows the essential rationality of the real, and Auguste Comte's society as an organism in which specific functions are eternally assigned to each organ, are instances in point. The same thing appears to have happened in Islam. But since Muslims have always sought the justification of their varying attitudes in the Qur'«n, even though at the expense of its plain meaning the fatalistic interpretation has had very far-reaching effects on Muslim peoples. I could, in this connexion, quote several instances of obvious misinterpretation; but the subject requires special treatment, and it is time now to turn to the question of immortality.

No age has produced so much literature on the question of immortality as our own, and this literature is continually increasing in spite of the victories of modern Materialism. Purely metaphysical arguments, however, cannot give us a positive belief in personal immortality. In the history of Muslim thought Ibn Rushd approached the question of immortality from a purely metaphysical point of view, and, I venture to think, achieved no results. He drew a distinction between sense and intelligence probably because of the expressions, *Nafs* and *Rëh*, used in the Qur'«n. These expressions, apparently suggesting a conflict between two opposing principles in man, have misled many a thinker in Islam. However, if Ibn Rushd's dualism was based on the Qur'«n, then I am afraid he was mistaken; for the word *Nafs* does not seem to have been used in the Qur'«n in any technical sense of the kind imagined by Muslim theologians. Intelligence, according to Ibn Rushd, is not a form of the body; it belongs to a different order of being, and transcends individuality. It is, therefore, one, universal, and eternal. This obviously means that, since unitary intellect transcends individuality, its appearance as so many unities in the multiplicity of human persons is a mere illusion. The eternal unity of intellect may mean, as Renan thinks, the everlastingness of humanity and civilization; it does not surely mean personal immortality.[38] In fact Ibn Rushd's view looks like William James's suggestion of a transcendental mechanism of consciousness which operates on a physical medium for a while, and then gives it up in pure sport [39]

In modern times the line of argument for personal immortality is on the whole ethical. But ethical arguments, such as that of Kant, and the modern revisions of his arguments, depend on a kind of faith in the fulfilment of the claims of justice, or in the irreplaceable and unique work of man as an individual pursuer of infinite ideals. With Kant immortality is beyond the scope of speculative reason; it is a postulate of practical reason, an axiom of man's moral consciousness. Man demands and pursues the supreme good which comprises both virtue and happiness. But virtue and happiness, duty and inclination, are, according to Kant, heterogeneous notions. Their unity cannot be achieved within the narrow span of the pursuer's life in this sensible world. We are, therefore, driven to postulate immortal life for the person's progressive completion of the unity of the mutually exclusive notions of virtue and happiness, and the existence of God eventually to effectuate this confluence. It is not clear, however, why the consummation of virtue and happiness should take infinite time, and how God can effectuate the confluence between mutually exclusive notions. This inconclusiveness of metaphysical arguments has led many thinkers to confine themselves to meeting the objections of modern Materialism which rejects immortality, holding that consciousness is merely a function of the brain, and therefore ceases with the cessation of the brain-process. William James thinks that this objection to immortality is valid only if the function in question is taken to be productive.[40] The mere fact that certain mental changes vary concomitantly with certain bodily changes, does not warrant the inference that mental changes are produced by bodily changes. The function is not necessarily productive; it may be permissive or transmissive like the function of the trigger of a crossbow or that of a reflecting lens.[41] This view which suggests that our inner life is due to the operation in us of a kind of transcendental mechanism of consciousness, somehow choosing a physical medium for a short period of sport, does not give us any assurance of the continuance of the content of our actual experience. I have already indicated in these lectures the proper way to meet Materialism.[42] Science must necessarily select for study certain specific aspects of Reality only and exclude others. It is pure dogmatism on the part of science to claim that the aspects of Reality selected by it are the only aspects to be studied. No doubt man has a spatial aspect; but this is not the only aspect of man. There are other aspects of man, such as evaluation, the unitary character of purposive experience, and the pursuit of truth which science must necessarily exclude from its study, and the understanding of which requires categories other than those employed by science.[43]

There is, however, in the history of modern thought one positive view of immortality - I mean Nietzsche's doctrine of Eternal Recurrence.[44] This view deserves some consideration, not only because Nietzsche has maintained it with a prophetical fervour, but also because it reveals a real tendency in the modern mind. The idea occurred to several minds about the time when it came to Nietzsche like a poetic inspiration, and the germs of its are also found in Herbert Spencer.[45] It was really the power of the idea rather than its logical demonstration that appealed to this modern prophet. This, in itself, is some evidence of the fact that positive views of ultimate things are the work rather of Inspiration than Metaphysics. However, Nietzsche has given his doctrine the form of a reasoned out theory, and as such I think we are entitled to examine it. The doctrine proceeds on the assumption that the quantity of energy in the universe is constant and consequently finite. Space is only a subjective form; there is no meaning in saying that the world is in space in the sense that it is situated in an absolute empty void. In his view of time, however, Nietzsche parts company with Kant and Schopenhauer. Time is not a subjective form; it is a real and infinite process which can be conceived only as 'Periodic'.[46] Thus it is clear that there can be no dissipation of energy in an infinite empty space. The centres of this energy are limited in number, and their combination perfectly calculable. There is no beginning or end of this ever-active energy, no equilibrium, no first or last change. Since time is infinite, therefore all possible combinations of energy-centres have already been exhausted. There is no new happening in the universe; whatever happens now has happened before an infinite number of times, and will continue to happen an infinite number of times in the future. On Nietzsche's view the order of happenings in the universe must be fixed and unalterable; for since an infinite time has passed, the energy-centres must have, by this time, formed certain definite modes of behaviour. The very word 'Recurrence' implies this fixity. Further, we must conclude that a combination of energy-centres which has once taken place must always return; otherwise there would be no guarantee for the return even of the superman.

'Everything has returned: Sirius and the spider, and thy thoughts at this moment and this last thought of thine that all things will return . . . . Fellow-man! your whole life, like a sand-glass, will always be reversed, and will ever run out again. This ring in which you are but a gain will glitter afresh for ever.'[47]

Such is Nietzsche's Eternal Recurrence. It is only a more rigid kind of mechanism, based not on an ascertained fact but only on a working hypothesis of science. Nor does Nietzsche seriously grapple with the question of time. He takes it objectively and regards it merely as an infinite series of events returning to itself over and over again. Now time, regarded as a perpetual circular movement, makes immortality absolutely intolerable. Nietzsche himself feels this, and describes his doctrine, not as one of immortality, but rather as a view of life which would make immortality endurable.[48] And what makes immortality bearable, according to Nietzsche? It is the expectation that a recurrence of the combination of energy-centres which constitutes my personal existence is a necessary factor in the birth of that ideal combination which he calls 'superman'. But the superman has been an infinite number of times before. His birth is inevitable; how can the prospect give me any aspiration? We can aspire only for what is absolutely new, and the absolutely new is unthinkable on Nietzsche's view which is nothing more than a Fatalism worse than the one summed up in the word *Qismat*. Such a doctrine, far from keying up the human organism for the fight of life, tends to destroy its action-tendencies and relaxes the tension of the ego.[49]

Passing now to the teaching of the Qur'«n. The Quranic view of the destiny of man is partly ethical, partly biological. I say partly biological because the Qur'«n makes in this connexion certain statements of a biological nature which we cannot understand without a deeper insight into the nature of life. It mentions, for instance, the fact of *Barzakh*[50] - a state, perhaps of some kind of suspense between Death and Resurrection. Resurrection, too, appears to have been differently conceived. The Qur'«n does not base its possibility, like Christianity, on the evidence of the actual resurrection of an historic person. It seems to take and argue resurrection as a universal phenomenon of life, in some sense, true even of birds and animals (6:38).

Before, however, we take the details of the Quranic doctrine of personal immortality we must note three things which are perfectly clear from the Qur'«n and regarding which there is, or ought to be, no difference of opinion:

(i) That the ego has a beginning in time, and did not pre-exist its emergence in the spatio-temporal order. This is clear from the verse which I cited a few minutes ago.[51]

(ii) That according to the Quranic view, there is no possibility of return to this earth. This is clear from the following verses:

'When death overtaketh one of them, he saith, "Lord! send me back again, that I may do the good that I have left undone!" By no means These are the very words which he shall speak. But behind them is a barrier (*Barzakh*), until the day when they shall be raised again' (23:99-100).

'And by the moon when at her full, that from state to state shall ye be surely carried onward' (84:18-19).

'The germs of life - Is it ye who create them? Or are We their Creator? It is We Who have decreed that death should be among you; yet We are not thereby hindered from replacing you with others, your likes, or from creating you again in forms which ye know not!' (56:58-61).

(iii) That finitude is not a misfortune:

'Verily there is none in the heavens and in the earth but shall approach the God of Mercy as a servant. He hath taken note of them and numbered them with exact numbering: and each of them shall come to Him on the Day of Resurrection as a single individual' (19:93-95).[52]

This is a very important point and must be properly understood with a view to secure a clear insight into the Islamic theory of salvation. It is with the irreplaceable singleness of his idividuality that the finite ego will approach the infinite ego to see for himself the consequences of his past action and to judge the possibilities of his future.

'And every man's fate have We fastened about his neck: and on the Day of Resurrection will We bring forthwith to him a book which shall be proffered to him wide open: "Read thy book: there needeth none but thyself to make out an account against thee this day" (17:13-14).

Whatever may be the final fate of man it does not mean the loss of individuality. The Qur'«n does not contemplate complete liberation from finitude as the highest state of human bliss. The 'unceasing reward'[53] of man consists in his gradual growth in self-possession, in uniqueness, and intensity of his activity as an ego. Even the scene of 'Universal Destruction' immediately preceding the Day of Judgement[54] cannot affect the perfect calm of a full-grown ego:

'And there shall be a blast on the trumpet, and all who are in the heavens and all who are in the earth shall faint away, save those in whose case God wills otherwise' (39:68).[55]

Who can be the subject of this exception but those in whom the ego has reached the very highest point of intensity? And the climax of this development is reached when the ego is able to retain full self-possession, even in the case of a direct contact with the all-embracing Ego. As the Qur'«n says of the Prophet's vision of the Ultimate Ego:

'His eye turned not aside, nor did it wander' (53:17).

This is the ideal of perfect manhood in Islam. Nowhere has it found a better literary expression than in a Persian verse which speaks of the Holy Prophet's experience of Divine illumination:

'Moses fainted away by a mere surface illumination of Reality. Thou seest the very substance of Reality with a smile!'[56]

Pantheistic Sufism obviously cannot favour such a view, and suggests difficulties of a philosophical nature. How can the Infinite and the finite egos mutually exclude each other? Can the finite ego, as such, retain its finitude besides the Infinite Ego? This difficulty is based on a misunderstanding of the true nature of the Infinite. True infinity does not mean infinite extension which cannot be conceived without embracing all available finite extensions. Its nature consists in intensity and not extensity; and the moment we fix our gaze on intensity, we begin to see that the finite ego must be distinct, though not isolated, from the Infinite. Extensively regarded I am absorbed by the spatio-temporal order to which I belong. Intensively regarded I consider the same spatio-temporal order as a confronting 'other' wholly alien to me. I am distinct from and yet intimately related to that on which I depend for my life and sustenance.

With these three points clearly grasped, the rest of the doctrine is easy to conceive. It is open to man, according to the Qur'«n, to belong to the meaning of the universe and become immortal.

'Thinketh man that he shall be left as a thing of no use? Was he not a mere embryo?

'Then he became thick blood of which God formed him and fashioned him; and made him twain, male and female. Is not God powerful enough to quicken the dead?' (75:36-40).

It is highly improbable that a being whose evolution has taken millions of years should be thrown away as a thing of no use. But it is only as an ever-growing ego that he can belong to the meaning of the universe:

'By the soul and He Who hath balanced it, and hath shown to it the ways of wickedness and piety, blessed is he who hath made it grow and undone is he who hath corrupted it' (91:7-9).

And how to make the soul grow and save it from corruption? By action:

'Blessed be He in Whose hand is the Kingdom! And over all things is He potent, who hath created death and life to test which of you is the best in point of deed; and He is the Mighty and Forgiving' (67:1-2).[57]

Life offers a scope for ego-activity, and death is the first test of the synthetic activity of the ego. There are no pleasure-giving and pain-giving acts; there are only ego-sustaining and ego-dissolving acts. It is the deed that prepares the ego for dissolution, or disciplines him for a future career. The principle of the ego-sustaining deed is respect for the ego in myself as well as in others. Personal immortality, then, is not ours as of right; it is to be achieved by personal effort. Man is only a candidate for it. The most depressing error of Materialism is the supposition that finite consciousness exhausts its object. Philosophy and science are only one way of approaching that object. There are other ways of approach open to us; and death, if present action has sufficiently fortified the ego against the shock that physical dissolution brings, is only a kind of passage to what the Qur'«n describes as *Barzakh*. The records of Sufistic experience indicate that *Barzakh* is a state of consciousness characterized by a change in the ego's attitude towards time and space. There is nothing improbable in it. It was Helmholtz who first discovered that nervous excitation takes time to reach consciousness.[58] If this is so, our present physiological structure is at the bottom of our present view of time, and if the ego survives the dissolution of this structure, a change in our attitude towards time and space seems perfectly natural. Nor is such a change wholly unknown to us. The enormous condensation of impressions which occurs in our dream-life, and the exaltation of memory, which sometimes takes place at the moment of death, disclose the ego's capacity for different standards of time. The state of *Barzakh*, therefore, does not seem to be merely a passive state of expectation; it is a state in which the ego catches a glimpse of fresh aspects of Reality, and prepares himself for adjustment to these aspects. It must be a state of great psychic unhingement, especially in the case of full-grown egos who have naturally developed fixed modes of operation on a specific spatio-temporal order, and may mean dissolution to less fortunate ones. However, the ego must continue to struggle until he is able to gather himself up, and win his resurrection. The resurrection, therefore, is not an external event. It is the consummation of a life-process within the ego. Whether individual or universal it is nothing more than a kind of stock-taking of the ego's past achievements and his future possibilities. The Qur'«n argues the phenomenon of re-emergence of the ego on the analogy of his first emergence:

'Man saith: "What! After I am dead, shall I in the end be brought forth alive?" Doth not man bear in mind that We made him at first when he was nought?' (19:66-67).

'It is We Who have decreed that death should be among you.

Yet We are not thereby hindered from replacing you with others your likes, or from producing you in a form which ye know not! Ye have known the first creation: will you not reflect?' (56:60-62).

How did man first emerge? This suggestive argument embodied in the last verses of the two passages quoted above did in fact open a new vista to Muslim philosophers. It was Jāḥiz (d. 255 A.H.) who first hinted at the changes in animal life caused by migrations and environment generally.[59] The association known as the 'Brethren of Purity' further amplified the views of Jāḥiz.[60] Ibn Maskawaih (d. 421 A.H.), however, was the first Muslim thinker to give a clear and in many respects thoroughly modern theory of the origin of man.[61] It was only natural and perfectly consistent with the spirit of the Qur'ān, that Rūmī regarded the question of immortality as one of biological evolution, and not a problem to be decided by arguments of purely metaphysical nature, as some philosophers of Islam had thought. The theory of evolution, however, has brought despair and anxiety, instead of hope and enthusiasm for life, to the modern world. The reason is to be found in the unwarranted modern assumption that man's present structure, mental as well as physiological, is the last word in biological evolution, and that death, regarded as a biological event, has no constructive meaning. The world of today needs a Rūmī to create an attitude of hope, and to kindle the fire of enthusiasm for life. His inimitable lines may be quoted here:

First man appeared in the class of inorganic things,
Next he passed therefrom into that of plants.
For years he lived as one of the plants,
Remembering naught of his inorganic state so different;
And when he passed from the vegetive to the animal state
He had no remembrance of his state as a plant,
Except the inclination he felt to the world of plants,
Especially at the time of spring and sweet flowers.
Like the inclination of infants towards their mothers,
Which know not the cause of their inclination to the breast.
Again the great Creator, as you know,
Drew man out of the animal into the human state.
Thus man passed from one order of nature to another,
Till he became wise and knowing and strong as he is now.
Of his first souls he has now no remembrance.
And he will be again changed from his present soul.[62]

The point, however, which has caused much difference of opinion among Muslim philosophers and theologians is whether the re-emergence of man involves the re-emergence of his former physical medium. Most of them, including Shāh Walīallāh, the last great theologian of Islam, are inclined to think that it does involve at least some kind of physical medium suitable to the ego's new environment. It seems to me that this view is mainly due to the fact that the ego, as an individual, is inconceivable without some kind of local reference or empirical background. The following verses, however, throw some light on the point:

'What! when dead and turned to dust, shall we rise again?

'Remote is such a return. Now know We what the Earth consumeth of them and with Us is a book in which account is kept ' (50:3-4).[63]

To my mind these verses clearly suggest that the nature of the universe is such that it is open to it to maintain in some other way the kind of individuality necessary for the final working out of human action, even after the disintegration of what appears to specify his individuality in his present environment. What that other way is we do not know. Nor do we gain any further insight into the nature of the 'second creation'[64] by associating it with some kind of body, however, subtle it may be. The analogies of the Qur'«n, only suggest it as a fact; they are not meant to reveal its nature and character. Philosophically speaking, therefore, we cannot go farther than this - that in view of the past history of man it is highly improbable that his career should come to an end with the dissolution of his body.

However, according to the teaching of the Qur'«n the ego's re-emergence brings him a 'sharp sight' (50:22) whereby he clearly sees his self-built 'fate fastened round his neck.'[65] Heaven and Hell are states, not localities. Their descriptions in the Qur'«n are visual representations[66] of an inner fact, i.e. character. Hell, in the words of the Qur'«n, is 'God's kindled fire which mounts above the hearts'[67] - the painful realization of one's failure as a man. Heaven is the joy of triumph over the forces of disintegration. There is no such thing as eternal damnation in Islam. The word 'eternity' used in certain verses, relating to Hell, is explained by the Qur'«n itself to mean only a period of time (78:23). Time cannot be wholly irrelevant to the development of personality. Character tends to become permanent; its reshaping must require time. Hell, therefore, as conceived by the Qur'«n, is not a pit of everlasting torture[68] inflicted by a revengeful God; it is a corrective experience[69] which may make a hardened ego once more sensitive to the living breeze of Divine Grace. Nor is heaven a holiday. Life is one and continuous. Man marches always onward to receive ever fresh illuminations from an Infinite Reality which 'every moment appears in a new glory'.[70] And the recipient of Divine illumination is not merely a passive recipient. Every act of a free ego creates a new situation, and thus offers further opportunities of creative unfolding.

Lecture IV Notes: THE HUMAN EGO - HIS FREEDOM AND IMMORTALITY

1. Cf. Qur'«n, 6:94, 19:80 and 19:93-95; see also p. 93 where Allama Iqbal, referring to these last verses, affirms that in the life hereafter the finite ego will approach the Infinite Ego 'with the irreplaceable singleness of his individually'.

2. This is, in fact translation of the Quranic text: *wa l«taziru w«zirat-unw wizra ukhr«* which appears in verses 6:164; 17:15; 35:18; 39:7 and 53:38. Chronologically the last verse 53:38 is the earliest on the subject. The implication of this supreme ethical principle or law is three-fold: a categorical rejection of the Christian doctrine of the 'original sin', refutation of the idea of 'vicarious atonement or redemption', and denial of the possibility of mediation between the sinner and God (cf. M. Asad, *The Message of the Qur'«n*, p. 816, note 31).

3. Again, translation of the Quranic verse 53:39 which is in continuation of the verse last referred to above.

4. Cf. O. Spengler, *The Decline of the West*, I, 306-07. Also Lecture V, p. 114 where Allama Iqbal makes the important statement: 'Indeed my main purpose in these lectures has been to secure a vision of the spirit of Islam as emancipated from its Magian overlayings' (italics mine). This may be read in conjunction with Allama's reply to a Parsi gentleman's letter published in *Statesman*. This reply makes it clear that: 'Magian thought and religious experience very much permeate Muslim theology, philosophy and Sufism. Indeed, there is evidence to show that certain schools of Sufism known as Islamic have only repeated the Magian type of religious experience . . . . There is definite evidence in the Qur'«n itself to show that Islam aimed at opening up new channels not only of thought but the religious experience as well. Our Magian inheritance, however, has stifled the life of Islam and never allowed the development of its real spirit and aspirations' (*Speeches, Writings and Statements of Iqbal*, ed. A.L. Sherwani, p. 170). It is important to note that, according to Allama Iqbal, Bahaism and Qadianism are 'the two forms which the modern revival of pre-Islamic Magianism has assumed', cf. his

article 'Qadianis and Orthodox Muslims', ibid., p. 162. This is reiterated in 'Introduction to the Study of Islam', a highly valuable synopsis of a book that Allama contemplated to write. Under section 'E' Sub-section (iii) one of the topics of this proposed book is: 'Babi, Ahmadiyya, etc. Prophecies. All More or Less Magian' (*Letters and Writings of Iqbal*, p. 93; italics mine). Earlier on pp. 87-88 there is an enlightening passage which reads: 'Empire brought men belonging to earlier ascetic cultures, which Spengler describes as Magian, within the fold of Islam. The result was the conversion of Islam to a pre-Islamic creed with all the philosophical controversies of these creeds: *Rēh*, *Nafs*; Qur'«n; *Àadâth* or *Qadâm*. Real Islam had very little chances.' This may be compared with Allama's impassioned statement in his article: 'Islam and Mysticism' (*Speeches, Writings and Statements of Iqbal*, p. 122): 'The Moslems of Spain, with their Aristotelian spirit, and away from the enervating influences of the thought of Western and Central Asia, were comparatively much closer to the spirit of Islam than the Moslem races of Asia, who let Arabian Islam pass through all the solvents of Ajam and finally divested it of its original character. The conquest of Persia meant not the conversion of Persia to Islam, but the conversion of Islam to Persianism. Read the intellectual history of the Moslems of Western and Central Asia from the 10th century downwards, and you will find therein verified every word that I have written above.' And Allama Iqbal wrote this, be it noted, in July 1917, i.e. before Spengler's magnum opus: *The Decline of the West* was published (Vol. I, 1918, revised 1923, Vol. II, 1922; English translation, Vol. I, 23 April 1926, Vol. II, 9 November 1928) and before the expressions such as 'Magian Soul', 'Magian Culture' and 'Magian Religion' came to be used by the philosophers of history and culture.

5. Cf. the Quranic verses 41:53 and 51:20-21, which make it incumbent on men to study signs of God in themselves as much as those in the world around them.

6. Cf. Husain b. Mansēr al-Àall«j, *Kit«b al-ñaw«sân*, English translation by Aisha Abd Ar-Rahman, also by Gilani Kamran, (*Ana al-Haqq Reconsidered*, pp. 55-108), *ñ«sân* VI, 23, containing al-Àall«j's ecstatic utterance: *an« al-Haqq*, and L. Massignon's explanatory notes on it translated by R.A. Butler in his article 'Kit«b al-Taw«sân of al-Hall«j' *Journal of the University of Baluchistan*, 1/2 (Autumn 1981), 79-85; cf. also A. Schimmel, *Mystical Dimensions of Islam*, pp. 66 ff.

It may be noted that Allama Iqbal in his, in many ways very valuable, article 'McTaggart's Philosophy' (*Speeches, Writings and Statements of Iqbal*, pp. 143-51), compares McTaggart to Àall«j (pp. 148-49). In the system of this 'philosopher-saint', 'mystical intuition, as a source of knowledge, is much more marked than in the system of Bradley . . . . In the case of McTaggart the mystic Reality came to him as a confirmation of his thought . . . . When the mystic Sultan Abē Sa'id met the philosopher Abē 'Alâ ibn Sân«, he is reported to have said, 'I see what he knows.' McTaggart both knew and saw' (pp. 145-46). The key to McTaggart's system indeed, is his mysticism as is borne out from the concluding sentence of his first work Studies in the Hegelian Dialectic: 'All true philosophy must be mystical, not indeed in its methods, but in its final conclusions.'

This in-depth article on 'McTaggart's Philosophy' also contains Allama Iqbal's own translation of two passages from his poem The New Garden of Mystery (*Gulshan-i R«z-i Jadâd*) dealing with Questions VI and VIII; the latter Question probes into the mystery of Àall«j's ecstatic utterance: 'I am the Truth'. Cf. B.A. Dar (tr.), *Iqbal's Gulshan-i R«z-i Jadâd and Bandagâ N«mah*, pp. 42-43, 51-54.

7. Cf. *The Muqaddimah*, trans. F. Rosenthal, II, 76-103.

8. Note Iqb«l significant observation that 'modern psychology has not yet touched even the outer fringe of religious life and is still far from the richness and variety of what is called religious experience' (Lecture VII, p. 152).

9. Cf. *Ethical Studies* (1876), pp. 80 f.

10. Cf. *The Principles of Logic* (1883), Vol. II, chapter ii.

11. Cf. *Appearance and Reality* (1893), pp. 90-103.

12. *Jâv«tm«* is the individual mind or consciousness of man or his soul distinguished from the cosmic mind, cosmic consciousness or world-soul; cf. 'Atman', *Encyclopaedia of Religion and Ethics*, II,195, also XII, 597.

13. Cf. *Appearance and Reality*, p. 89; also 'Appendix', p. 497.

14. Misprinted as, mutual, states in the previous editions.

15. For Ghazâlâ's conception of the soul, cf. M. Saeed Sheikh, 'Al-Ghazâlâ: *Mysticism'*, *A History of Muslim Philosophy*, ed. M.M. Sharif, I, 619-21.

16. Reference here is to what Kant named 'Paralogisms of Pure Reason', i.e. fallacious arguments which allege to prove substantiality, simplicity, numerical identity and eternality of the human soul; cf. *Critique of Pure Reason*, pp. 328-83.

17. *Ibid.*, pp. 329-30.

18. *Ibid.*, pp. 372-73; this is, in fact, Kant's argument in refutation of the German Jewish philosopher Moses Mendelssohn's 'Proof of the Permanence of the Soul'; cf. Kemp Smith, *Commentary to Kant's Critique of Pure Reason*, pp. 470-71.

19. Cf. *Principles of Psychology*, Vol. I, chapter ix, especially pp. 237-48.

20. Ibid., p. 340.

21. Ibid., p. 339; cf. *Critique of Pure Reason*, p. 342, note (a) where Kant gives an illustration of a series of elastic balls in connection with the third paralogism to establish the numerical identity of the ego. Kemp Smith in his Commentary p. 461, has rightly observed that William James's psychological description of self-consciousness is simply an extension of this illustration.

22. Qur'ân, 7:54.

23. Cf. pp. 84-85, where Allama Iqbal gives a philosophical answer to this question in terms of contemporary theory of emergent evolution as expounded by S. Alexander (*Space, Time and Deity*, 2 vols., 1920) and C.L. Morgan (*Emergent Evolution*, 1923). The theory distinguishes between two kinds of effects: 'resultants' which are the predictable outcome of previously existing conditions and 'emergents' which are specifically new and not completely predictable. According to Alexander, who in his original conception of emergence was indebted to Morgan (cf. *Space, Time and Deity*, II, 14), mind is 'an 'emergent' from life, and life an emergent from a lower physico-chemical level of existence' (ibid.). When physico-chemical processes attain a certain degree of Gestalt-like structural complexity life emerges out of it. Life is not an epiphenomenon, nor is it an entelechy as with Hans Driesch but an 'emergent' - there is no cleft between life and matter. At the next stage of 'configurations' when neural processes in living organisms attain a certain level of structural complexity, mind appears as a novel emergent. By reasonable extrapolation it may be assumed that there are emergents (or 'qualities') higher than mind.

This is very close to Maulânâ Rûmî's 'biological future of man', 'Abd al-Karâm al-Jâlâ's 'Perfect Man' and Nietzsche's 'Superman'. No wonder that Allama Iqbal in his letter dated 24 January 1921 to R.A. Nicholson (*Letters of Iqbal*, pp. 141-42), while taking a strict notice of E.M. Forster's review of *The Secrets of the Self* (translation of his epoch-making *Asrâr-i Khudâ*) and particularly of the Nietzschean allegation against him (cf. Forster's review in Dr Riffat Hassan, The *Sword and the Sceptre*, p. 284) writes: 'Nor does he rightly understand my idea of the Perfect Man which he confounds with the German thinker's Superman. I wrote on the Sufi doctrine of the Perfect Man more than twenty years ago, long before I had read or heard anything of Nietzsche . . . . The English reader ought to approach this idea, not through the German thinker, but through an English *thinker of great merit* (italics mine) - I mean Alexander - whose Gifford Lectures (1916-18) delivered at Glasgow were published last year.' This is followed by a quotation from Alexander's chapter on 'Deity and God' (op. cit., II, 347, II, 1-8) ending in a significant admission: '*Alexander's thought is much bolder than mine* (italics mine).

24. More generally known as James-Lange theory of emotions. This theory was propounded by the Danish physician and psychologist, Carl George Lange in a pamphlet *Om Sindsbevaegelser* in 1885, while William James had already set forth similar views in an article published in *Mind* in 1884. For a full statement of the theory, see William James, Principles of Psychology, II, 449 ff. and for its refutation (as hinted at by Allama Iqbal), Encyclopaedia Britanica, s.v., XII, 885-86.

25. For Iqbal's very clear and definitive verdict of body-mind dualism, cf. Lecture VI, p. 122.

26. Reference is to the Quranic verse (7:54) quoted on p. 82.

27. Cf. Lecture II, p. 28.

28. Qur'«n, 57:3.

29. Cf. William James, *op. cit.*, II, 549.

30. More generally known as Gestalt Psychology, this German school of psychology was the result of the combined work of M. Wertheimer, K. Koffka and W. Kö hler during 1912-14. It came as a reaction against the psychic elements of analytic or associationistic psychology, insisting upon the concept of gestalt, configuration, or organized whole which, if analyzed, it was averred, would lose its distinctive quality. Thus it is impossible to consider the phenomenon of perception as in any way made up of a number of isolable elements, sensory or of any other origin, for what we perceive are 'forms', 'shapes' or 'configurations'. From 'perception' the gestalt-principle has been extended throughout psychology and into biology and physics. Important for Iqbal scholars are the suggestions recently made to discern some 'points of contact' between the Gestalt and the philosophies of J. C. Smuts (holism) and A.N. Whitehead (philosophy of organism); cf. K. Koffka, 'Gestalt', *Encyclopaedia of the Social Sciences*, VI, 642-46; also J. C. Smuts, 'Holism', *Encyclopaedia Britannica*, XI, 643.

31. The concept of 'insight' was first elaborately expounded by W. Kö hler in his famous work: *The Mentality of Apes* (first English translation in 1924 of his *Intelligerprufù ngen an Menschenaffen*, 1917); cf. C.S. Peyser, 'Kohler, Wolfgang (1887-1967)', *Encyclopedia of Psychology*, II, 271.

32. In the history of Islamic thought, this is one of the finest arguments to resolve the age-long controversy between determinism and indeterminism and to establish the soundest basis for self-determinism.

33. Cf. *The Decline of the West*, II, 240, where Spengler says: 'But it is precisely the impossibility of an Ego as a free power in the face of the divine that constitutes Islam. (italics by Spengler); earlier on p. 235 speaking of Magian religions (and for him Islam is one of them) Spengler observes: 'the impossibility of a thinking, believing, and knowing Ego is the presupposition inherent in all the fundamentals of all these religions'.

34. Cf. Lecture II, p. 40.

35. Cf. Introduction to the *Secrets of the Self* (English translation of Allama Iqbal's 'philosophical poem': *Asr«r-i Khudâ*), pp. xviii-xix.

36. See Ibn Qutaibah, *Kit«b al-Ma'«rif*, ed. 'Ukashah, p. 441; cf. also Obermann, 'Political Theology in Early Islam': Àasan al-Basrâ's Treatise on qadar', *Journal of the American Oriental Society*, LV (1935), 138-62.

37. Cf. D. B. Macdonald, *Development of Muslim Theology*, pp. 123-24, for a brief mention of 'the origin of the theory of the accomplished fact' with reference to the political attitude of the Murjâ'ites, and Khuda Bukhsh, *Politics in Islam*, p. 150, for Ibn Jam«'ah's view on the subject as contained in his work on constitutional law of Islam: *TaÁrâr al-Ahk«m fâ Tadbâr Ahl al-Isl«m* (ed. Hans Kofler), p. 357. It may be added that Allama Iqbal did take notice of Ibn Jama''ah's view (of bai'ah through force) and observed: 'This opportunist view has no support in the law of Islam': cf. his article 'Political Thought in Islam' *Sociological Review*, I (1908), 256, II, 15-16; reproduced in *Speeches, Writings and Statements of Iqbal*, ed. A. L. Sherwani, p. 115.

38. Cf. Renan, *Averrö es et l'averroisme* (pp. 136f.) as quoted in R.A. Tsanoff, *The Problem of Immortality*, p. 76.

39. Cf. William James, *Human Immortality*, p. 32.

40. *Ibid.*, p. 28.

41. *Ibid.*, p. 29.

42. Cf. Lecture II, pp. 26-28; also p. 83.

43. This passage in its entire import seems to be quite close to the one quoted from Eddington's widely read *Nature of the Physical World* (p. 323) in Lecture VII, p. 147.

44. Cf. R. A. Tsanoff, *op. cit.*, pp. 143-78, for a commendable account of Nietzsche's doctrine of Eternal Recurrence.

45. Cf. H. Spencer, *First Principles*, pp. 549 ff.

46. Cf. Tsanoff, *op. cit.*, pp. 162-63.

47. Cf. Oscar Levy (ed.), *Complete Works of Friedrich Nietzsche*, XIV, 248 and 250, quoted in Tsanoff, *op. cit.*, p. 163.

48. Cf. Levy, *op. cit.*, XVI, 274, and Tsanoff, *op. cit.*, p. 177.

49. Cf. Lecture V, p. 113 where Iqbal says: 'Whatever may be the criterion by which to judge the forward steps of creative movement, the movement itself, if conceived as cyclic, ceases to be creative. Eternal recurrence is not eternal creation, it is eternal repetition'.

50. *Barzakh*, according to Lane's *Arabic-English Lexicon*, means 'a thing that intervenes between any two things, or a bar, an obstruction, or a thing that makes a separation between two things'. As signifying the state between death and resurrection the word barzakh occurs in the Qur'«n, 23:99-100.

51. Reference is to the Quranic verses 23:12-14 quoted on p. 83.

52. See also verses 6:94 and 19:80.

53. Translation of the Quranic expression *ajr-un ghairu mamnun-in* found in verses 41:8; 84:25 and 95:6.

54. Reference here is among others to the Quranic verses 69:13-18; 77:8-11.

55. Cf. also the Quranic verses 20:112; 21:103; 101:6-7.

56. This alludes to the difference of the Prophet's encounter with God as stated in the Quranic verse 53:17 from that of Prophet Moses' as given in verses 7:143. Referring to the Persian verse (ascribed by some to the Sufä poet Jam«lâ of Delhi who died in 942/1535), Iqbal in his letter to Dr Hadi Hasan of Aligarh Muslim University observes: 'In the whole range of Muslim literature there is not one verse like it and these two lines enclose a whole infinitude of ideas'. See B.A. Dar (ed.), *Letters and Writings of Iqbal*, pp. 2-3.

57. So important is 'action' or 'deed' according to the Qur'«n that there are more than one hundred verses urging the believers to act righteously - hence, the opening line of Allama Iqbal's Preface to the Lectures; see M. Fu'«d 'Abd al-B«qâ's al-Mu'jam al-Mufahras li Alf«z al-Qur'«n al Karâm, verses under the radicals: ml, slh and hsn.

58. This, according to Helmholtz, one of the greatest scientists of the nineteenth century, was about thirty metres per second. Before Helmholtz the conduction of neural impulse was thought to be instantareous, too fast to be measured. After he had demonstrated its measurement through his experimental studies; his researches came to be used in experiments on reaction time (cf. Gardner Murphy, *Historical Introduction to Modern Psychology*, p. 138 and N. A. Haynie's article: 'Helmholtz, Hermann von (1821-1894)' in *Encyclopedia of Psychology*, II, 103. Allama Iqbal's Hypothetical statement with reference to Helmholtz's discovery: 'If this is so, our present physiological structure is at the bottom of our present view of time' is highly suggestive of new physiological or biological studies of time. It is to be noted that some useful research in this direction seems to have been undertaken already; cf. articles: 'Time' and 'Time Perception' in *The New Encyclopaedia Britannica* (Macropaedia), XVIII, 420-22.

59. See George Sarton, *Introduction to the History of Science*, I, 597, where it is said that the Kitāb al-Hayawān of al-Jāḥiẓ contains the germs of many later theories: evolution adaptation, animal psychology. Cf. also M. Plessner, 'Al-Jāḥiẓ' in *Dictionary of Scientific Biography*, VII, 63-65.

60. For a statement of the views of 'Brethren of Purity' with regard to the hypothesis of evolution, cf. Seyyed Hossein Nasr, *An Introduction to Islamic Cosmological Doctrines*, pp. 72-74.

61. See Lecture V, p. 107, for Ibn Maskawaih's very clear conception of biological evolution, which later found expression in the 'inimitable lines' of 'the excellent Rūmā' quoted in the next passage as well as in Lecture VII, pp. 147-48.

62. Cf. E. H. Whinfield (tr.), *Masnavi*, pp. 216-17; this is translation of verses 3637-41 and 3646-48 of Book iv of Rūmā' s *Mathnawā*- cf. Allama Iqbal's observation on these verses in his *Development of Metaphysics in Persia*, p. 91.

63. For the keeping of a book or record of whatever man does in life here, there is repeated mention in the Qur'a`n; see, for example, verses 18:49; 21:94; 43:80 and 45:29.

64. Reference seems here to be to the Quranic verse 29:20 though 'second creation' is also alluded to in such verses as 10:4; 27:64; 30:11. See also 56:61.

65. Qur'ān, 17:13.

66. Reference here is to the Quranic description of life hereafter such as is to be found in verses 37:41-49 and 44:51-55 for the state of life promised to the righteous, and 37:62-68 and 44:43-49 for the kind of life to be suffered by the wicked. See also 32:17.

67. Qur'ān, 104:6-7.

68. Reference is to the Quranic expression hāwâyah (for hell) in 101:9.

69. See the Quranic verse 57:15 where the fire of hell is spoken of as man's friend (*maulā*), i.e. 'the only thing by which he may hope to be purified and redeemed' (cf. M. Asad, *The Message of the Qur'ān*, p. 838, note 21).

70. Qur'ān, 55:29.

Home   **The Spirit of Muslim Culture**

by Dr. Muhammad Iqbal

'Muhammad of Arabia ascended the highest Heaven and returned. I swear by God that if I had reached that point, I should never have returned.'[1] These are the words of a great Muslim saint, 'AbdulQuddēs of Gangoh. In the whole range of Sufi literature it will be probably difficult to find words which, in a single sentence, disclose such an acute perception of the psychological difference between the prophetic and the mystic types of consciousness. The mystic does not wish to return from the repose of 'unitary experience'; and even when he does return, as he must, his return does not mean much for mankind at large. The prophet's return is creative. He returns to insert himself into the sweep of time with a view to control the forces of history, and thereby to create a fresh world of ideals. For the mystic the repose of 'unitary experience' is something final; for the prophet it is the awakening, within him, of world-shaking psychological forces, calculated to completely transform the human world. The desire to see his religious experience transformed into a living world-force is supreme in the prophet. Thus his return amounts to a kind of pragmatic test of the value of his religious experience. In its creative act the prophet's will judges both itself and the world of concrete fact in which it endeavours to objectify itself. In penetrating the impervious material before him the prophet discovers himself for himself, and unveils himself to the eye of history. Another way of judging the value of a prophet's religious experience, therefore, would be to examine the type of manhood that he has created, and the cultural world that has sprung out of the spirit of his message. In this lecture I want to confine myself to the latter alone. The idea is not to give you a description of the achievements of Islam in the domain of knowledge. I want rather to fix your gaze on some of the ruling concepts of the culture of Islam in order to gain an insight into the process of ideation that underlies them, and thus to catch a glimpse of the soul that found expression through them. Before, however, I proceed to do so it is necessary to understand the cultural value of a great idea in Islam - I mean the finality of the institution of prophethood.[2]

A prophet may be defined as a type of mystic consciousness in which 'unitary experience' tends to overflow its boundaries, and seeks opportunities of redirecting or refashioning the forces of collective life. In his personality the finite centre of life sinks into his own infinite depths only to spring up again, with fresh vigour, to destroy the old, and to disclose the new directions of life. This contact with the root of his own being is by no means peculiar to man. Indeed the way in which the word WaÁâ (inspiration) is used in the Qur'«n shows that the Qur'«n regards it as a universal property of life;[3] though its nature and character are different at different stages of the evolution of life. The plant growing freely in space, the animal developing a new organ to suit a new environment, and a human being receiving light from the inner depths of life, are all cases of inspiration varying in character according to the needs of the recipient, or the needs of the species to which the recipient belongs. Now during the minority of mankind psychic energy develops what I call prophetic consciousness - a mode of economizing individual thought and choice by providing ready-made judgements, choices, and ways of action. With the birth of reason and critical faculty, however, life, in its own interest, inhibits the formation and growth of non-rational modes of consciousness through which psychic energy flowed at an earlier stage of human evolution. Man is primarily governed by passion and instinct. Inductive reason, which alone makes man master of his environment, is an achievement; and when once born it must be reinforced by inhibiting the growth of other modes of knowledge. There is no doubt that the ancient world produced some great systems of philosophy at a time when man was comparatively primitive and governed more or less by suggestion. But we must not forget that this system-building in the ancient world was the work of abstract thought which cannot go beyond the systematization of vague religious beliefs and traditions, and gives us no hold on the concrete situations of life.

Looking at the matter from this point of view, then, the Prophet of Islam seems to stand between the ancient and the modern world. In so far as the source of his revelation is concerned he belongs to the ancient world; in so far as the spirit of his revelation is concerned he belongs to the modern world. In him life discovers other sources of knowledge suitable to its new direction. The birth of Islam, as I hope to be able presently to prove to your satisfaction, is the birth of inductive intellect. In Islam prophecy reaches its perfection in discovering the need of its own abolition.[4] This involves the keen perception that life cannot for ever be kept in leading strings; that, in order to achieve full self-consciousness, man must finally be thrown back on his own resources. The abolition of priesthood and hereditary kingship in Islam, the constant appeal to reason and experience in the Qur'«n, and the emphasis that it lays on Nature and History as sources of human knowledge, are all different aspects of the same idea of finality. The idea, however, does not mean that mystic experience, which qualitatively does not differ from the experience of the prophet, has now ceased to exist as a vital fact. Indeed the Qur'«n regards both *Anfus* (self) and *ÿf«q* (world) as sources of knowledge.[5] God reveals His signs in inner as well as outer experience, and it is the duty of man to judge the knowledge-yielding capacity of all aspects of experience. The idea of finality, therefore, should not be taken to suggest that the ultimate fate of life is complete displacement of emotion by reason. Such a thing is neither possible nor desirable. The intellectual value of the idea is that it tends to create an independent critical attitude towards mystic experience by generating the belief that all personal authority, claiming a supernatural origin, has come to an end in the history of man. This kind of belief is a psychological force which inhibits the growth of such authority. The function of the idea is to open up fresh vistas of knowledge in the domain of man's inner experience. Just as the first half of the formula of Islam[6] has created and fostered the spirit of a critical observation of man's outer experience by divesting the forces of nature of that Divine character with which earlier cultures had clothed them. Mystic experience, then, however unusual and abnormal, must now be regarded by a Muslim as a perfectly natural experience, open to critical scrutiny like other aspects of human experience. This is clear from the Prophet's own attitude towards Ibn Âayy«d's psychic experiences.[7] The function of Sufism in Islam has been to systematize mystic experience; though it must be admitted that Ibn Khaldën was the only Muslim who approached it in a thoroughly scientific spirit.[8]

But inner experience is only one source of human knowledge. According to the Qur'«n, there are two other sources of knowledge - Nature and History; and it is in tapping these sources of knowledge that the spirit of Islam is seen at its best. The Qur'«n sees signs of the Ultimate Reality in the 'sun', the 'moon', 'the lengthening out of shadows', 'the alternation of day and night', 'the variety of human colours and tongues',10 'the alternation of the days of success and reverse among peoples' - in fact in the whole of Nature as revealed to the sense-perception of man. And the Muslim's duty is to reflect on these signs and not to pass by them 'as if he is dead and blind', for he 'who does not see these signs in this life will remain blind to the realities of the life to come'.[9] This appeal to the concrete combined with the slow realization that, according to the teachings of the Qur'«n, the universe is dynamic in its origin, finite and capable of increase, eventually brought Muslim thinkers into conflict with Greek thought which, in the beginning of their intellectual career, they had studied with so much enthusiasm. Not realizing that the spirit of the Qur'«n was essentially anti-classical, and putting full confidence in Greek thinkers, their first impulse was to understand the Qur'«n in the light of Greek philosophy. In view of the concrete spirit of the Qur'«n, and the speculative nature of Greek philosophy which enjoyed theory and was neglectful of fact, this attempt was foredoomed to failure. And it is what follows their failure that brings out the real spirit of the culture of Islam, and lays the foundation of modern culture in some of its most important aspects.

This intellectual revolt against Greek philosophy manifests itself in all departments of thought. I am afraid I am not competent enough to deal with it as it discloses itself in Mathematics, Astronomy, and Medicine. It is clearly visible in the metaphysical thought of the Ash'arite, but appears as a most well-defined phenomenon in the Muslim criticism of Greek Logic. This was only natural; for dissatisfaction with purely speculative philosophy means the search for a surer method of knowledge. It was, I think, Naïï«m who first formulated the principle of 'doubt' as the beginning of all knowledge. Ghazz«lâ further amplified it in his 'Revivification of the Sciences of Religion',[10] and prepared the way for 'Descartes' Method'. But Ghazz«lâ remained on the whole a follower of Aristotle in Logic. In his *Qist«s* he puts some of the Quranic arguments in the form of Aristotelian figures,[11] but forgets the Quranic *Sërah* known as *Shu'ar«'* where the proposition that retribution follows the gainsaying of prophets is established by the method of simple enumeration of historical instances. It was Ishr«qâ and Ibn Taimâyyah who undertook a systematic refutation of Greek Logic.[12] Abë Bakr R«zâ was perhaps the first to criticize Aristotle's first figure,[13] and in our own times his objection, conceived in a thoroughly inductive spirit, has been reformulated by John Stuart Mill. Ibn Àazm, in his 'Scope of Logic',[14] emphasizes sense-perception as a source of knowledge; and Ibn Taimâyyah in his 'Refutation of Logic', shows that induction is the only form of reliable argument. Thus arose the method of observation and experiment. It was not a merely theoretical affair. Al-Bârënâ's discovery of what we call reaction-time and al-Kindâ's discovery that sensation is proportionate to the stimulus, are instances of its application in psychology.[15] It is a mistake to suppose that the experimental method is a European discovery. Dü hring tells us that Roger Bacon's conceptions of science are more just and clear than those of his celebrated namesake. And where did Roger Bacon receive his scientific training? - In the Muslim universities of Spain. Indeed Part V of his *Opus Majus* which is devoted to 'Perspective' is practically a copy of Ibn Haitham's *Optics*.[16] Nor is the book, as a whole, lacking in evidences of Ibn Hazm's influence on its author.[17] Europe has been rather slow to recognize the Islamic origin of her scientific method. But full recognition of the fact has at last come. Let me quote one or two passages from Briffault's *Making of Humanity*,

'. . . it was under their successors at that Oxford school that Roger Bacon learned Arabic and Arabic science. Neither Roger Bacon nor his later namesake has any title to be credited with having introduced the experimental method. Roger Bacon was no more than one of the apostles of Muslim science and method to Christian Europe; and he never wearied of declaring that a knowledge of Arabic and Arabian science was for his contemporaries the only way to true knowledge. Discussions as to who was the originator of the experimental method . . . are part of the colossal misrepresentation of the origins of European civilization. The experimental method of the Arabs was by Bacon's time widespread and eagerly cultivated throughout Europe' (pp. 200-01). . . .

'Science is the most momentous contribution of Arab civilization to the modern world, but its fruits were slow in ripening. Not until long after Moorish culture had sunk back into darkness did the giant to which it had given birth rise in his might. It was not science which brought Europe back to life. Other and manifold influences from the civilization of Islam communicated its first glow to European life' (p. 202).

'For although there is not a single aspect of European growth in which the decisive influence of Islamic culture is not traceable, nowhere is it so clear and momentous as in the genesis of that power which constitutes the paramount distinctive force of the modern world, and the supreme source of its victory - natural science and the scientific spirit' (p. 190).

'The debt of our science to that of the Arabs does not consist in startling discoveries or revolutionary theories; science owes a great deal more to Arab culture, it owes its existence. The ancient world was, as we saw, pre-scientific. The astronomy and mathematics of the Greek were a foreign importation never thoroughly acclimatized in Greek culture. The Greeks systematized, generalized, and theorized, but the patient ways of investigation, the accumulation of positive knowledge, the minute methods of science, detailed and prolonged observation, experimental inquiry, were altogether alien to the Greek temperament. Only in Hellenistic Alexandria was any approach to scientific work conducted in the ancient classical world. What we call science arose in Europe as a result of a new spirit of inquiry, of new methods of investigation, of the method of experiment, observation, measurement, of the development of mathematics in a form unknown to the Greeks. That spirit and those methods were introduced into the European world by the Arabs' (p. 191).

The first important point to note about the spirit of Muslim culture then is that, for purposes of knowledge, it fixes its gaze on the concrete, the finite. It is further clear that the birth of the method of observation and experiment in Islam was due not to a compromise with Greek thought but to a prolonged intellectual warfare with it. In fact, the influence of the Greeks who, as Briffault says, were interested chiefly in theory, not in fact, tended rather to obscure the Muslims' vision of the Qur'«n, and for at least two centuries kept the practical Arab temperament from asserting itself and coming to its own. I want, therefore, definitely to eradicate the misunderstanding that Greek thought, in any way, determined the character of Muslim culture. Part of my argument you have seen; part you will see presently.

Knowledge must begin with the concrete. It is the intellectual capture of and power over the concrete that makes it possible for the intellect of man to pass beyond the concrete. As the Qur'«n says:

'O company of djinn and men, if you can overpass the bounds of the heaven and the earth, then overpass them. But by power alone shall ye overpass them' (55:33).

But the universe, as a collection of finite things, presents itself as a kind of island situated in a pure vacuity to which time, regarded as a series of mutually exclusive moments, is nothing and does nothing. Such a vision of the universe leads the reflecting mind nowhere. The thought of a limit to perceptual space and time staggers the mind. The finite, as such, is an idol obstructing the movement of the mind; or, in order to overpass its bounds, the mind must overcome serial time and the pure vacuity of perceptual space. 'And verily towards thy God is the limit', says the Qur'«n.[18] This verse embodies one of the deepest thoughts in the Qur'«n; for it definitely suggests that the ultimate limit is to be sought not in the direction of stars, but in an infinite cosmic life and spirituality. Now the intellectual journey towards this ultimate limit is long and arduous; and in this effort, too, the thought of Islam appears to have moved in a direction entirely different to the Greeks. The ideal of the Greeks, as Spengler tells us, was proportion, not infinity. The physical presentness of the finite with its well-defined limits alone absorbed the mind of the Greeks. In the history of Muslim culture, on the other hand, we find that both in the realms of pure intellect and religious psychology, by which term I mean higher Sufism, the ideal revealed is the possession and enjoyment of the Infinite. In a culture, with such an attitude, the problem of space and time becomes a question of life and death. In one of these lectures I have already given you some idea of the way in which the problem of time and space presented itself to Muslim thinkers, especially the Ash'arite. One reason why the atomism of Democritus never became popular in the world of Islam is that it involves the assumption of an absolute space. The Ash'arite were, therefore, driven to develop a different kind of atomism, and tried to overcome the difficulties of perceptual space in a manner similar to modern atomism. On the side of Mathematics it must be remembered that since the days of Ptolemy (A.D. 87-165) till the time of NaÄâr ñësâ (A.D. 120-74) nobody gave serious thought to the difficulties of demonstrating the certitude of Euclid's parallel postulate on the basis of perceptual space.[19] It was ñësâ who first disturbed the calm which had prevailed in the world of Mathematics for a thousand years; and in his effort to improve the postulate realized the necessity of abandoning perceptual space. He thus furnished a basis, however slight, for the hyperspace movement of our time.[20] It was, however, al-Bârënâ who, in his approach to the modern mathematical idea of function saw, from a purely scientific point of view, the insufficiency of a static view of the universe. This again is a clear departure from the Greek view. The function-idea introduces the element of time in our world-picture. It turns the fixed into the variable, and sees the universe not as being but as becoming. Spengler thinks that the mathematical idea of function is the symbol of the West of which 'no other culture gives even a hint'.[21] In view of al-Bârënâ, generalizing Newton's formula of interpolation from trignometrical function to any function whatever.[22] Spengler's claim has no foundation in fact. The transformation of the Greek concept of number from pure magnitude to pure relation really began with Khw«rizmâs movement from Arithmetic to Algebra.[23] al-Bârënâ took a definite step forward towards what Spengler describes as chronological number which signifies the mind's passage from being to becoming. Indeed, more recent developments in European mathematics tend rather to deprive time of its living historical character, and to reduce it to a mere representation of space. That is why Whitehead's view of Relativity is likely to appeal to Muslim students more than that of Einstein in whose theory time loses its character of passage and mysteriously translates itself into utter space.[24a]

Side by side with the progress of mathematical thought in Islam we find the idea of evolution gradually shaping itself. It was Ja`hiz who was the first to note the changes in bird-life caused by migrations. Later Ibn Maskawaih who was a contemporary of al-Bârënâ gave it the shape of a more definite theory, and adopted it in his theological work - *al-Fauz al-Asghar*. I reproduce here the substance of his evolutionary hypothesis, not because of its scientific value, but because of the light which it throws on the direction in which Muslim thought was moving.

According to Ibn Maskawaih plant-life at the lowest stage of evolution does not need any seed for its birth and growth. Nor does it perpetuate its species by means of the seed. This kind of plant-life differs from minerals only in some little power of movement which grows in higher forms, and reveals itself further in that the plant spreads out its branches, and perpetuates its species by means of the seed. The power of movement gradually grows farther until we reach trees which possess a trunk, leaves, and fruit. At a higher stage of evolution stand forms of plant-life which need better soil and climate for their growth. The last stage of development is reached in vine and date-palm which stand, as it were, on the threshold of animal life. In the date-palm a clear sex-distinction appears. Besides roots and fibres it develops something which functions like the animal brain, on the integrity of which depends the life of the date-palm. This is the highest stage in the development of plant-life, and a prelude to animal life. The first forward step towards animal life is freedom from earth-rootedness which is the germ of conscious movement. This is the initial state of animality in which the sense of touch is the first, and the sense of sight is the last to appear. With the development of the senses of animal acquires freedom of movement, as in the case of worms, reptiles, ants, and bees. Animality reaches its perfection in the horse among quadrupeds and the falcon among birds, and finally arrives at the frontier of humanity in the ape which is just a degree below man in the scale of evolution. Further evolution brings physiological changes with a growing power of discrimination and spirituality until humanity passes from barbarism to civilization.[24b]

But it is really religious psychology, as in 'Ir«qâ and Khw«jah Muhammad P«rs«,[25] which brings us much nearer to our modern ways of looking at the problem of space and time. 'Ir«qâ's view of time-stratifications I have given you before.[26] I will now give you the substance of his view of space.

According to 'Ir«qâ the existence of some kind of space in relation to God is clear from the following verses of the Qur'«n:

'Dost thou not see that God knoweth all that is in the heavens and all that is in the earth? Three persons speak not privately together, but He is their fourth; nor five, but He is their sixth; nor fewer nor more, but wherever they be He is with them' (58:7).

'Ye shall not be employed in affairs, nor shall ye read a text out of the Qur'«n, nor shall ye do any work, but We will be witness over you when you are engaged therein; and the weight of an atom on earth or in heaven escapeth not thy Lord; nor is there aught[27] that is less than this or greater, but it is in the Perspicuous Book' (10:61).

'We created man, and We know what his soul whispereth to him, and We are closer to him than his neck-vein' (50:16).

But we must not forget that the words proximity, contact, and mutual separation which apply to material bodies do not apply to God. Divine life is in touch with the whole universe on the analogy of the soul's contact with the body.[28] The soul is neither inside nor outside the body; neither proximate to nor separate from it. Yet its contact with every atom of the body is real, and it is impossible to conceive this contact except by positing some kind of space which befits the subtleness of the soul. The existence of space in relation to the life of God, therefore, cannot be denied;[29] only we should carefully define the kind of space which may be predicated of the Absoluteness of God. Now, there are three kinds of space - the space of material bodies, the space of immaterial beings, and the space of God.[30] The space of material bodies is further divided into three kinds. First, the space of gross bodies of which we predicate roominess. In this space movement takes time, bodies occupy their respective places and resist displacement. Secondly, the space of subtle bodies, e.g. air and sound. In this space too bodies resist each other, and their movement is measurable in terms of time which, however, appears to be different to the time of gross bodies. The air in a tube must be displaced before other air can enter into it; and the time of sound-waves is practically nothing compared to the time of gross bodies. Thirdly, we have the space of light. The light of the sun instantly reaches the remotest limits of the earth. Thus in the velocity of light and sound time is reduced almost to zero. It is, therefore, clear that the space of light is different to the space of air and sound. There is, however, a more effective argument than this. The light of a candle spreads in all directions in a room without displacing the air in the room; and this shows that the space of light is more subtle than the space of air which has no entry into the space of light.[31] In view of the close proximity of these spaces, however, it is not possible to distinguish the one from the other except by purely intellectual analysis and spiritual experience. Again, in the hot water the two opposites - fire and water - which appear to interpenetrate each other cannot, in view of their respective natures, exist in the same space.[32] The fact cannot be explained except on the supposition that the spaces of the two substances, though closely proximate to each other, are nevertheless distinct. But while the element of distance is not entirely absent, there is no possibility of mutual resistance in the space of light. The light of a candle reaches up to a certain point only, and the lights of a hundred candles intermingle in the same room without displacing one another.

Having thus described the spaces of physical bodies possessing various degrees of subtleness 'Ir«qâ proceeds briefly to describe the main varieties of space operated upon by the various classes of immaterial beings, e.g. angels. The element of distance is not entirely absent from these spaces; for immaterial beings, while they can easily pass through stone walls, cannot altogether dispense with motion which, according to 'Ir«qâ, is evidence of imperfection in spirituality.[33] The highest point in the scale of spatial freedom is reached by the human soul which, in its unique essence, is neither at rest nor in motion.[34] Thus passing through the infinite varieties of space we reach the Divine space which is absolutely free from all dimensions and constitutes the meeting point of all infinities.[35]

From this summary of 'Ir«qâ's view you will see how a cultured Muslim Sufi`intellectually interpreted his spiritual experience of time and space in an age which had no idea of the theories and concepts of modern Mathematics and Physics. 'Ir«qâ is really trying to reach the concept of space as a dynamic appearance. His mind seems to be vaguely struggling with the concept of space as an infinite continuum; yet he was unable to see the full implications of his thought partly because he was not a mathematician and partly because of his natural prejudice in favour of the traditional Aristotelian idea of a fixed universe. Again, the interpenetration of the super-spatial 'here' and super-eternal 'now' in the Ultimate Reality suggests the modern notion of space-time which Professor Alexander, in his lectures on 'Space, Time, and Deity', regards as the matrix of all things.[36] A keener insight into the nature of time would have led 'Ir«qâ to see that time is more fundamental of the two; and that it is not a mere metaphor to say, as Professor Alexander does say, that time is the mind of space.[37] 'Ir«qâ conceives God's relation to the universe on the analogy of the relation of the human soul to the body;[38] but, instead of philosophically reaching this position through a criticism of the spatial and temporal aspects of experience, he simply postulates it on the basis of his spiritual experience. It is not sufficient merely to reduce space and time to a vanishing point-instant. The philosophical path that leads to God as the omnipsyche of the universe lies through the discovery of living thought as the ultimate principle of space-time. 'Ir«qâ's mind, no doubt, moved in the right direction, but his Aristotelian prejudices, coupled with a lack of psychological analysis, blocked his progress. With his view that Divine Time is utterly devoid of change[39] - a view obviously based on an inadequate analysis of conscious experience - it was not possible for him to discover the relation between Divine Time and serial time, and to reach, through this discovery, the essentially Islamic idea of continuous creation which means a growing universe.

Thus all lines of Muslim thought converge on a dynamic conception of the universe. This view is further reinforced by Ibn Maskawaih's theory of life as an evolutionary movement, and Ibn Khaldën's view of history. History or, in the language of the Qur'«n, 'the days of God', is the third source of human knowledge according to the Qur'«n. It is one of the most essential teachings of the Qur'«n that nations are collectively judged, and suffer for their misdeeds here and now.[40] In order to establish this proposition, the Qur'«n constantly cites historical instances, and urges upon the reader to reflect on the past and present experience of mankind.

"Of old did We send Moses with Our signs, and said to him: 'Bring forth thy people from the darkness into the light, and remind them of the days of God." Verily, in this are signs for every patient, grateful person' (14:5).

'And among those whom We had created are a people who guide others with truth, and in accordance therewith act justly. But as for those who treat Our signs as lies, We gradually ring them down by means of which they know not; and though I lengthen their days, verily, My stratagem is effectual' (7:181-83).

'Already, before your time, have precedents been made. Traverse the Earth then, and see what hath been the end of those who falsify the signs of God!' (3:137).

'If a wound hath befallen you, a wound like it hath already befallen others; We alternate the days of successes and reverses among peoples' (3:140).

'Every nation hath its fixed period' (7:34).[41]

The last verse is rather an instance of a more specific historical generalization which, in its epigrammatic formulation, suggests the possibility of a scientific treatment of the life of human societies regarded as organisms. It is, therefore, a gross error to think that the Qur'«n has no germs of a historical doctrine. The truth is that the whole spirit of the 'Prolegomena' of Ibn Khaldën appears to have been mainly due to the inspiration which the author must have received from the Qur'«n. Even in his judgements of character he is, in no small degree, indebted to the Qur'«n. An instance in point is his long paragraph devoted to an estimate of the character of the Arabs as a people. The whole paragraph is a mere amplification of the following verses of the Qur'«n:

'The Arabs of the desert are most stout in unbelief and dissimulation; and likelier it is that they should be unaware of the laws which God hath sent down to His Apostle; and God is Knowing, Wise.

'Of the Arabs of the desert there are some who reckon what they expend in the cause of God as tribute, and wait for some change of fortune to befall you: a change for evil shall befall them! God is the Hearer, the Knower' (9:97-98).

However, the interest of the Qur'«n in history, regarded as a source of human knowledge, extends farther than mere indications of historical generalizations. It has given us one of the most fundamental principles of historical criticism: Since accuracy in recording facts which constitute the material of history is an indispensable condition of history as a science, and an accurate knowledge of facts ultimately depends on those who report them, the very first principle of historical criticism is that the reporter's personal character is an important factor in judging his testimony. The Qur'«n says:

'O believers! if any bad man comes to you with a report, clear it up at once' (49:6).

It is the application of the principle embodied in this verse to the reporters of the Prophet's traditions out of which were gradually evolved the canons of historical criticism. The growth of historical sense in Islam is a fascinating subject.[42] The Quranic appeal to experience, the necessity to ascertain the exact sayings of the Prophet, and the desire to furnish permanent sources of inspiration to posterity - all these forces contributed to produce such men as Ibn Ish«q,[43] ñabarâ,[44] and Mas'ëdâ.[45] But history, as an art of firing the reader's imagination, is only a stage in the development of history as a genuine science. The possibility of a scientific treatment of history means a wider experience, a greater maturity of practical reason, and finally a fuller realization of certain basic ideas regarding the nature of life and time. These ideas are in the main two; and both form the foundation of the Quranic teaching.

1. The Unity of Human Origin. 'And We have created you all from one breath of life', says the Qur'«n.[46] But the perception of life as an organic unity is a slow achievement, and depends for its growth on a people's entry into the main current of world-events. This opportunity was brought to Islam by the rapid development of a vast empire. No doubt, Christianity, long before Islam, brought the message of equality to mankind; but Christian Rome did not rise to the full apprehension of the idea of humanity as a single organism. As

Flint rightly says, 'No Christian writer and still less, of course, any other in the Roman Empire, can be credited with having had more than a general and abstract conception of human unity.' And since the days of Rome the idea does not seem to have gained much in depth and rootage in Europe. On the other hand, the growth of territorial nationalism, with its emphasis on what is called national characteristics, has tended rather to kill the broad human element in the art and literature of Europe. It was quite otherwise with Islam. Here the idea was neither a concept of philosophy nor a dream of poetry. As a social movement the aim of Islam was to make the idea a living factor in the Muslim's daily life, and thus silently and imperceptibly to carry it towards fuller fruition.

2. *A Keen Sense of the Reality of Time, and the Concept of Life as a Continuous Movement in Time.* It is this conception of life and time which is the main point of interest in Ibn Khaldūn's view of history, and which justifies Flint's eulogy that 'Plato, Aristotle, and Augustine were not his peers, and all others were unworthy of being even mentioned along with him'.[47] From the remarks that I have made above I do not mean to throw doubt on the originality of Ibn Khaldūn. All that I mean to say is that, considering the direction in which the culture of Islam had unfolded itself, only a Muslim could have viewed history as a continuous, collective movement, a real inevitable development in time. The point of interest in this view of history is the way in which Ibn Khaldūn conceives the process of change. His conception is of infinite importance because of the implication that history, as a continuous movement in time, is a genuinely creative movement and not a movement whose path is already determined. Ibn Khaldūn was not a metaphysician. Indeed he was hostile to Metaphysics.[48] But in view of the nature of his conception of time he may fairly be regarded as a forerunner of Bergson. I have already discussed the intellectual antecedents of this conception in the cultural history of Islam. The Quranic view of the 'alternation of day and night'[49] as a symbol of the Ultimate Reality which 'appears in a fresh glory every moment',[50] the tendency in Muslim Metaphysics to regard time as objective, Ibn Maskawaih's view of life as an evolutionary movement,[51] and lastly al-Bârenâ's definite approach to the conception of Nature as a process of becoming[52] - all this constituted the intellectual inheritance of Ibn Khaldūn. His chief merit lies in his acute perception of, and systematic expression to, the spirit of the cultural movement of which he was a most brilliant product. In the work of this genius the anti-classical spirit of the Qur'«n scores its final victory over Greek thought; for with the Greeks time was either unreal, as in Plato and Zeno, or moved in a circle, as in Heraclitus and the Stoics.[53] Whatever may be the criterion by which to judge the forward steps of a creative movement, the movement itself, if conceived as cyclic, ceases to be creative. Eternal recurrence is not eternal creation; it is eternal repetition.

We are now in a position to see the true significance of the intellectual revolt of Islam against Greek philosophy. The fact that this revolt originated in a purely theological interest shows that the anti-classical spirit of the Qur'«n asserted itself in spite of those who began with a desire to interpret Islam in the light of Greek thought.

It now remains to eradicate a grave misunderstanding created by Spengler's widely read book, *The Decline of the West*. His two chapters devoted to the problem of Arabian culture[54] constitute a most important contribution to the cultural history of Asia. They are, however, based on a complete misconception of the nature of Islam as a religious movement, and of the cultural activity which it initiated. Spengler's main thesis is that each culture is a specific organism, having no point of contact with cultures that historically precede or follow it. Indeed, according to him, each culture has its own peculiar way of looking at things which is entirely inaccessible to men belonging to a different culture. In his anxiety to prove this thesis he marshals an overwhelming array of facts and interpretations to show that the spirit of European culture is through and through anti-classical. And this anti-classical spirit of European culture is entirely due to the specific genius of Europe, and not to any inspiration she may have received from the culture of Islam which, according to Spengler, is thoroughly 'Magian' in spirit and character. Spengler's view of the spirit of modern culture is, in my opinion, perfectly correct. I have, however, tried to show in these lectures that the anti-classical spirit of the modern world has really arisen out of the revolt of Islam against Greek thought.[55] It is obvious that such a view cannot be acceptable to Spengler; for, if it is possible to show that the anti-classical spirit of modern culture is due to the inspiration which it received from the culture immediately preceding it, the whole argument of Spengler regarding the complete mutual independence of cultural growths would collapse. I am afraid Spengler's anxiety to establish this thesis has completely perverted his vision of Islam as a cultural movement.

By the expression 'Magian culture' Spengler means the common culture associated with what he calls 'Magian group of religions',[56] i.e. Judaism, ancient Chaldean religion, early Christianity, Zoroastrianism, and Islam. That a Magian crust has grown over Islam, I do not deny. Indeed my main purpose in these lectures has been to secure a vision of the spirit of Islam as emancipated from its Magian overlayings which, in my opinion, have misled Spengler. His ignorance of Muslim thought on the problem of time, as well as of the way in which the 'I', as a free centre of experience, has found expression in the religious experience of Islam, is simply appalling.[57] Instead of seeking light from the history of Muslim thought and experience, he prefers to base his judgement on vulgar beliefs as to the beginning and end of time. Just imagine a man of overwhelming learning finding support for the supposed fatalism of Islam in such Eastern expressions and proverbs as the 'vault of time',[58] and 'everything has a time!'[59] However, on the origin and growth of the concept of time in Islam, and on the human ego as a free power, I have said enough in these lectures. It is obvious that a full examination of Spengler's view of Islam, and of the culture that grew out of it, will require a whole volume. In addition to what I have said before, I shall offer here one more observation of a general nature.

'The kernel of the prophetic teaching,' says Spengler, 'is already Magian. There is one God - be He called *Yahweh*,[60] *Ahuramazda*, or *Marduk-Baal* - who is the principle of good, and all other deities are either impotent or evil. To this doctrine there attached itself the hope of a Messiah, very clear in Isaiah, but also bursting out everywhere during the next centuries, under pressure of an inner necessity. It is the basic idea of Magian religion, for it contains implicitly the conception of the world-historical struggle between Good and Evil, with the power of Evil prevailing in the middle period, and the Good finally triumphant on the Day of Judgement.'60 If this view of the prophetic teaching is meant to apply to Islam it is obviously a misrepresentation. The point to note is that the Magian admitted the existence of false gods; only they did not turn to worship them. Islam denies the very existence of false gods. In this connexion Spengler fails to appreciate the cultural value of the idea of the finality of prophethood in Islam. No doubt, one important feature of Magian culture is a perpetual attitude of expectation, a constant looking forward to the coming of Zoroaster's unborn sons, the Messiah, or the Paraclete of the fourth gospel. I have already indicated the direction in which the student of Islam should seek the cultural meaning of the doctrine of finality in Islam. It may further be regarded as a psychological cure for the Magian attitude of constant expectation which tends to give a false view of history. Ibn Khaldēn, seeing the spirit of his own view of history, has fully criticized and, I believe, finally demolished the alleged revelational basis in Islam of an idea similar, at least in its psychological effects, to the original Magian idea which had reappeared in Islam under the pressure of Magian thought.[61]

Lecture V Notes: THE SPIRIT OF MUSLIM CULTURE

1. Cf. 'Abd al-Quddës Gangàhâ, *Lat« 'if-i Quddësâ*, ed. Shaikh Rukn al-Di`n, *LaÇâfah* 79; the Persian text rendered into English here is:

Reference may also be made here to very pithy and profound jottings of Allama Iqbal on the back cover of his own copy of William James's *Varieties of Religious Experience*, especially to those under the sub-heading: 'Mystical and Prophetic Consciousness' with explicit mention of 'Abd al-Quddu`s Gango`hi'; see Muhammad Siddiq, *Descriptive Catalogue of Allama Iqbal's Personal Library*, Plate No. 8.

2. This great idea is embodied in the Quranic verse 33:40, i.e. 'Muhammad... is All«h's Apostle and the Seal of all Prophets, (*Muhammad-un rasël All«h wa kh«tam-un nabâyyân*). It has also been variously enunciated in the Àadâth literature (i) *y« Muhammad-u anta rasël Ull«h-i wa kh«tam al-anbiy«'* : 'O Muhammad! you are Allah's Apostle and the Seal of all Prophets'; this is what other Prophets would proclaim on the Day of Resurrection (Bukh«râ, *Tafsâr*: 17). (ii) *Wa 'an«kh«tim-un-nabâyyân*: 'And I am the last of the Prophets' (ibid., *Man«qib*: 7; Muslim, *¥m«n*: 327). (iii) *Laisa nabâyyu ba'dâ*: 'There is no Prophet after me' (Bukh«râ, *Magh«zâ*: 77). (iv) *L«nabâyya badâ*: 'There is no Prophet after me' (ibid., Anbâya: 50; Muslim, *Im«rah*: 44; *Fad« 'il al-Sah«bah*: 30-31). (v) *Wa l«nabâyya ba'dahë*: 'And there is no Prophet after him', said so by Abë Awf« as narrated by Ism«`âl (Bukh«râ, *ÿd«b*: 109). (vi) *L«nubuwwah ba'dâ*: 'There is no prophethood after me (Muslim, *Fad« ' al-Sah«bah*: 30-32).

3. Though *wahy matluww* (revelation which is recited or worded revelation) is specific to the Prophets, the Qur'«n speaks of revelation in connection with earth (99:5), heavens (41:12), honey-bee (16:68-69), angels (8:12), mother of Moses (28:7) and disciples of Jesus (5:111). As to the different modes of revelation see 42:51.

4. Reference here is to the last but one passage of the Quranic verse 5:3 which reads: 'This day have I perfected your religion for you and completed My favour unto you and have chosen for you as religion *al-Isl«m'*. This passage, according to all available *aÁ«dâth* on the testimony of the Prophet's contemporaries, was revealed at 'Araf«t in the afternoon of Friday, the 9th of Dhu'l-Àijjah 10 A.H., the year of the Prophet's last pilgrimage to Makkah (cf. Bukha`ri`, *¥m«n*: 34, where this fact is authenticated by Haîrat 'Umar b. al-Khatta`b). It is to be noted that the Prophet's death took place eighty-one of eighty-two days after the revelation of this verse and as it speaks of the perfection of religion in Islam, no precept of legal import whatsoever was revealed after it; cf. R«zâ, *al-Tafsâr al-Kabâr*.

5. Qur'«n, 41:53.

6. The first half of the formula of Islam is: *l«il«h ill All«h*, i.e. there is no god but Allah, or nothing whatever is worthy of worship except Allah. The other half is *Muhammad-un Rasëlull«h*, i.e. Muhammad is the Messenger of Allah. The expression 'formula of Islam' signifies that by bearing witness to the truth of these two simple propositions a man enters the fold of Islam.

7. Cf. Bukh«râ, *Jan« 'iz*: 78; *Shah«dah*: 3; and *Jih«d*: 160 and 178 (Eng. trans. M. Muhsin Khan, II, 244-45; III, 488-89, and IV, 168-69 and 184-86) and Muslim: *Fitan*: 95-96 (Eng. trans. A.H. Siddiqi, IV, 1510-15).

8. Cf. *Muqaddimah*, trans. Rosenthal, Vol. III, Section vi, Discourse: 'The Science of Sufism'; D. B. Macdonald, *Religious Attitude and Life in Islam*, pp. 165-74, and M. Syrier, 'Ibn Khaldu`n and Mysticism', *Islamic Culture*, XXI/ii (1947), 264-302.

9. Reference here is to the Quranic verses: 41:37; 25:45; 10:6; 30:22 and 3:140 bearing on the phenomena of Nature which have quite often been named in the Qur'«n as «y«t All«h, i.e. the 'apparent signs of God' (R«ghib, *al-Mufrad«t*, pp. 32-33); this is followed by reference to verses 25:73 and 17:72 which in the present context clearly make it as much a religious duty of the 'true servants of the Most Gracious God 'Iba`d-ur-Rahma`n' to ponder over these apparent signs of God 'as revealed to the sense-perception of man' as to ponder over the Divine communications («y«t al-Qur'«n) revealed to the Holy Prophet - this two-way God-consciousness alone ensures man's physical and spiritual prosperity in this life as well as in the life hereafter.

10. Cf. G. H. Lewes, *The Biographical History of Philosophy* (1857), p. 306, lines, 4-8, where Lewes says: 'It is this work ('Revivification of the Sciences of Religion') which A. Schmö lders has translated; it bears so remarkable a resemblance to the *Discours de la mé thod*' of Descartes, that had any translation of it existed in the days of Descartes, everyone would have cried against the plagiarism'. The second sentence of this passage was quoted by Allama Iqbal in his doctoral dissertation: *The Development of Metaphysics in Persia* (1908), p. 73, note (1), in support of his statement that Ghazz«lâ anticipated Descartes in his philosophical method'.

It is to be noted that Schmö lders' *Essai sur les é coles philosophiques chez les Arabes* (Paris, 1842) was not the French translation of Ghazz«lâ's voluminous 'Revivification' (*Ihy«* ' *'Ulëm al-Dân* in forty books) but that of his autobiographical work *Al-Munqidh min al-Dal«l* with its earliest edited Arabic text. It seems that the remarkable originality and boldness of Ghazz«lâ's thought in the French version of *al-Munqidh* led Lewes to confuse it with the greater, the more famous 'Revivification' (*Ihy«*). For the 'amazing resemblance' between Ghazz«lâ's *Al-Munqidh min al-Dal«l* (Liberation from Error) and Descartes' *Discours de la method'* (Discourse on Method), see Professor M. M. Sharif, 'The Influence of Muslim Thought on the West', 'Section: D', *A History of Muslim Philosophy*, II, 1382-84.

11. Cf. *al-QisÇ«s al-Mustaqâm*, trans. D.P. Brewster (*The Just Balance*), chapters ii-vi and translator's Appendix III: 'Al-Ghazz«lâ and the Syllogism', pp. 126-30; cf. also Michael E. Marmura, 'Ghaza`li`'s Attitude to the Secular Sciences and Logic', *Essays on Islamic Philosophy and Science*, ed. G. F. Hourani, Section II, pp. 102-03, and Susanna Diwald's detailed review on *al-QisÇ«s* in *Der Islam* (1961), pp. 171-74.

12. For an account of Ishra`qi`'s criticism of Greek logic contained in his *Hikmat al-Ishr«q*, cf. S. Hossein Nasr, 'Shiha`b al-Di`n Suhrawardi`Maqtu`l', *A History of Muslim Philosophy*, I, 384-85; a fuller account of Ishra`qi`'s logic, according to Nicholas Rescher, is to be found in his extant but unpublished (?) *Kit«b al-Talwâh«t and Kit«b al-Lamah«t* (cf. *Development of Arabic Logic*, p. 185). It is to be noted that the earliest explanation of Ishra`qi`'s disagreement with Aristotle that logical definition is genus plus differentia, in terms of modern (Bosanquet's) logic, was given by Allama Iqbal in his *Development of Metaphysics in Persia*, pp. 97-98.

For an expose of Ibn Taimâyyah's logical masterpiece *al-Radd 'ala 'l-Mantâqâyin* (Refutation of the Logicians') cf. Serajul Haque, 'Ibn Taimi`yyah' in *A History of Muslim Philosophy*, II, 805-12; also Majid Fakhry, *A History of Islamic Philosophy* (pp. 352-53) for a lucid summing up. A valuable study of Ibn Taimi`yyah's logical ideas is that by 'Alâ S«mâ al-Nashsh«r in *Man«hij al-Bahth 'inda Mufakkiri'l-Isl«m wa Naqd al-Muslimân li'l-Mantiq al-Aristat«lâsâ*, chapter III, sections ii and iii. Al-Nashsh«r has also edited Suyëtâ's *Jahd al-Qarih«h fi tajrâd al-Nasâhah*, an abridgment of ibn Taimâyyah's *Al-Radd 'ala 'l-Mantiqiyân*.

13. Aristotle's first figure, *al-shakl al-awwal* or *al-qiyas al-k«mil* of the Muslim logicians, is a form of syllogism in which the middle term occurs as a subject in the first premiss and as a predicate in the second premiss. It is the only form of syllogism in which the conclusion becomes available in the form of a general (universal - proposition needed for scientific purposes; cf. M. Saeed Sheikh, *A Dictionary of Muslim Philosophy*, s.v.

As to the criticism of the first figure referred to here, it is more rightly to be ascribed to Fakhr al-Dân R«zâ, who, besides his own now available logical works, wrote quite a few critical commentaries on the works of Ibn Sân«, rather than to the eminent physician of Islam, Abë Bakr Zakarâya R«zâ, none of whose short treatises on some parts of the Aristotelian *Organon* seems to have survived; cf. Nicholas Rescher, *The Development of Arabic Logic*, pp. 117-18. Happily this stands confirmed by Allama Iqbal's Presidential comments (almost all of which have been incorporated in the present passage) on Khwajah Kamal's Lecture (in Urdu) on 'Islam and Modern Sciences' in the third session of the All-India Muhammadan Educational Conference, 1911, in Delhi; see S.'A.'Vahid (ed.), Maq«l«t-i Iqb«l, pp. 239-40; cf. also Allama's letter dated 1st February 1924 to Sayyid Sulaim«n Nadvâ, Iqb«ln«mah, I, 127-28; reference in both cases is to Fakhr al-Dân al-R«zâ and not to Abë Bakr R«zâ.

It is to be noted that of all the writings of Allama Iqbal including his more than 1200 letters Abë Bakr R«zi`is mentioned only in *Development of Metaphysics in Persia*: 'as a physician and as a thinker who admitted the eternity of matter, space and time and possibly looked upon light as the first creation' (pp. 24, 96). In a significant passage on p. 96 of this work Allama has listed about ten Muslim thinkers who were highly critical either of Greek philosophy in general or Greek logic in particular – Abë Bakr R«zâ's name does not appear in this list.

14. This is Ibn Hazm's *Àudëd al-Mantiq* referred to in his well-known *Kit«b al-Fisal* (I, 4 and 20; V, 70 and 128) under somewhat varied titles; also mentioned by his contemporary and compatriot Sa`id b. Ahmad al-Andalusâ in his *ñabaq«t al-Umam* (p.'118) and later listed by Brockelmann in *GAL*; Supplementbände (I, 696). C. van Arendonk, however, in his article on 'Ibn Hazm' in *The Encyclopaedia of Islam* (II, 385) and I. Goldziher, s.v. in Encyclopaedia of Religion and Ethics, VII, 71 have declared that 'the work has not survived'. And certainly very little was heard of this work until Dr Ihsan 'Abba`s of the University of Khartoum discovered possibly the only MS and published it under the title: *al-ñaqrâb li-Àadd al-Mantiq* (The Approach to the Limits of Logic) in 1959. Allama's comments on Ibn Àazm's 'Scope of Logic' *(Hudëd al-Mantiq)* at a time when it was generally considered to have been lost is a proof of his extraordinary knowledge of Muslim writers and their works.

15. Cf. *Development of Metaphysics in Persia* (1964), p. 64, where it is stated that 'Al-Birënâand Ibn Haitham (d. 1038) . . . anticipated modern empirical psychology in recognizing what is called reaction-time': in the two footnotes to this statement Allama Iqb«l quotes from de Boer's *History of Philosophy in Islam*, pp. 146 and 150, to establish the positivism, i.e. sense-empiricism respectively of both al-Birënâ and Ibn Haitham. On pp. 151-52 of this work is a passage (possibly referred to by Allama Iqbal here) which describes reaction-time very much in the modern sense: 'not only is every sensation attended by a corresponding change localized in the sense-organ, which demands a certain time, but also, between the stimulation of the organ and consciousness of the perception an interval of time must elapse, corresponding to the transmission of stimulus for some distance along the nerves.'

As to al-Kindâ's discovery that sensation is proportionate to stimulus, cf. de Boer, *op. cit.*, p. 101, where he speaks of 'the proportional relation existing between stimulus and sensation' in connection with al-Kindâ's mathematized theory of compound remedies. This is given in al-Kindâ's celebrated treatise: *Ris«lah fi Ma'rifah Quwwat-Adwâyat al-Murakkabah* which was at least twice translated into Latin (Sarton, *Introduction to the History of Science*, II, 342 and 896).

16. Cf. *Opus Majus, trans.* Robert Belle Burke, Vol. II, Part V (pp. 419-82). It is important to note that Sarton's observation on Roger Bacon's work on optics is very close to that of Allama Iqbal. 'His optics', says Sarton, 'was essentially based upon that of Ibn al-Haitham, with small additions and practical applications' *(op. cit.*, II, 957). As reported by Dr M. S. N«mës, Allama Iqbal helped him in understanding the rotographs of the only MS (No. 2460 in Bibliothéque Nationale, Paris) of Ibn Haitham's *T«hrâr al-Man«zir* for a number of days; cf. *Ibn al-Haitham: Proceedings of the Celebrations of 1000th Anniversary* (held in November 1969 under the auspices of Hamdard National Foundation Pakistan, Karachi), p. 128.

See, however, Professor A. I. Sabra's scholarly article: 'Ibn al-Haytham' in *Dictionary of Scientific Biography*, VI, 189-210, especially p 205 where he gives an up-to-date information about the MSS of Ibn Haitham's *Kit«b al-Man«zir*. According to Professor Sabra, 'The reference in Brockelmann to a recension of this work in the Paris MS, ar. 2460 (Brockelmann has 2640) is mistaken; the MS is a recension of Euclid's *Optics* which is attributed on the title page to Hasan ibn (Mës«ibn) Sh«kir'.

17. 'Ibn Hazm' here is a palpable misprint for 'ibn Haitham' - the context of the passage more fittingly demands and latter rather than the former name. Ibn Hazm's influence on Roger Bacon's *Opus Majus*, a predominantly science-oriented work, looks somewhat odd. There seems to be no evidence of it in the text of *Opus Majus* - Ibn Hazm is not even so much as mentioned by name in this work. Sarton, despite his great praise for Ibn Hazm's scholarship *(op. cit.* I, 713), nowhere hints at his contributions to 'science' or his influence of Roger Bacon, nor is this to be found in other standard works, for example, in the sixteen-volume *Dictionary of Scientific Biography*.

18. Qur'«n, 53:42.

19. For ñësâ's discussion of the parallel postulate (also named 'axiom of parallelism'), see his *'Al-Ris«lat al-Sh«fâyan 'an al-Shakk fi 'l-Khutët al-Mutaw«zâyah'* in (ñësâ's) *Ras« 'il*, Vol. II, Pt. viii, pp. 1-40. Commenting on this work Sarton observes *(op. cit.*, II, 1003): 'NaÂâr al-Dân's discussion was remarkably elaborate'. Cf. also Cajori, *A History of Elementary Mathematics*, p. 127, Q. À«fiz ñauq«`n, *Tur«th al-'Arab al-'Ilmâ*, pp. 97-98, R. Bonola, *Non-Euclidean Geometry*, pp. 12-13 and 37-38 and Dr S. H. Nasr's article: 'Al-ñësâ' in *Dictionary of Scientific Biography*, XIII, 508-14 especially p. 510.

20. This passage may be read in conjunction with Allama Iqbal's observation on ñĕsâ in his Sectional Presidential Address (delivered at the Fifth Oriental Conference, Lahore, on 20 November 1928): 'A Plea for the Deeper Study of Muslim Scientists': 'It is Tusi's effort to improve the parallel postulate of Euclid that is believed to have furnished a basis in Europe for the problem of space which eventually led to the theories of Gauss and Riemann' (*Speeches, Writings and Statements of Iqbal*, p. 138). Euclid's parallel postulate is Postulate V of the first book of his *Elements*. What it means to say is that through a given point 'P' there can be only one straight line 'L' parallel to a given straight line. It is to be noted that to Euclid's successors this postulate had signally failed to appear self-evident, and had equally failed to appear indemonstrable - hence, Allama Iqbal's generalized statement that 'since the days of Ptolemy (87-165 A.D.) till the time of NaÃâr ñĕsâ nobody gave serious thought' to the postulate. Deeper and wider implication of the postulate, however, cannot be denied. 'The innumerable attempts to prove this fifth postulate on the one hand and the development of the non-Euclidean geometries on the other are as many tributes to Euclid's wisdom', says Sarton (*op. cit.*, I, 153). A long note on the postulate by Spengler - well versed in mathematics - in his *Decline of the West*, 1, 176, admirably brings out its deep philosophical import.

These non-Euclidean geometries were developed in the nineteenth century by certain European mathematicians: Gauss (1777-1855) in Germany, Lobachevski (1792-1856) in Russia, Bolyai (1802-1860) in Hungary and Riemann (1826-1866) in Germany. They abandoned the attempt to prove Euclid's parallel postulate for they discovered that Euclid's postulates of geometry were not the only possible postulates and that other sets of postulates could be formulated arbitrarily and self-consistent geometries based on them. They further discovered that the space assumed in Euclidean geometry is only a special case of a more general type. These non-Euclidean geometries assumed immense scientific significance when it was found that the space-time continuum required by Einstein's theory of gravitation is non-Euclidean.

This in short is the movement of the idea of parallel postulate from Euclid to Einstein. Allama Iqbal with his seer-like vision for ideas was very much perceptive of this 'movement' and also of the scientific and philosophical significance of the non-Euclidean geometries. It is to be noted that Allama's keenly perceptive mind took full notice of the scientific developments of his days, for example, of anti-mechanistic biology (neo-vitalism) of Hans Driesch and J. S. Haldane and of quantum theory as well as of relativity-physics especially as expounded by Eddington, Louis Rougier, Lord Haldane, Wildon Carr and other philosopher-scientists. Among other things, one may notice a score of books on the 'Philosophy of Contemporary Science, more than half of which are on relativity-physics (mostly published between 1920 and 1928) in his personal library alone. See M. Siddiq, *Descriptive Catalogue of Allama Iqbal's Personal Library*, pp. 4-7 and 71-76, as well as Plates Nos. 22 and 23 giving the facsimiles of Allama's signatures dated July 1921 and September 1921 on his own copies of Einstein's work: *Relativity: The Special and the General Theory: A Popular Exposition* (1920) and Edwin E. Slosson's *Easy Lessons in Einstein* (1920); cf. also Dr Ahmad Nabi Khan, *Relics of Allama Iqbal (Catalogue)*, books listed at IV. 41 and IV. 46. The first book The *Mystery of Space* by Robert T. Browne by its very sub-title: 'A Study of the Hyperspace Movement in the Light of the Evolution of New Psychic Faculties and an Inquiry into the Genesis and Essential Nature of Space' suggests that it was probably this book which was foremost in Allama's mind when he spoke of highly mathematical notion of 'hyperspace movement' in connection with Tusi's effort to improve the parallel postulate here as well as in his 'Plea for Deeper Study' (*Speeches, Writings and Statements of Iqbal*, p. 141). Allama's keen interest in higher mathematics is evinced by his references in the present rather compact discussion on Newton's interpolation formula, recent developments in European mathematics and Whitehead's view of relativity as distinguished from that of Einstein. For the development of Allama's interest in certain mathematical key-concepts and in sciences in general see M. Saeed Sheikh, 'Allama Iqbal's interest in the Sciences', *Iqbal Review*, XXX/i (April-June, 1989), 31-43.

21. Cf. a fairy long passage from Spengler's *Decline of the West* (I, 75) quoted in Allama's Address: 'A Plea for Deeper Study of the Muslim Scientists' and an account of the way he went into the authentication of al-Bârĕnâ's view of mathematical function (*Speeches, Writings and Statements of Iqbal*, pp. 135-36). Allama's interest in 'mathematical idea of function' seems to be two-fold: religio-philosophical and scientific. The function-idea, he says, 'turns the fixed into the variable, and sees the universe not as being but as becoming'. This is in full accord with the Quranic view of the universe which God has built with power and it is He Who is steadily expanding it (cf. M. Asad, *The Message of the Qur'«n*, p. 805, note 31) and again 'He adds to his creation whatever He wills: for verily, God has the power to will anything' (35:1). The Quranic view of the growing universe is thus 'a clear departure' from the Aristotelian view of the fixed universe. Aristotle's doctrine of potentiality passing into actuality fails to resolve the mystery of becoming, in its living historicity and novelty or, as W. D. Ross has put it: 'The conception of potentiality has often been used to cover mere barrenness of thought' (cf. his Aristotle, p. 176). Hence, Allama's repeated pronouncement, that the spirit of the Qur'«n is essentially anti-classical. Philosophically speaking, time, which in the present context has been linked up with the notion of functionality

and rightly so, is the most indispensable condition for the very possibility and reality of human experience, cognitive or moral. This explains, partly at least, why 'Time' is the recurring theme in Allama's works in both prose and verse.

In mathematics function is a relationship of correspondence between two variables called independent variable and dependent variable and is expressed by saying 'y is a function of x' which means y change with x , so that for a certain value of x, y has a certain value (or values). In Europe though the term 'function' in its full mathematical sense was first used by Leibniz in 1694, the theory of functions had already emerged with the analytic geometry of Pierce Fermat in 1629 and that of the father of modern philosophy Ré ne Descartes - Descartes' *La Geometrie* appeared along with his better *known Discours de la mé thode* in 1637. After that such rapid advances took place in mathematics that within, say, fifty years it was completely metamorphosed into its modern form or, as Spengler puts it: 'Once this immense creation found wings, its rise was miraculous'. Being well versed in mathematics, Spengler gives an exciting account of the new discoveries of the Western mathematicians and their impact of European science and arts (*op. cit.*, I, 74-90). Two of his statements are to be noted. Not until the theory of functions was fully evolved, says Spengler, 'could this mathematics be unreservedly brought to bear in the parallel sphere of our dynamic Western physics'. Generally speaking, this means that Nature speaks the subtle and complex language of mathematics and that without the use of this language the breath-taking progress of science in the West, since the seventeenth century, would have been a sheer impossibility. Spengler, however, did not care to know that the mathematical idea of function originated, not in the West, but in the East, more particularly with the most brilliant al-Bârënâ's Al-Qnën al Mas'ëdâ in 1030, i.e. six hundred years before Fermat and Descartes.

The second statement to be noted is that, according to Spengler, 'The history of Western knowledge is thus one of progressive emancipation from classical thought' (*ibid*, p. 76). As it is, Allama Iqbal has the least quarrel with Spengler on the truth of this statement for he says: 'The most remarkable phenomenon of modern history, however, is the enormous rapidity with which the world of Islam is spiritually moving towards the West. There is nothing wrong in this movement, for European culture, on its intellectual side, is only a further development of some of the most important phases of the culture of Islam' (Lecture I, p. 6: italics mine). And further, 'Spengler's view of the spirit of modern culture is, in my opinion, perfectly correct' (p. 114). What Allama Iqbal, however, rightly insists is 'that the anticlassical spirit of the modern world has really arisen out of the revolt of Islam against Greek thought' (*ibid*). This revolt consists in Islam's focusing its vision on 'the concrete', 'the particular' and 'the becoming as against the Greeks' search for 'the ideal' 'the universal' and 'the being'. Spengler failed to see these Islamic ingredients of modern culture because of his self-evolved thesis 'that each culture is a specific organism, having no point of contact with cultures that historically precede or follow it'. Spengler's thesis has its roots, not in any scientifically established dynamics of history, but in his uncompromising theory of cultural holism (note the sub-title of the first volume of his work: *Gestalt und Wirklichkeit*). Cf. W. H. Dray's article, 'Spengler, Oswald', in *Encyclopedia of Philosophy*, VII, 527-30 for critical evaluation of Spengler's philosophical position.

22. Cf. M. A. Kazim, 'al-Bârënâ and Trignometry', al-Bârënâ Commemoration Volume, esp. pp. 167-68, for the English translation of the passage from al-Bârënâ's *al-Q«nën al-Mas'ëdâ* wherein al-Bârënâ generalizes his interpolation formula 'from trignometrical function to any function whatever'. This is likely the passage pointedly referred to by Allama Iqbal in his 'A Plea for Deeper Study of the Muslim Scientists' (*Speeches, Writings and Statements of Iqbal*, p. 136). See, however, Professor E. S. Kennedy's highly commendable article on 'al-Bârënâ' in *Dictionary of Scientific Biography*, II, 147-58. He bases al- Bârënâ's theory of function on his 'Treatise on Shadows' already translated by him.

23. Cf. M. R. Siddiqi, 'Mathematics and Astronomy', *A History of Muslim Philosophy*, ed. M. M. Sharif, II, 1280, and Juan Vernet, 'Mathematics, Astronomy, Optics', *The Legacy of Islam* ed. Joseph Schacht and C. E. Bosworth, pp. 466-68. According to Sarton, al-Khaw«rizmâ may be called one of the founders of analysis or algebra as distinct from geometry' and that his astronomical and trignometric tables were the first Muslim tables which contained, not simply the sine function, but also the tangent' (*op. cit.*, I, 563).

24. Cf. *Al-Fauz al-Asghar*, pp. 78-83; also *Development of Metaphysics in Persia*, p. 29 where an account of Ibn Maskawaih's theory of evolution is given as summed up by Shiblâ Nu'm«ni in his *'Ilm al-Kal«m*, pp. 141-43.

25. This is a reference to the views of Khw«jah Muhammad P«rs«as contained in his short but valuable tractate on time and space: *Ris«lah dar Zam«n-o-Mak«n*, the only extant MS (6 folios) of which, perhaps, is the one listed by A. Monzavi in his *Catalogue of Persian Manuscripts*, Vol II, Part I, p. 800. I am greatly indebted to

Q«zâ Mahmëd ul Haq of British Library, London, for the microfilm of this MS. This resulted as a preliminary in the publication of Urdu translation of Khw«jah Muhammad P«rs«'s *Ris«lah dar Zam«n-o-Mak«n* along with a brief account of his life and works by Dr Khw«ja Hamâd Yazd«nâ in *Al-Ma'«rif* (Lahore), XVII/vii, July 1984), 31-42, 56. Cf. Nadhr S«birâ, *Gh«yat al-Imk«n fi Ma'rifat al-Zam«n* by Shaikh Mahmëd Ashnawâ, 'Introduction', p. 'r' where it is alleged that Khw«jah P«rs«made an extensive use of Ashnawâ's said tractate on space and time, which is not very unlikely seeing the close resemblance between the two tractates; yet at places Khw«jah P«rs«'s treatment of the subject is sufistically more sophisticated.

26. Cf. Lecture II, pp. 60-61.

27. Misprinted as 'weight' in previous editions; see also the significant Quranic text repeated in verse 34:3.

28. Cf. *Gh«yat al-Imk«n fi Dirayat al-Mak«n*, ed. Rahâm Farmanâsh, pp. 16-17; English trans. A. H. Kamali, p. 13. On the authorship of this sufistic tractate on space and time, see note 34 in Lecture III.

29. *Ibid.*, p. 17; English trans., p. 13.

30. *Ibid.*, p. 23; English trans., p. 17.

31. *Ibid.*, pp. 24-25; English trans., pp. 18-19.

32. *Ibid.*, p. 25; English trans., p. 19.

33. *Ibid.*, p. 17; English trans., pp. 20-21.

34. *Ibid.*, pp. 27-28; English trans., p. 21.

35. *Ibid.*, pp. 28-29; English trans., pp. 21-22.

36. Cf. Space, *Time and Deity*, II, 41; also R. Metz, *A Hundred Years of British Philosophy*, pp. 634-38, and article 'S. Alexander' in *The Dictionary of Philosophy*, ed. D. D. Runes, wherein it is made clear that the term 'deity' is not used by Alexander in any theological sense but in terms of his doctrine of emergent evolution: 'The quality next above any given level (of evolution) is deity to the beings on that level'.

37. Alexander's metaphor that time is mind of space is to be found in statements such as this: 'It is that Time as a whole and in its parts bears to space as a whole and its corresponding parts a relation analogous to the relation of mind . . . or to put the matter shortly that Time is the mind of Space and Space the body of Time' (*Space, Time and Deity*, II, 38). Allama Iqbal's references to Alexander's *Space, Time and Deity*, in the sufistic account of space and time in the present Lecture as also in his address earlier: 'A Plea for Deeper Study of Muslim Scientists' (*Speeches, Writings and Statements*, p. 142) coupled with his commendatory observations on Alexander's work in his letter dated 24 January 1921 addressed to R. A. Nicholson (*Letters of Iqbal*, p. 141) are suggestive of Allama's keen interest in the metaphysical views of Alexander.

Of all the British philosophers, contemporaries of Allama Iqbal, Alexander can be singled out for laying equal emphasis on space and time as central to all philosophy. 'All the vital problems of philosophy', says Alexander, 'depend for their solution on the solution of the problem what Space and Time are and, more particularly, in how they are related to each other'. According to Allama Iqbal, 'In [Muslim] . . . culture the problem of space and time becomes a question of life and death' (p. 105). 'Space and Time in Muslim Thought' was the subject selected by Allama for his proposed Rhodes Memorial Lectures at Oxford (1934-1935) (cf. *Letters of Iqbal*, pp.135-36 and 183; also *Relics of Allama Iqbal: Catalogue*, Letter II, 70 dated 27 May 1935 from Secretary, Rhodes Trust) which very unfortunately he could not deliver owing to his increasing ill health. A letter dated 6 May 1937 addressed to Dr Syed Zafarul Hasan of Aligarh Muslim University (author of the well-known *Realism*, 1928), discovered only recently, shows that Allama Iqbal had already gathered 'material' for his Rhodes Memorial Lectures; cf. Rafãal-Dân Ha`shimi`, 'Allamah Iqbal ke Chand Ghair Mudawwan KhuÇëÇ', *Iqbal Review*, XXIII/iv (January 1983), 41-43.

Attention may be called here also to an obviously unfinished two-page draft on 'The Problem of Time in Muslim Philosophy' in Allama's own hand preserved in the Allama Iqbal Museum, Lahore; cf. Dr Ahmad Nabi Khan, *Relics of Allama Iqbal: Catalogue*, I, 37.

38. Cf. *Ghāyat al-Imkān fī Dirāyat al-Makān*, pp. 16-17; English trans., p. 13.

39. *Ibid.*, p. 50; English trans., p. 36.

40. This is a reference to the Quranic verses: 6:6; 9:39; 17:16-17; 18:59; 21:11; 22:45; 36:31.

God's judgment on nations, also called 'judgment in history', according to the Qur'ān is said to be more relentless than God's judgment on individuals - in the latter case God is forgiving and compassionate. Nations are destroyed only for their transgression and evil doings. And when a nation perishes, its good members meet the same doom as its bad ones for the former failed to check the spread of evil (11:116), cf. F. Rahman, *Major Themes of the Qur'ān*, p. 53.

41. See also Quranic verses 15:5 and 24:43.

42. For very special circumstances under which a keen sense of history grew in Islam, see I. H. Qureshi, 'Historiography', *A History of Muslim Philosophy*, II, 1197-1203.

43. Abē 'Abdullah Muhammad b. Ishāq (d. c. 150/767) has the distinction of being the first biographer of the Holy Prophet. His work *Kitāb Sirat Rasēl Allāh* ('The Life of the Apostle of God') has, however, been lost and is now known only through Ibn Hishām's recension of it.

44. Abē Ja'far Muhammad b. Jarâr al-ñabarâ is one of the greatest Muslim historians. His remarkably accurate monumental history *Kitāb Akhbār al-Rusēl wa'l-Mulēk* ('Annals of the Apostles and the Kings'), the first comprehensive work in the Arabic language, has been edited M. J. de Goeje and others in 15 volumes (Leiden, 1879-1901). Al-Tabarâ is equally well known for his commendable commentary on the Qur'ān: *Jāmi' al-Bayān 'an Tāwâl al-Qur'ān* in 30 volumes - a primal work for the later commentators because of its earliest and largest collection of the exegetical traditions.

45. Abē'l-Hasan 'Ali b. al-Husain b. 'Alâ al-Mas'ēdi (d. c. 346/957), after al-Tabari`, is the next greatest historian in Islam - rightly named as the 'Herodotus of the Arabs'. He inaugurated a new method in the writing of history: instead of grouping events around years (annalistic method) he grouped them around kings, dynasties and topics (topical method); a method adopted also by Ibn Khaldu`n. His historico-geographical work *Murëj al-Dhahab wa'l-Ma'ādin al-Jauhar* ('Meadows of Gold and Mines of Gems') also deals with Persian, Roman and Jewish history and religion.

46. Reference is to the Quranic verses 4:1; 6:98; 7:189; 39:6.

47. See Robert Flint, *History of the Philosophy of History*, p. 86. Flint's eulogy of Ibn Khaldēn, expressive of his sentiment of a discovery of a genius, now stands more or less confirmed by the realistic assessments made of Ibn Khaldēn by eminent scholars such as A. Toynbee, *A Study of History*, III, 322; Sarton, *op. cit.*, III, 1262; Gaston Bouthoul in his Preface to de Slane's *Les Prolegomenes d'Ibn Khaldoun* (second edition, Paris, 1934-38) and R. Brunschvig, *La Berberie orientale sous les Hafsides*, II, 391.

48. Cf. *Muqaddimah*, trans. F. Rosenthal, III, 246-58, also M. Fakhry, *A History of Islamic Philosophy*, pp. 361-64.

49. Phenomenon of the alternation of day and night is spoken of in many verses of the Qur'ān such as 2:164; 3:190; 10:6; 23:80; 45:5.

50. *Ibid.*, 55:29.

51. Cf. p. 107.

52. Cf. p. 106.

53. On the notion of time as held by Zeno, Plato, Heraclitus and Stoics, cf. A. J. Gunn, *The Problem of Time*, pp. 19-22.

54. Cf. O. Spengler, *The Decline of the West*, II, 189-323.

55. Cf. Lecture I, p. 3, Lecture III, p. 56 and p. 102.

56. Cf. Spengler, *op. cit.*, II, 248-55.

57. *Ibid.*, pp. 235, 240; cf. also note 33 in Lecture IV.

58. *Ibid.*, p. 238.

59. *Ibid.*

60. *Ibid.*, pp. 206-07.

61. Cf. *Muqaddimah*, Chapter III, section 51: 'The Fatimid . . . ', trans. Rosenthal, II, 156-200. Ibn Khaldu`n recounts formally twenty-four traditions bearing upon the belief in Mahdi (none of which is from Bukh«râ or Muslim) and questions the authenticity of them all. Cf. also the article 'al-Mahdi'' in *Shorter Encyclopaedia of Islam* and P. K. Hitti, *History of the Arabs*, pp. 439-49, for the religio-political background of the *imam-mahdi* idea.

Reference may also be made to Allama Iqbal's letter dated 7 April 1932 to Muhammad Ahsan wherein, among other things, he states that, according to his firm belief (*'aqâdah*), all traditions relating to *mahdâ*, *masâhâyat* and *mujaddidâyat* are the product of Persian and non-Arab imagination; and he adds that certainly they have nothing to do with the true spirit of the Qur'«n (*Iqb«ln«mah*, II, 231).

And finally it shall be rewarding to read this last paragraph in conjunction with Allama's important notes on the back cover of his own copy of Spengler's *Decline of the West*, facsimile of which is reproduced in *Descriptive Catalogue of Allama Iqbal's Personal Library*, Plate No. 33.

The Principle of Movement in the Structure of Islam

by Dr. Muhammad Iqbal

As a cultural movement Islam rejects the old static view of the universe, and reaches a dynamic view. As an emotional system of unification it recognizes the worth of the individual as such, and rejects blood-relationship as a basis of human unity. Blood-relationship is earth-rootedness. The search for a purely psychological foundation of human unity becomes possible only with the perception that all human life is spiritual in its origin.[1] Such a perception is creative of fresh loyalties without any ceremonial to keep them alive, and makes it possible for man to emancipate himself from the earth. Christianity which had originally appeared as a monastic order was tried by Constantine as a system of unification.[2] Its failure to work as such a system drove the Emperor Julian[3] to return to the old gods of Rome on which he attempted to put philosophical interpretations. A modern historian of civilization has thus depicted the state of the civilized world about the time when Islam appeared on the stage of History:

It seemed then that the great civilization that it had taken four thousand years to construct was on the verge of disintegration, and that mankind was likely to return to that condition of barbarism where every tribe and sect was against the next, and law and order were unknown . . . The old tribal sanctions had lost their power. Hence the old imperial methods would no longer operate. The new sanctions created by Christianity were working division and destruction instead of unity and order. It was a time fraught with tragedy. Civilization, like a gigantic tree whose foliage had overarched the world and whose branches had borne the golden fruits of art and science and literature, stood tottering, its trunk no longer alive with the flowing sap of devotion and reverence, but rotted to the core, riven by the storms of war, and held together only by the cords of ancient customs and laws, that might snap at any moment. Was there any emotional culture that could be brought in, to gather mankind once more into unity and to save civilization? This culture must be something of a new type, for the old sanctions and ceremonials were dead, and to build up others of the same kind would be the work of centuries.'[4]

The writer then proceeds to tell us that the world stood in need of a new culture to take the place of the culture of the throne, and the systems of unification which were based on blood-relationship. It is amazing, he adds, that such a culture should have arisen from Arabia just at the time when it was most needed. There is, however, nothing amazing in the phenomenon. The world-life intuitively sees its own needs, and at critical moments defines its own direction. This is what, in the language of religion, we call prophetic revelation. It is only natural that Islam should have flashed across the consciousness of a simple people untouched by any of the ancient cultures, and occupying a geographical position where three continents meet together. The new culture finds the foundation of world-unity in the principle of Tauhâd.'[5] Islam, as a polity, is only a practical means of making this principle a living factor in the intellectual and emotional life of mankind. It demands loyalty to God, not to thrones. And since God is the ultimate spiritual basis of all life, loyalty to God virtually amounts to man's loyalty to his own ideal nature. The ultimate spiritual basis of all life, as conceived by Islam, is eternal and reveals itself in variety and change. A society based on such a conception of Reality must reconcile, in its life, the categories of permanence and change. It must possess eternal principles to regulate its collective life, for the eternal gives us a foothold in the world of perpetual change. But eternal principles when they are understood to exclude all possibilities of change which, according to the Qur'«n, is one of the greatest 'signs' of God, tend to immobilize what is essentially mobile in its nature. The failure of the Europe in political and social sciences illustrates the former principle, the immobility of Islam during the last five hundred years illustrates the latter. What then is the principle of movement in the structure of Islam? This is known as *Ijtih«d*.

The word literally means to exert. In the terminology of Islamic law it means to exert with a view to form an independent judgement on a legal question. The idea, I believe, has its origin in a well-known verse of the Qur'«n - 'And to those who exert We show Our path'.[6] We find it more definitely adumbrated in a tradition of the Holy Prophet. When Mu'«dh was appointed ruler of Yemen, the Prophet is reported to have asked him as to how he would decide matters coming up before him. 'I will judge matters according to the Book of God,' said Mu'«dh. 'But if the Book of God contains nothing to guide you?' 'Then I will act on the precedents of the Prophet of God.' 'But if the precedents fail?' 'Then I will exert to form my own judgement.'[7] The student of the history of Islam, however, is well aware that with the political expansion of Islam systematic legal thought became an absolute necessity, and our early doctors of law, both of Arabian and non-Arabian descent, worked ceaselessly until all the accumulated wealth of legal thought found a final expression in our recognized schools of

Law. These schools of Law recognize three degrees of *Ijtih«d*: (1) complete authority in legislation which is practically confined to be founders of the schools, (2) relative authority which is to be exercised within the limits of a particular school, and (3) special authority which relates to the determining of the law applicable to a particular case left undetermined by the founders.[8] In this paper I am concerned with the first degree of *Ijtih«d* only, i.e. complete authority in legislation. The theoretical possibility of this degree of *Ijtih«d* is admitted by the Sunni`s, but in practice it has always been denied ever since the establishment of the schools, inasmuch as the idea of complete *Ijtih«d* is hedged round by conditions which are well-nigh impossible of realization in a single individual. Such an attitude seems exceedingly strange in a system of law based mainly on the groundwork provided by the Qur'«n which embodies an essentially dynamic outlook on life. It is, therefore, necessary, before we proceed farther, to discover the cause of this intellectual attitude which has reduced the Law of Islam practically to a state of immobility. Some European writers think that the stationary character of the Law of Islam is due to the influence of the Turks. This is an entirely superficial view, for the legal schools of Islam had been finally established long before the Turkish influence began to work in the history of Islam. The real causes are, in my opinion, as follows:

1. We are all familiar with the Rationalist movement which appeared in the church of Islam during the early days of the Abbasids and the bitter controversies which it raised. Take for instance the one important point of controversy between the two camps - the conservative dogma of the eternity of the Qur'«n. The Rationalists denied it because they thought that this was only another form of the Christian dogma of the eternity of the word; on the other hand, the conservative thinkers whom the later Abbasids, fearing the political implications of Rationalism, gave their full support, thought that by denying the eternity of the Qur'«n the Rationalists were undermining the very foundations of Muslim society.[9] Naïï«m, for instance, practically rejected the traditions, and openly declared Abë Hurairah to be an untrustworthy reporter.[10] Thus, partly owing to a misunderstanding of the ultimate motives of Rationalism, and partly owing to the unrestrained thought of particular Rationalists, conservative thinkers regarded this movement as a force of disintegration, and considered it a danger to the stability of Islam as a social polity.[11] Their main purpose, therefore, was to preserve the social integrity of Islam, and to realize this the only course open to them was to utilize the binding force of Sharâ'ah, and to make the structure of their legal system as rigorous as possible.

2. The rise and growth of ascetic Sufism, which gradually developed under influences of a non-Islamic character, a purely speculative side, is to a large extent responsible for this attitude. On its purely religious side Sufism fostered a kind of revolt against the verbal quibbles of our early doctors. The case of Sufy«n Thaurâ is an instance in point. He was one of the acutest legal minds of his time, and was nearly the founder of a school of law,[12] but being also intensely spiritual, the dry-as-dust subtleties of contemporary legists drove him to ascetic Sufism. On its speculative side which developed later, Sufism is a form of freethought and in alliance with Rationalism. The emphasis that it laid on the distinction of *ï«hir* and *b«Çin* (Appearance and Reality) created an attitude of indifference to all that applies to Appearance and not to Reality.[13]

This spirit of total other-wordliness in later Sufism obscured men's vision of a very important aspect of Islam as a social polity, and, offering the prospect of unrestrained thought on its speculative side, it attracted and finally absorbed the best minds in Islam. The Muslim state was thus left generally in the hands of intellectual mediocrities, and the unthinking masses of

Islam, having no personalities of a higher calibre to guide them, found their security only in blindly following the schools.

3. On the top of all this came the destruction of Baghdad - the centre of Muslim intellectual life - in the middle of the thirteenth century. This was indeed a great blow, and all the contemporary historians of the invasion of Tartars describe the havoc of Baghdad with a half-suppressed pessimism about the future of Islam. For fear of further disintegration, which is only natural in such a period of political decay, the conservative thinkers of Islam focused all their efforts on the one point of preserving a uniform social life for the people by a jealous exclusion of all innovations in the law of Sharâ'ah as expounded by the early doctors of Islam. Their leading idea was social order, and there is no doubt that they were partly right, because organization does to a certain extent counteract the forces of decay. But they did not see, and our modern 'Ulem« do not see, that the ultimate fate of a people does not depend so much on organization as on the worth and power of individual men. In an over-organized society the individual is altogether crushed out of existence. He gains the whole wealth of social thought around him and loses his own soul. Thus a false reverence for past history and its artificial resurrection constitute no remedy for a people's decay. 'The verdict of history', as a modern writer has happily put it, 'is that worn-out ideas have never risen to power among a people who have worn them out.' The only effective power, therefore, that counteracts the forces of decay in a people is the rearing of self-concentrated individuals. Such individuals alone reveal the depth of life. They disclose new standards in the light of which we begin to see that our environment is not wholly inviolable and requires revision. The tendency to over-organization by a false reverence of the past, as manifested in the legists of Islam in the thirteenth century and later, was contrary to the inner impulse of Islam, and consequently invoked the powerful reaction of Ibn Taimâyyah, one of the most indefatigable writers and preachers of Islam, who was born in 1263, five years after the destruction of Baghdad.

Ibn Taimâyyah was brought up in Hanbalite tradition. Claiming freedom of *Ijtih«d* for himself he rose in revolt against the finality of the schools, and went back to first principles in order to make a fresh start. Like Ibn Àazm - the founder of Ê«hirâschool of law[14] - he rejected the Hanafite principle of reasoning by analogy and *Ijm«'* as understood by older legists;[15] for he thought agreement was the basis of all superstition.[16] And there is no doubt that, considering the moral and intellectual decrepitude of his times, he was right in doing so. In the sixteenth century Suyëtâ claimed the same privilege of *Ijtih«d* to which he added the idea of a renovator at the beginning of each century.[17] But the spirit of Ibn Taimâyyah's teaching found a fuller expression in a movement of immense potentialities which arose in the eighteenth century, from the sands of Nejd, described by Macdonald as the 'cleanest spot in the decadent world of Islam'. It is really the first throb of life in modern Islam. To the inspiration of this movement are traceable, directly or indirectly, nearly all the great modern movements of Muslim Asia and Africa, e.g. the Sanâsâ movement, the Pan-Islamic movement,[18] and the B«bâ movement, which is only a Persian reflex of Arabian Protestantism. The great puritan reformer, Muhammad Ibn 'Abd al-Wahh«h, who was born in 1700,[19] studied in Medina, travelled in Persia, and finally succeeded in spreading the fire of his restless soul throughout the whole world of Islam. He was similar in spirit to Ghazz«lâ's disciple, Muhammad Ibn Tëmart[20] - the Berber puritan reformer of Islam who appeared amidst the decay of Muslim Spain, and gave her a fresh inspiration. We are, however, not concerned with the political career of this movement which was terminated by the armies of Muhammad 'Alâ P«sh«. The essential thing to note is the spirit of freedom manifested in it, though inwardly this movement, too, is conservative in its own fashion. While it rises in revolt against the finality of the schools, and vigorously asserts the right of private judgement, its vision of the past is wholly uncritical, and in matters of law it mainly falls back on the traditions of the Prophet.

Passing on to Turkey, we find that the idea of *Ijtih«d*, reinforced and broadened by modern philosophical ideas, has long been working in the religious and political thought of the Turkish nation. This is clear from Àalim S«bit's new theory of Muhammadan Law, grounded on modern sociological concepts. If the renaissance of Islam is a fact, and I believe it is a fact, we too one day, like the Turks, will have to re-evaluate our intellectual inheritance. And if we cannot make any original contribution to the general thought of Islam, we may, by healthy conservative criticism, serve at least as a check on the rapid movement of liberalism in the world of Islam.

I now proceed to give you some idea of religio-political thought in Turkey which will indicate to you how the power of *Ijtih«d* is manifested in recent thought and activity in that country. There were, a short time ago, two main lines of thought in Turkey represented by the Nationalist Party and the Party of Religious Reform. The point of supreme interest with the Nationalist Party is above all the State and not Religion. With these thinkers religion as such has no independent function. The state is the essential factor in national life which determines the character and function of all other factors. They, therefore, reject old ideas about the function of State and Religion, and accentuate the separation of Church and State. Now the structure of Islam as a religio-political system, no doubt, does permit such a view, though personally I think it is a mistake to suppose that the idea of state is more dominant and rules all other ideas embodied in the system of Islam. In Islam the spiritual and the temporal are not two distinct domains, and the nature of an act, however secular in its import, is determined by the attitude of mind with which the agent does it. It is the invisible mental background of the act which ultimately determines its character.[21] An act is temporal or profane if it is done in a spirit of detachment from the infinite complexity of life behind it; it is spiritual if it is inspired by that complexity. In Islam it is the same reality which appears as Church looked at from one point of view and State from another. It is not true to say that Church and State are two sides or facets of the same thing. Islam is a single unanalysable reality which is one or the other as your point of view varies. The point is extremely far-reaching and a full elucidation of it will involve us in a highly philosophical discussion. Suffice it to say that this ancient mistake arose out of the bifurcation of the unity of man into two distinct and separate realities which somehow have a point of contact, but which are in essence opposed to each other. The truth, however, is that matter is spirit in space-time reference. The unity called man is body when you look at it as acting in regard to what we call the external world; it is mind or soul when you look at it as acting in regard to the ultimate aim and ideal of such acting. The essence of Tauhâd, as a working idea, is equality, solidarity, and freedom. The state, from the Islamic standpoint, is an endeavour to transform these ideal principles into space-time forces, an aspiration to realize them in a definite human organization. It is in this sense alone that the state in Islam is a theocracy, not in the sense that it is headed by a representative of God on earth who can always screen his despotic will behind his supposed infallibility. The critics of Islam have lost sight of this important consideration. The Ultimate Reality, according to the Qur'«n, is spiritual, and its life consists in its temporal activity. The spirit finds its opportunities in the natural, the material, the secular. All that is secular is, therefore, sacred in the roots of its being. The greatest service that modern thought has rendered to Islam, and as a matter of fact to all religion, consists in its criticism of what we call material or natural - a criticism which discloses that the merely material has no substance until we discover it rooted in the spiritual. There is no such thing as a profane world. All this immensity of matter constitutes a scope for the self-realization of spirit. All is holy ground. As the Prophet so beautifully puts it: 'The whole of this earth is a mosque.'[22] The state, according to Islam, is only an effort to realize the spiritual in a human organization. But in this sense all state, not based on mere domination and aiming at the realization of ideal principles, is theocratic.

The truth is that the Turkish Nationalists assimilated the idea of the separation of Church and State from the history of European political ideas. Primitive Christianity was founded, not as a political or civil unit, but as a monastic order in a profane world, having nothing to do with civil affairs, and obeying the Roman authority practically in all matters. The result of this was that when the State became Christian, State and Church confronted each other as distinct powers with interminable boundary disputes between them. Such a thing could never happen in Islam; for Islam was from the very beginning a civil society, having received from the Qur'«n a set of simple legal principles which, like the twelve tables of the Romans, carried, as experience subsequently proved, great potentialities of expansion and development by interpretation. The Nationalist theory of state, therefore, is misleading inasmuch as it suggests a dualism which does not exist in Islam.

The Religious Reform Party, on the other hand, led by Sa'âd Àalâm P«sh«, insisted on the fundamental fact that Islam is a harmony of idealism and positivism; and, as a unity of the eternal verities of freedom, equality, and solidarity, has no fatherland. 'As there is no English Mathematics, German Astronomy or French Chemistry,' says the Grand Vizier, 'so there is no Turkish, Arabian, Persian or Indian Islam. Just as the universal character of scientific truths engenders varieties of scientific national cultures which in their totality represent human knowledge, much in the same way the universal character of Islamic verities creates varieties of national, moral and social ideals.' Modern culture based as it is on national egoism is, according to this keen-sighted writer, only another form of barbarism. It is the result of an over-developed industrialism through which men satisfy their primitive instincts and inclinations. He, however, deplores that during the course of history the moral and social ideals of Islam have been gradually deislamized through the influence of local character, and pre-Islamic superstitions of Muslim nations. These ideals today are more Iranian, Turkish, or Arabian than Islamic. The pure brow of the principle of Tauhâd has received more or less an impress of heathenism, and the universal and impersonal character of the ethical ideals of Islam has been lost through a process of localization. The only alternative open to us, then, is to tear off from Islam the hard crust which has immobilized an essentially dynamic outlook on life, and to rediscover the original verities of freedom, equality, and solidarity with a view to rebuild our moral, social, and political ideals out of their original simplicity and universality. Such are the views of the Grand Vizier of Turkey. You will see that following a line of thought more in tune with the spirit of Islam, he reaches practically the same conclusion as the Nationalist Party, that is to say, the freedom of *Ijtih«d* with a view to rebuild the laws of Sharâ'ah in the light of modern thought and experience.

Let us now see how the Grand National Assembly has exercised this power of *Ijtih«d* in regard to the institution of Khil«fat. According to Sunni Law, the appointment of an Imam or Khalâfah is absolutely indispensable. The first question that arises in this connexion is this - Should the Caliphate be vested in a single person? Turkey's *Ijtih«d* is that according to the spirit of Islam the Caliphate or Imamate can be vested in a body of persons, or an elected Assembly. The religious doctors of Islam in Egypt and India, as far as I know, have not yet expressed themselves on this point. Personally, I believe the Turkish view is perfectly sound. It is hardly necessary to argue this point. The republican form of government is not only thoroughly consistent with the spirit of Islam, but has also become a necessity in view of the new forces that are set free in the world of Islam.

In order to understand the Turkish view let us seek the guidance of Ibn Khaldën - the first philosophical historian of Islam. Ibn Khaldën, in his famous 'Prolegomena', mentions three distinct views of the idea of Universal Caliphate in Islam[23]: (1) That Universal Imamate is a Divine institution, and is consequently indispensable. (2) That it is merely a matter of expediency. (3) That there is no need of such an institution. The last view was taken by the Khaw«rij.[24] It seems that modern Turkey has shifted from the first to the second view, i.e. to the view of the Mu'tazilah who regarded Universal Imamate as a matter of expediency only. The Turks argue that in our political thinking we must be guided by our past political experience which points unmistakably to the fact that the idea of Universal Imamate has failed in practice. It was a workable idea when the Empire of Islam was intact. Since the break-up of this Empire independent political units have arisen. The idea has ceased to be operative and cannot work as a living factor in the organization of modern Islam. Far from serving any useful purpose it has really stood in the way of a reunion of independent Muslim States. Persia has stood aloof from the Turks in view of her doctrinal differences regarding the Khil«fat; Morocco has always looked askance at them, and Arabia has cherished private ambition. And all these ruptures in Islam for the sake of a mere symbol of a power which departed long ago. Why should we not, they can further argue, learn from experience in our political thinking? Did not Q«dâ Abë Bakr B«qil«nâ drop the condition of Qarshâyat in the *Khalâfah* in view of the facts of experience, i.e. the political fall of the Quraish and their consequent inability to rule the world of Islam? Centuries ago Ibn Khaldën, who personally believed in the condition of Qarshâyat in the *Khali`fah*, argued much in the same way. Since the power of the Quraish, he says, has gone, there is no alternative but to accept the most powerful man as Ima`m in the country where he happens to be powerful. Thus Ibn Khaldën, realizing the hard logic of facts, suggests a view which may be regarded as the first dim vision of an International Islam fairly in sight today. Such is the attitude of the modern Turk, inspired as he is by the realities of experience, and not by the scholastic reasoning of jurists who lived and thought under different conditions of life.

To my mind these arguments, if rightly appreciated, indicate the birth of an International ideal which, though forming the very essence of Islam, has been hitherto over-shadowed or rather displaced by Arabian Imperialism of the earlier centuries of Islam. This new ideal is clearly reflected in the work of the great nationalist poet Êiy« whose songs, inspired by the philosophy of Auguste Comte, have done a great deal in shaping the present thought of Turkey. I reproduce the substance of one of his poems from Professor Fischer's German translation:

In order to create a really effective political unity of Islam, all Muslim countries must first become independent: and then in their totality they should range themselves under one Caliph. Is such a thing possible at the present moment? If not today, one must wait. In the meantime the Caliph must reduce his own house to order and lay the foundations of a workable modern State.

'In the International world the weak find no sympathy; power alone deserves respect.'[25]

These lines clearly indicate the trend of modern Islam. For the present every Muslim nation must sink into her own deeper self, temporarily focus her vision on herself alone, until all are strong and powerful to form a living family of republics. A true and living unity, according to the nationalist thinkers, is not so easy as to be achieved by a merely symbolical overlordship. It is truly manifested in a multiplicity of free independent units whose racial rivalries are adjusted and harmonized by the unifying bond of a common spiritual aspiration. It seems to me that God is slowly bringing home to us the truth that Islam is neither Nationalism nor Imperialism but a League of Nations which recognizes artificial boundaries and racial distinctions for facility of reference only,[26] and not for restricting the social horizon of its members.

From the same poet the following passage from a poem called 'Religion and Science' will throw some further light on the general religious outlook which is being gradually shaped in the world of Islam today:

"Who were the first spiritual leaders of mankind? Without doubt the prophets and holy men. In every period religion has led philosophy; From it alone morality and art receive light. But then religion grows weak, and loses her original ardour! Holy men disappear, and spiritual leadership becomes, in name, the heritage of the Doctors of Law! The leading star of the Doctors of Law is tradition; They drag religion with force on this track; but philosophy says: 'My leading star is reason: you go right, I go left."

'Both religion and philosophy claim the soul of man and draw it on either side!'

'When this struggle is going on pregnant experience delivers up positive science, and this young leader of thought says, "Tradition is history and Reason is the method of history! Both interpret and desire to reach the same indefinable something!"

'But what is this something?'
'Is it a spiritualized heart?'

'If so, then take my last word - Religion is positive science, the purpose of which is to spiritualize the heart of man!'[27]

It is clear from these lines how beautifully the poet has adopted the Comtian idea of the three stages of man's intellectual development, i.e. theological, metaphysical and scientific - to the religious outlook of Islam. And the view of religion embodied in these lines determines the poet's attitude towards the position of Arabic in the educational system of Turkey. He says:

'The land where the call to prayer resounds in Turkish; where those who pray understand the meaning of their religion; the land where the Qur'«n is learnt in Turkish; where every man, big or small, knows full well the command of God; O! Son of Turkey! that land is thy fatherland!'[28]

If the aim of religion is the spiritualization of the heart, then it must penetrate the soul of man, and it can best penetrate the inner man, according to the poet, only if its spiritualizing ideas are clothed in his mother tongue. Most people in India will condemn this displacement of Arabic by Turkish. For reasons which will appear later the poet's *Ijtih«d* is open to grave objections, but it must be admitted that the reform suggested by him is not without a parallel in the past history of Islam. We find that when Muhammad Ibn Tëmart - the Mahdi of Muslim Spain - who was Berber by nationality, came to power, and established the pontifical rule of the MuwaÁÁidën, he ordered for the sake of the illiterate Berbers, that the Çur'«n should be translated and read in the Berber language; that the call to prayer should be given in Berber;[29] and that all the functionaries of the Church must know the Berber language.

In another passage the poet gives his ideal of womanhood. In his zeal for the equality of man and woman he wishes to see radical changes in the family law of Islam as it is understood and practised today:

'There is the woman, my mother, my sister, or my daughter; it is she who calls up the most sacred emotions from the depths of my life! There is my beloved, my sun, my moon and my star; it is she who makes me understand the poetry of life! How could the Holy Law of God regard these beautiful creatures as despicable beings? Surely there is an error in the interpretation of the Qur'«n by the learned?[30]

'The foundation of the nation and the state is the family!'
'As long as the full worth of the woman is not realized, national life remains incomplete.'
'The upbringing of the family must correspond with justice;'
'Therefore equality is necessary in three things - in divorce, in separation, and in inheritance.'
'As long as the woman is counted half the man as regards inheritance and one-fourth of man in matrimony, neither the family nor the country will be elevated. For other rights we have opened national courts of justice;'
'he family, on the other hand, we have left in the hands of schools.'
I do not know why we have left the woman in the lurch?
Does she not work for the land? Or, will she turn her needle into a sharp bayonet to tear off her rights from our hands through a revolution?[31]

The truth is that among the Muslim nations of today, Turkey alone has shaken off its dogmatic slumber, and attained to self-consciousness. She alone has claimed her right of intellectual freedom; she alone has passed from the ideal to the real - a transition which entails keen intellectual and moral struggle. To her the growing complexities of a mobile and broadening life are sure to bring new situations suggesting new points of view, and necessitating fresh interpretations of principles which are only of an academic interest to a people who have never experienced the joy of spiritual expansion. It is, I think, the English thinker Hobbes who makes this acute observation that to have a succession of identical thoughts and feelings is to have no thoughts and feelings at all. Such is the lot of most Muslim countries today. They are mechanically repeating old values, whereas the Turk is on the way to creating new values. He has passed through great experiences which have revealed his deeper self to him. In him life has begun to move, change, and amplify, giving birth to new desires, bringing new difficulties and suggesting new interpretations. The question which confronts him today, and which is likely to confront other Muslim countries in the near future is whether the Law of Islam is capable of evolution - a question which will require great intellectual effort, and is sure to be answered in the affirmative, provided the world of Islam approaches it in the spirit of 'Umar - the first critical and independent mind in Islam who, at the last moments of the Prophet, had the moral courage to utter these remarkable words: 'The Book of God is sufficient for us.'[32]

We heartily welcome the liberal movement in modern Islam, but it must also be admitted that the appearance of liberal ideas in Islam constitutes also the most critical moment in the history of Islam. Liberalism has a tendency to act as a force of disintegration, and the race-idea which appears to be working in modern Islam with greater force than ever may ultimately wipe off the broad human outlook which Muslim people have imbibed from their religion. Further, our religious and political reformers in their zeal for liberalism may overstep the proper limits of reform in the absence of check on their youthful fervour. We are today passing through a period similar to that of the Protestant revolution in Europe, and the lesson which the rise and outcome of Luther's movement teaches should not be lost on us. A careful reading of history shows that the Reformation was essentially a political movement, and the net result of it in Europe was a gradual displacement of the universal ethics of Christianity by systems of national ethics.[33] The result of this tendency we have seen with our own eyes in the Great European War which, far from bringing any workable synthesis of the two opposing systems of ethics, has made the European situation still more intolerable. It is the duty of the leaders of the world of Islam today to understand the real meaning of what has happened in Europe, and then to move forward with self-control and a clear insight into the ultimate aims of Islam as a social polity.

I have given you some idea of the history and working of *Ijtih«d* in modern Islam. I now proceed to see whether the history and structure of the Law of Islam indicate the possibility of any fresh interpretation of its principles. In other words, the question that I want to raise is - Is the Law of Islam capable of evolution? Horten, Professor of Semitic Philology at the University of Bonn, raises the same question in connexion with the Philosophy and Theology of Islam. Reviewing the work of Muslim thinkers in the sphere of purely religious thought he points out that the history of Islam may aptly be described as a gradual interaction, harmony, and mutual deepening of two distinct forces, i.e. the element of Aryan culture and knowledge on the one hand, and a Semitic religion on the other. The Muslim has always adjusted his religious outlook to the elements of culture which he assimilated from the peoples that surrounded him. From 800 to 1100, says Horten, not less than one hundred systems of theology appeared in Islam, a fact which bears ample testimony to the elasticity of Islamic thought as well as to the ceaseless activity of our early thinkers. Thus, in view of the revelations of a deeper study of Muslim literature and thought, this living European Orientalist has been driven to the following conclusion:

The spirit of Islam is so broad that it is practically boundless. With the exception of atheistic ideas alone it has assimilated all the attainable ideas of surrounding peoples, and given them its own peculiar direction of development.'

The assimilative spirit of Islam is even more manifest in the sphere of law. Says Professor Hurgronje - the Dutch critic of Islam:

When we read the history of the development of Mohammadan Law we find that, on the one hand, the doctors of every age, on the slightest stimulus, condemn one another to the point of mutual accusations of heresy; and, on the other hand, the very same people, with greater and greater unity of purpose, try to reconcile the similar quarrels of their predecessors.'

These views of modern European critics of Islam make it perfectly clear that, with the return of new life, the inner catholicity of the spirit of Islam is bound to work itself out in spite of the rigorous conservatism of our doctors. And I have no doubt that a deeper study of the enormous legal literature of Islam is sure to rid the modern critic of the superficial opinion that the Law of Islam is stationary and incapable of development. Unfortunately, the conservative Muslim public of this country is not yet quite ready for a critical discussion of *Fiqh*, which, if undertaken, is likely to displease most people, and raise sectarian controversies; yet I venture to offer a few remarks on the point before us.

1. In the first place, we should bear in mind that from the earliest times practically up to the rise of the Abbasids, there was no written law of Islam apart from the Qur'«n.

2. Secondly, it is worthy of note that from about the middle of the first century up to the beginning of the fourth not less than nineteen schools of law and legal opinion appeared in Islam.[34] This fact alone is sufficient to show how incessantly our early doctors of law worked in order to meet the necessities of a growing civilization. With the expansion of conquest and the consequent widening of the outlook of Islam these early legists had to take a wider view of things, and to study local conditions of life and habits of new peoples that came within the fold of Islam. A careful study of the various schools of legal opinion, in the light of contemporary social and political history, reveals that they gradually passed from the deductive to the inductive attitude in their efforts at interpretation.[35]

3. Thirdly, when we study the four accepted sources of Muhammadan Law and the controversies which they invoked, the supposed rigidity of our recognized schools evaporates and the possibility of a further evolution becomes perfectly clear. Let us briefly discuss these sources.

(a) The Qur'«n. The primary source of the Law of Islam is the Qur'«n. The Qur'«n, however, is not a legal code. Its main purpose, as I have said before, is to awaken in man the higher consciousness of his relation with God and the universe.[36] No doubt, the Qur'«n does lay down a few general principles and rules of a legal nature, especially relating to the family[37] - the ultimate basis of social life. But why are these rules made part of a revelation the ultimate aim of which is man's higher life? The answer to this question is furnished by the history of Christianity which appeared as a powerful reaction against the spirit of legality manifested in Judaism. By setting up an ideal of otherworldliness it no doubt did succeed in spiritualizing life, but its individualism could see no spiritual value in the complexity of human social relations. 'Primitive Christianity', says Naumann in his *Briefe Ü ber Religion*, 'attached no value to the preservation of the State, law, organization, production. It simply does not reflect on the conditions of human society.' And Naumann concludes: 'Hence we either dare to aim at being without a state, and thus throwing ourselves deliberately into the arms of anarchy, or we decide to possess, alongside of our religious creed, a political creed as well.'[38] Thus the Qur'«n considers it necessary to unite religion and state, ethics and politics in a single revelation much in the same way as Plato does in his Republic.

The important point to note in this connexion, however, is the dynamic outlook of the Qur'«n. I have fully discussed its origin and history. It is obvious that with such an outlook the Holy Book of Islam cannot be inimical to the idea of evolution. Only we should not forget that life is not change, pure and simple. It has within it elements of conservation also. While enjoying his creative activity, and always focusing his energies of the discovery of new vistas of life, man has a feeling of uneasiness in the presence of his own unfoldment. In his forward movement he cannot help looking back to his past, and faces his own inward expansion with a certain amount of fear. The spirit of man in its forward movement is restrained by forces which seem to be working in the opposite direction. This is only another way of saying that life moves with the weight of its own past on its back, and that in any view of social change the value and function of the forces of conservatism cannot be lost sight of. It is with this organic insight into the essential teaching of the Qur'«n that to approach our existing institutions. No people can afford to reject their past entirely, for it is their past that has made their personal identity. And in a society like Islam the problem of a revision of old institutions becomes still more delicate, and the responsibility of the reformer assumes a far more serious aspect. Islam is non-territorial in its character, and its aim is to furnish a model for the final combination of humanity by drawing its adherents from a variety of mutually repellent races, and then transforming this atomic aggregate into a people possessing a self-consciousness of their own. This was not an easy task to accomplish. Yet Islam, by means of its well-conceived institutions, has succeeded to a very great extent in creating something like a collective will and conscience in this heterogeneous mass. In the evolution of such a society even the immutability of socially harmless rules relating to eating and drinking, purity or impurity, has a life-value of its own, inasmuch as it tends to give such society a specific inwardness, and further secures that external and internal uniformity which counteracts the forces of heterogeneity always latent in a society of a composite character. The critic of these institutions must, therefore, try to secure, before he undertakes to handle them, a clear insight into the ultimate significance of the social experiment embodied in Islam. He must look at their structure, not from the standpoint of social advantage or disadvantage to this or that country, but from the point of view of the larger purpose which is being gradually worked out in the life of mankind as a whole.

Turning now to the groundwork of legal principles in the Qur'«n, it is perfectly clear that far from leaving no scope for human thought and legislative activity the intensive breadth of these principles virtually acts as an awakener of human thought. Our early doctors of law taking their clue mainly from this groundwork evolved a number of legal systems; and the student of Muhammadan history knows very well that nearly half the triumphs of Islam as a social and political power were due to the legal acuteness of these doctors. 'Next to the Romans', says von Kremer, 'there is no other nation besides the Arabs which could call its own a system of law so carefully worked out.' But with all their comprehensiveness these systems are after all individual interpretations, and as such cannot claim any finality. I know the *'Ulem«* of Islam claim finality for the popular schools of Muhammadan Law, though they never found it possible to deny the theoretical possibility of a complete *Ijtih«d*. I have tried to explain the causes which, in my opinion, determined this attitude of the *'Ulem«*; but since things have changed and the world of Islam is confronted and affected today by new forces set free by the extraordinary development of human thought in all its directions, I see no reason why this attitude should be maintained any longer. Did the founders of our schools ever claim finality for their reasonings and interpretations? Never. The claim of the present generation of Muslim liberals to reinterpret the foundational legal principles, in the light of their own experience and the altered conditions of modern life is, in my opinion, perfectly justified. The teaching of the Qur'«n that life is a process of progressive creation necessitates that each generation, guided but unhampered by the work of its predecessors, should be permitted to solve its own problems.

You will, I think, remind me here of the Turkish poet Êiy« whom I quoted a moment ago, and ask whether the equality of man and woman demanded by him, equality, that is to say, in point of divorce, separation, and inheritance, is possible according to Muhammadan Law. I do not know whether the awakening of women in Turkey has created demands which cannot be met with without a fresh interpretation of foundational principles. In the Punjab, as everybody knows, there have been cases in which Muslim women wishing to get rid of undesirable husbands have been driven to apostasy.[39] Nothing could be more distant from the aims of a missionary religion. The Law of Islam, says the great Spanish jurist Im«m Sh«tibâin his al-Muwafiq«t, aims at protecting five things - *Dân, Nafs, 'Aql, M«l,* and *Nasl*.[40] Applying this test I venture to ask: 'Does the working of the rule relating to apostasy, as laid down in the *Hed«yah* tend to protect the interests of the Faith in this country?'[41] In view of the intense conservatism of the Muslims of India, Indian judges cannot but stick to what are called standard works. The result is that while the peoples are moving the law remains stationary.

With regard to the Turkish poet's demand, I am afraid he does not seem to know much about the family law of Islam. Nor does he seem to understand the economic significance of the Quranic rule of inheritance.[42] Marriage, according to Muhammadan Law, is a civil contract.[43] The wife at the time of marriage is at liberty to get the husband's power of divorce delegated to her on stated conditions, and thus secure equality of divorce with her husband. The reform suggested by the poet relating to the rule of inheritance is based on a misunderstanding. From the inequality of their legal shares it must not be supposed that the rule assumes the superiority of males over females. Such an assumption would be contrary to the spirit of Islam. The Qur'«n says:

And for women are rights over men similar to those for men over women' (2:228).

The share of the daughter is determined not by any inferiority inherent in her, but in view of her economic opportunities, and the place she occupies in the social structure of which she is a part and parcel. Further, according to the poet's own theory of society, the rule of inheritance must be regarded not as an isolated factor in the distribution of wealth, but as one factor among others working together for the same end. While the daughter, according to Muhammadan Law, is held to be full owner of the property given to her by both the father and the husband at the time of her marriage; while, further, she absolutely owns her dower-money which may be prompt or deferred according to her own choice, and in lieu of which she can hold possession of the whole of her husband's property till payment, the responsibility of maintaining her throughout her life is wholly thrown on the husband. If you judge the working of the rule of inheritance from this point of view, you will find that there is no material difference between the economic position of sons and daughters, and it is really by this apparent inequality of their legal shares that the law secures the equality demanded by the Turkish poet. The truth is that the principles underlying the Quranic law of inheritance - this supremely original branch of Muhammadan Law as von Kremer describes it - have not yet received from Muslim lawyers the attention they deserve.[44] Modern society with its bitter class-struggles ought to set us thinking; and if we study our laws in reference to the impending revolution in modern economic life, we are likely to discover, in the foundational principles, hitherto unrevealed aspects which we can work out with a renewed faith in the wisdom of these principles.

(b) The Àadâth. The second great source of Muhammadan Law is the traditions of the Holy Prophet. These have been the subject of great discussion both in ancient and modern times. Among their modern critics Professor Goldziher has subjected them to a searching examination in the light of modern canons of historical criticism, and arrives at the conclusion that they are, on the whole, untrustworthy.[45] Another European writer, after examining the Muslim methods of determining the genuineness of a tradition, and pointing out the theoretical possibilities of error, arrives at the following conclusion:

'It must be said in conclusion that the preceding considerations represent only theoretical possibilities and that the question whether and how far these possibilities have become actualities is largely a matter of how far the actual circumstances offered inducements for making use of the possibilities. Doubtless, the latter, relatively speaking, were few and affected only a small proportion of the entire Sunnah. It may therefore be said that . . . for the most part the collections of Sunnah considered by the Moslems as canonical are genuine records of the rise and early growth of Islam' (*Mohammedan Theories of Finance*).[46]

For our present purposes, however, we must distinguish traditions of a purely legal import from those which are of a non-legal character. With regard to the former, there arises a very important question as to how far they embody the pre-Islamic usages of Arabia which were in some cases left intact, and in others modified by the Prophet. It is difficult to make this discovery, for our early writers do not always refer to pre-Islamic usages. Nor is it possible to discover that usages, left intact by express or tacit approval of the Prophet, were intended to be universal in their application. Sh«h Walâ All«h has a very illuminating discussion on the point. I reproduce here the substance of his view. The prophetic method of teaching, according to Sh«h Walâ All«h, is that, generally speaking, the law revealed by a prophet takes especial notice of the habits, ways, and peculiarities of the people to whom he is specifically sent. The prophet who aims at all-embracing principles, however, can neither reveal different principles for different peoples, nor leaves them to work out their own rules of conduct. His method is to train one particular people, and to use them as a nucleus for the building up of a universal Sharâ'ah. In doing so he accentuates the principles underlying the social life of all mankind, and applies them to concrete cases in the light of the specific habits of the people immediately before him. The Sharâ'ah values (AÁk«m) resulting from this application (e.g. rules relating to penalties for crimes) are in a sense specific to that people; and since their observance is not an end in itself they cannot be strictly enforced in the case of future generations.[47] It was perhaps in view of this that Abë Àanâfah, who had, a keen insight into the universal character of Islam, made practically no use of these traditions. The fact that he introduced the principle of IstiÁs«n, i.e. juristic preference, which necessitates a careful study of actual conditions in legal thinking, throws further light on the motives which determined his attitude towards this source of Muhammadan Law. It is said that Abë Àanâfah made no use of traditions because there were no regular collections in his day. In the first place, it is not true to say that there were no collections in his day, as the collections of 'Abd al-M«lik and Zuhrâ were made not less than thirty years before the death of Abë Àanâfah. But even if we suppose that these collections never reached him, or that they did not contain traditions of a legal import, Abë Àanâfah, like M«lik and AÁmad Ibn Àanbal after him, could have easily made his own collection if he had deemed such a thing necessary. On the whole, then, the attitude of Abë Àanâfah towards the traditions of a purely legal import is to my mind perfectly sound; and if modern Liberalism considers it safer not to make any indiscriminate use of them as a source of law, it will be only following one of the greatest exponents of Muhammadan Law in Sunni Islam. It is, however, impossible to deny the fact that the traditionists, by insisting on the value of the concrete case as against the tendency to abstract thinking in law, have done the greatest service to the Law of Islam. And a further intelligent study of the literature of traditions, if used as indicative of the spirit in which the Prophet himself interpreted his Revelation, may still be of great help in understanding the life-value of the legal principles enunciated in the Qur'«n. A complete grasp of their life-value alone can equip us in our endeavour to reinterpret the foundational principles.

(c) The *Ijm«'*. The third source of Muhammadan Law is *Ijm«'* which is, in my opinion, perhaps the most important legal notion in Islam. It is, however, strange that this important notion, while invoking great academic discussions in early Islam, remained practically a mere idea, and rarely assumed the form of a permanent institution in any Muhammadan country. Possibly its transformation into a permanent legislative institution was contrary to the political interests of the kind of absolute monarchy that grew up in Islam immediately after the fourth Caliph. It was, I think, favourable to the interest of the Umayyad and the Abbasid Caliphs to leave the power of *Ijtih«d* to individual *Mujtahids* rather than encourage the formation of a permanent assembly which might become too powerful for them. It is, however, extremely satisfactory to note that the pressure of new world-forces and the political experience of

European nations are impressing on the mind of modern Islam the value and possibilities of the idea of *Ijm«'*. The growth of republican spirit and the gradual formation of legislative assemblies in Muslim lands constitute a great step in advance. The transfer of the power of *Ijtih«d* from individual representatives of schools to a Muslim legislative assembly which, in view of the growth of opposing sects, is the only possible form *Ijm«'* can take in modern times, will secure contributions to legal discussion from laymen who happen to possess a keen insight into affairs. In this way alone can we stir into activity the dormant spirit of life in our legal system, and give it an evolutionary outlook. In India, however, difficulties are likely to arise for it is doubtful whether a non-Muslim legislative assembly can exercise the power of *Ijtih«d*.

But there are one or two questions which must be raised and answered in regard to the *Ijm«'*. Can the *Ijm«'* repeal the Qur'«n? It is unnecessary to raise this question before a Muslim audience, but I consider it necessary to do so in view of a very misleading statement by a European critic in a book called *Mohammedan Theories of Finance* - published by the Columbia University. The author of this book says, without citing any authority, that according to some Hanafâ and Mu'tazilah writers the *Ijm«'* can repeal the Qur'«n.[48] There is not the slightest justification for such a statement in the legal literature of Islam. Not even a tradition of the Prophet can have any such effect. It seems to me that the author is misled by the word Naskh in the writings of our early doctors to whom, as Im«m Sh«Çibâê points out in al-Muwaffiq«t, vol. iii, p. 65, this word, when used in discussions relating to the *Ijm«'* of the companions, meant only the power to extend or limit the application of a Quranic rule of law, and not the power to repeal or supersede it by another rule of law. And even in the exercise of this power the legal theory, as 'Amâdâ- a Sh«fi'â doctor of law who died about the middle of the seventh century, and whose work is recently published in Egypt - tells us, is that the companions must have been in possession of a Sharâ'ah value (*Äukm*) entitling them to such a limitation or extension.[49]

But supposing the companions have unanimously decided a certain point, the further question is whether later generations are bound by their decision. Shauk«nâ has fully discussed this point, and cited the views held by writers belonging to different schools.[50] I think it is necessary in this connexion to discriminate between a decision relating to a question of fact and the one relating to a question of law. In the former case, as for instance, when the question arose whether the two small *Sërahs* known as *Mu'awwidhat«n*[51] formed part of the Qur'«n or not, and the companions unanimously decided that they did, we are bound by their decision, obviously because the companions alone were in a position to know the fact. In the latter case the question is one of interpretation only, and I venture to think, on the authority of Karkhâ, that later generations are not bound by the decision of the companions. Says Karkhâ: 'The Sunnah of the companions is binding in matters which cannot be cleared up by Qiy«s, but it is not so in matters which can be established by Qiy«s.'[52]

One more question may be asked as to the legislative activity of a modern Muslim assembly which must consist, at least for the present, mostly of men possessing no knowledge of the subtleties of Muhammadan Law. Such an assembly may make grave mistakes in their interpretation of law. How can we exclude or at least reduce the possibilities of erroneous interpretation? The Persian constitution of 1906 provided a separate ecclesiastical committee of '*Ulem«* - 'conversant with the affairs of the world' - having power to supervise the legislative activity of the *Mejlis*. This, in my opinion, dangerous arrangement is probably necessary in view of the Persian constitutional theory. According to that theory, I believe, the king is a mere custodian of the realm which really belongs to the Absent *Im«m*. The '*Ulem«*, as representatives of the *Im«m*, consider themselves entitled to supervise the whole life of the community, though I fail to understand how, in the absence of an apostolic succession, they establish their claim to represent the *Im«m*. But whatever may be the Persian constitutional theory, the arrangement is not free from danger, and may be tried, if at all, only as a temporary measure in Sunnâ countries.[53] The *'Ulem«* should form a vital part of a Muslim legislative assembly helping and guiding free discussion on questions relating to law. The only effective remedy for the possibilities of erroneous interpretations is to reform the present system of legal education in Muhammadan countries, to extend its sphere, and to combine it with an intelligent study of modern jurisprudence.[54]

(d) The *Qiy«s*. The fourth basis of *Fiqh* is *Qiy«s*, i.e. the use of analogical reasoning in legislation. In view of different social and agricultural conditions prevailing in the countries conquered by Islam, the school of Abë Àanâfah seem to have found, on the whole, little or no guidance from the precedents recorded in the literature of traditions. The only alternative open to them was to resort to speculative reason in their interpretations. The application of Aristotelian logic, however, though suggested by the discovery of new conditions in Iraq, was likely to prove exceedingly harmful in the preliminary stages of legal development. The intricate behaviour of life cannot be subjected to hard and fast rules logically deducible from certain general notions. Yet, looked at through the spectacles of Aristotle's logic, it appears to be a mechanism pure and simple with no internal principle of movement. Thus, the school of Abë Àanâfah tended to ignore the creative freedom and arbitrariness of life, and hoped to build a logically perfect legal system on the lines of pure reason. The legists of Àij«z, however, true to the practical genius of their race, raised strong protests against the scholastic subtleties of the legalists of Iraq, and their tendency to imagine unreal cases which they rightly thought would turn the Law of Islam into a kind of lifeless mechanism. These bitter controversies among the early doctors of Islam led to a critical definition of the limitations, conditions, and correctives of *Qiy«s* which, though originally appeared as a mere disguise for *Mujtahid's* personal opinion, eventually became a source of life and movement in the Law of Islam. The spirit of the acute criticism of M«lik and Sh«fi'â on Abë Àanâfah's principle of *Qiy«s*, as a source of law, constitutes really an effective Semitic restraint on the Aryan tendency to seize the abstract in preference to the concrete, to enjoy the idea rather than the event. This was really a controversy between the advocates of deductive and inductive methods in legal research. The legists of Iraq originally emphasized the eternal aspect of the 'notion', while those of Àij«z laid stress on its temporal aspect. The latter, however, did not see the full significance of their own position, and their instinctive partiality to the legal tradition of Àij«z narrowed their vision to the 'precedents' that had actually happened in the days of the Prophet and his companions. No doubt they recognized the value of the concrete, but at the same time they eternalized it, rarely resorting to *Qiy«s* based on the study of the concrete as such. Their criticism of Abë Àanâfah and his school, however, emancipated the concrete as it were, and brought out the necessity of observing the actual movement and variety of life in the interpretation of juristic principles. Thus the school of Abë Àanâfah which fully assimilated the results of this controversy is absolutely free in its essential principle and possesses much greater power of creative adaptation than any other school of Muhammadan Law. But, contrary to the spirit of his own school, the modern Hanafâ legist has eternalized the interpretations of the founder or his immediate followers much in the same way as the early critics of Abë Àanâfah eternalized the decisions given on concrete cases. Properly understood and applied, the essential principle of this school, i.e. *Qiy«s*, as Sh«fi'â rightly says, is only another name for *Ijtih«d*[55] which, within the limits of the revealed texts, is absolutely free; and its importance as a principle can be seen from the fact that, according to most of the doctors, as Q«dâ Shauk«nâ tells us, it was permitted even in the lifetime of the

Holy Prophet.[56] The closing of the door of *Ijtih«d* is pure fiction suggested partly by the crystallization of legal thought in Islam, and partly by that intellectual laziness which, especially in the period of spiritual decay, turns great thinkers into idols. If some of the later doctors have upheld this fiction, modern Islam is not bound by this voluntary surrender of intellectual independence. Zarkashâ writing in the eighth century of the Hijrah rightly observes:

'If the upholders of this fiction mean that the previous writers had more facilities, while the later writers had more difficulties, in their way, it is, nonsense; for it does not require much understanding to see that *Ijtih«d* for later doctors is easier than for the earlier doctors. Indeed the commentaries on the Kor«n and *sunnah* have been compiled and multiplied to such an extent that the mujtahid of today has more material for interpretation than he needs'.[57]

This brief discussion, I hope, will make it clear to you that neither in the foundational principles nor in the structure of our systems, as we find them today, is there anything to justify the present attitude. Equipped with penetrative thought and fresh experience the world of Islam should courageously proceed to the work of reconstruction before them. This work of reconstruction, however, has a far more serious aspect than mere adjustment to modern conditions of life. The Great European War bringing in its wake the awakening on Turkey - the element of stability in the world of Islam - as a French writer has recently described her, and the new economic experiment tried in the neighbourhood of Muslim Asia, must open our eyes to the inner meaning and destiny of Islam.[58] Humanity needs three things today - a spiritual interpretation of the universe, spiritual emancipation of the individual, and basic principles of a universal import directing the evolution of human society on a spiritual basis. Modern Europe has, no doubt, built idealistic systems on these lines, but experience shows that truth revealed through pure reason is incapable of bringing that fire of living conviction which personal revelation alone can bring. This is the reason why pure thought has so little influenced men, while religion has always elevated individuals, and transformed whole societies. The idealism of Europe never became a living factor in her life, and the result is a perverted ego seeking itself through mutually intolerant democracies whose sole function is to exploit the poor in the interest of the rich. Believe me, Europe today is the greatest hindrance in the way of man's ethical advancement. The Muslim, on the other hand, is in possession of these ultimate ideas of the basis of a revelation, which, speaking from the inmost depths of life, internalizes its own apparent externality. With him the spiritual basis of life is a matter of conviction for which even the least enlightened man among us can easily lay down his life; and in view of the basic idea of Islam that there can be no further revelation binding on man, we ought to be spiritually one of the most emancipated peoples on earth. Early Muslims emerging out of the spiritual slavery of pre-Islamic Asia were not in a position to realize the true significance of this basic idea. Let the Muslim of today appreciate his position, reconstruct his social life in the light of ultimate principles, and evolve, out of the hitherto partially revealed purpose of Islam, that spiritual democracy which is the ultimate aim of Islam.[59]

Lecture VI Notes: THE PRINCIPLE OF MOVEMENT IN THE STRUCTURE OF ISLAM

1. The Qur'«n maintains the divine origin of man by affirming that God breathed of His own spirit unto him as in verses 15:29; 32:9; and 38:72.

2. Constantine the Great was Roman Emperor from 306 to 337. He was converted to Christianity, it is said, by seeing a luminous cross in the sky. By his celebrated Edict of Toleration in 313 he raised Christianity to equality

with the public pagan cults in the Empire. For his attempt at the unification of Christianity, cf. Will Durant, *Caesar and Christ*, pp. 655-61, and *The Cambridge Medieval History*, vol.1, chapter i.

3. Flavius Claudius Julianus (331-363), nephew of Constantine, traditionally known as Julian the Apostate, ruled the Roman Empire from 361 to 363. Studying in Athens in 355, he frequented pagan Neoplatonist circles. As emperor, he at once proclaimed himself a pagan, restored freedom of worship for pagans and began a campaign against the orthodox church. Cf. Alice Gardner, *Julian and the Last Struggle of Paganism against Christianity*, and Will Durant, *The Age of Faith*, pp. 10-19.

4. See J. H. Denison, *Emotion as the Basis of Civilization*, pp. 267-68.

5. The principle of Divine Unity as embodied in the Quranic proclamation: *l«il«ha illa-All«h*: there is no God except All«h. It is a constant theme of the Qur'«n and is repeatedly mentioned as the basic principle not only of Islam but of every religion revealed by God.

6. Reference is to the Quranic verse 29:69. During the course of his conversation with one of his admirers, Allama Iqbal is reported to have made the following general observation with reference to this verse: 'All efforts in the pursuit of sciences and for attainment of perfections and high goals in life which in one way or other are beneficial to humanity are man's exerting in the way of Allah (*Malfëz«t-i Iqb«l*, ed. and annotated Dr Abë'l-Laith Siddâqâ, p. 67).

Translating this verse thus: 'But as for those who strive hard in Our cause - We shall most certainly guide them onto paths that lead unto us', Muhammad Asad adds in a footnote that the plural 'used here is obviously meant to stress the fact - alluded to often in the Qur'«n - that there are many paths which lead to a cognizance (*ma'rifah*) of God' (*The Message of the Qur'«n*, p. 616, note 61).

7. Cf. Abë D«wëd, *Aqdáya*: 11; Tirmidhâ, *AÁk«m*: 3, and D«rimâ, *Kit«b al-Sunan*, I, 60; this hadâth is generally regarded as the very basis of *Ijtih«d* in Islam. On the view expressed by certain scholars that this *hadâth* is to be ranked as *al-mursal*, cf. 'Abd al-Q«dir, Nazarah, *ÿ mmah fi T«rikh al-Fiqh al-Isl«mâ*, I, 70 and 210, and Sayyid Muhammad Yësuf Binorâas quoted by Dr Kh«lid Mas'ëd, *'Khutub«t-i Iqb«l men Ijtih«d kt Ta'râf: Ijtih«d k« T«râkhâ Pas-i Manzar'*, *Fikr-o-Nazar*, XV/vii-viii (Islamabad, Jan-Feb. 1978), 50-51. See also Ahmad Hasan (tr.), *Sunan Abë D«wëd*, III, 109, note 3034 based on Shams al-Haqq, *'Aun al-Ma'bëd li-hall-i Mushkil«t Sunan Abë D«wëd*, III, 331.

8. These three degrees of legislation in the language of the later jurists of Islam are: *ijtih«d fi'l-shar'*, *ijtih«d fi'l-madhhab* and *ijtih«d fi'l-mas«'il*; cf. Subhâ Mahmas«nâ, *Falsafat al-Tashrâ' fi'l-Islam*, English trans. F. J. Ziadeh, p. 94, and N. P. Aghnides, *Mohammeden Theories of Finance*, pp. 121-22. For somewhat different schemes of gradation of the jurists (for example the one laid down by the Ottoman scholar and Shaikh al-Isla`m Kem«l P«shaza`deh (d. 940/1534) in his (*Tabaq«t al-Fuqah«'*) and minor differences in nomenclature in different schools of law (Hanafis, Sh«fâ'â's and others), cf. Z«hid al-Kautharâ, *Husn al-Taq«dâfâ Sârat al-Im«m abâYësuf al-Q«îâ*, pp. 24-25.

It is the possibilities anew of the first degree of *Ijtih«d* - complete authority in legislation - that Allama Iqbal proposes to consider in what he calls (and this is to be noted) 'this paper' rather than 'this lecture' as everywhere else in the present work. This is a manifest reference to a 'paper on *Ijtih«d*' that he read on 13 December 1924 at the annual session of Anjuman-i Him«yat-i Isl«m. Cf. M. Khalid Mas'ëd, 'Iqbal's Lecture on Ijtih«d', *Iqbal Review*, XIX/iii (October 1978), p. 8, quoting in English the announcement about this Lecture published in the Daily *Zamând«r* Lahore, 12 December 1924; and also S. M. Ikram, *Modern Muslim India and the Birth of Pakistan*, p. 183, note 19 where the worthy author tells us that he 'was present at this meeting as a young student'.

Among Allama Iqbal's letters discovered only recently are the four of them addressed to Professor M. Muhammad Shafi' of University Oriental College, Lahore (later Chairman: *Urdu Encyclopaedia of Islam*). These letters dating from 13 March 1924 to 1 May 1924, reproduced with their facsimiles in Dr Rana M. N. Ehsan Elahie, 'Iqbal on the Freedom of Ijtiha`d', *Oriental College Magazine* (Allama Iqba Centenary Number), LIII (1977), 295-300, throw light, among other things, on the authors and movements that Allama Iqbal thought it was necessary for him to study anew for the writing of what he calls in one of these letters a paper on the 'freedom of *Ijtih«d* in Modern Islam'. A few months later when the courts were closed for summer vacation

Allama Iqbal in his letter dated 13 August 1924 to M. Sa'âd al-Dân Ja'farâ informed him that he was writing an elaborate paper on 'The Idea of *Ijtih«d*, in the Law of Islam' (cf. *Aur«q-i Gumgashtah*, ed. Rahâm Bakhsh Shaheen, p. 118). This is the paper which when finally written was read in the above-mentioned session of the Anjuman-i Àim«yat-i Isl«m in December 1924; the present Lecture, it is now generally believed, is a revised and enlarged form of this very paper.

9. Cf. M. Hanâf Nadvâ, 'Mas'alah Khalq-i Qur'«n' in *'Aqliy«t-i Ibn Taimâyyah* (Urdu), pp. 231-53, and A. J. Arberry, *Revelation and Reason in Islam*, pp. 23-27.

References to this hotly debated issue of the eternity or createdness of the Qur'«n are also to be found in Allama Iqbal's private notes, for example those on the back cover of his own copy of Spengler's *Decline of the West* (cf. *Descriptive Catalogue of Allama Iqbal's Personal Library*, Plate No. 33) or his highly valuable one-page private study notes preserved in Allama Iqbal Museum, Lahore (cf. *Relics of Allama Iqbal: Catalogue*, I, 26). It is, however, in one of his greatest poems 'Iblâs ki Majlis-i Shër« ('Satan's Parliament') included in the posthumous *Armugh«n-i Hij«z* that one is to find his final verdict on this baseless scholastic controversy:

Are the words of the Qur'«n created or uncreated?

In which belief does lie the salvation of the ummah?

Are the idols of L«t and Man«t chiselled by Muslim theology

Not sufficeint for the Muslims of today?

10. Cf. Ibn Qutaibah, Ta'wâ l Mukhtalif al-Àadâth, p.19.

11. Cf. *Development of Metaphysics in Persia*, p. 54, where it is stated that rationalism 'tended to disintegrate the solidarity of the Islamic Church'; also W. M. Watt, 'The Political Attitudes of the Mu'tazilah', *Journal of the Royal Asiatic Society* (1962), pp. 38-54.

12. Cf. Muhammad al-Khudari, *T«rákh al-Tashrâ' al-Isl«mâ*, Urdu trans. 'Abd al-Sal«m Nadvâ, p. 323; Ibn Qutaibah, *Ma'«rif*, p. 217, and J. Schacht, *The Origins of Muhammadan Jurisprudence*, p. 242. According to A. J. Arberry, Sufy«n al-Thaurâ's school of jurisprudence survive for about two centuries; cf. *Muslim Saints and Mystics*, p. 129 translator's prefatory remarks.

13. On the distinction of *z«hir* and *b«tin*, see Allama Iqbal's article 'Ilm-i Za`hir wa 'Ilm-i Ba`tin (*Anw«r-i Iqb«l*, ed. B. A. Dar, pp. 268-77) and also the following passage from Allama Iqbal's article captioned as 'Self in the Light of Relativity' (*Thoughts and Reflections of Iqbal*, ed. S. A. Vahid, pp. 113-14): 'The mystic method has attracted some of the best minds in the history of mankind. Probably there is something in it. But I am inclined to think that it is detrimental to some of the equally important interests of life, and is prompted by a desire to escape from the arduous task of the conquest of matter through intellect. The surest way to realise the potentialities of the world is to associate with its shifting actualities. I believe that Empirical Science - association with the visible - is an indispensable stage in the life of contemplation. In the words of the Qur'«n, the Universe that confronts us is not ba`til. It has its uses, and the most important use of it is that the effort to overcome the obstruction offered by it sharpens our insight and prepared us for an insertion into what lies below the surface of phenomena.

14. The founder of Z«hirâ school of law was D«wëd b. 'Alâb. Khalaf (c. 200-270/c. 815-884) who flourished in Baghdad; Ibn Haïm (384-456/994-1064) was its founder in Muslim Spain and its most illustrious representative in Islam. According to Goldziher, Ibn Hazm was the first to apply the principles of the Z«hirite school to dogmatics (*The Z«hiris: Their Doctrine and Their History*, p. 112); cf. also Goldziher's articles: 'D«wëd B. 'Alâ B. Khalf' and 'Ibn Hazm' in *Encyclopaedia of Religion and Ethics*, V, 406 b and VII, 71 a.

15. Cf. Serajul Haque, 'Ibn Taimiyya's Conception of Analogy and Consensus', *Islamic Culture*, XVII (1943), 77-78; Ahmad Hasan, *The Doctrine of Ijm«' in Islam*, pp. 189-92, and H. Laoust, 'Ibn Taymiyya', *Encyclopaedia of Islam* (New edition), III, 954.

16. Cf. D.'B. Macdonald, *Development of Muslim Theology*, p. 275.

17. Suyëtâ, *Husn al-Mëh«darah* 1, 183; also *'Abd Muta'«l al-Sa'idâ, Al-Mujaddidën fi'l-Isl«m*, pp. 8-12. Cf. also Allama Iqbal's 'Rejoinder to The Light' (*Speeches, Writings and Statements of Iqbal*, pp. 167-68) wherein, commenting on the tradition that mujaddids appear at the head of every century (Abë Dawëd, *Mal«him*: 1), he observed that the tradition 'was probably popularised by Jal«lud-Dân Suyëti in his own interest and much importance cannot be attached to it.'

Reference may also be made here to Allama's letter dated 7 April 1932 addressed to Muhammad Ahsan wherein, among other things, he observes that, according to his firm belief ('*aqâdh*), all traditions relating to *mujaddidiyat* are the product of Persian and non-Arab imagination and they certainly are foreign to the true spirit of the Qur'«n (cf. *Iqb«ln«mah*, II, 231).

18. For Allama Iqbal's statements issued from time to time in clarification on meanings and intentions of pan-Islamic movement or pan-Islamism see: *Letters and Writings of Iqbal*, pp. 55-57; *Speeches, Writings and Statements of Iqbal*, p. 237; *Guft«r-i Iqb«l*, ed. M. Rafâq Afial, pp. 177-79 and 226 - the earliest of these statements is contained in Allama's letter dated 22 August 1910 to Editor: *Paisa Akhb«r* reproduced in Riaz Hussain, '1910 men Duny«-i Isl«m kü H«l«t' (Political Conditions of the Islamic World in 1910), *Iqbal Review*, XIX/ii (July 1978), 88-90.

In three of these statements Allama Iqbal has approvingly referred to Professor E. G. Browne's well-grounded views on 'Pan-Islamism', the earliest of which were published (s.v.) in Lectures on the *History of the Nineteenth Century*, ed. F. Kirpatrick (Cambridge, 1904).

It may be added that Allama's article 'Political Thought in Islam', *Sociological Review*, I (1908), 249-61 (reproduced in *Speeches, Writings and Statements*, pp. 107-21), was originally a lecture delivered by him in a meeting of the Pan-Islamic Society, London, founded by Abdullah Suhrawardy in 1903 - the Society also had its own journal: Pan-Islam. Incidentally, there is a mention of Allama's six lectures on Islamic subjects in London by his biographers (cf. Abdullah Anwar Beg, *The Poet of the East*, p. 28, and Dr Abdus Sal«m Khurshâd, *Sargudhasht-i Iqb«l*, pp. 60-61) which is supported by Allama's letter dated 10 February 1908 to Khwa`jah Hasan Niz«mâ, listing the 'topics' of four of these lectures as (i) 'Islamic Mysticism', (ii) 'Influence of Muslim Thought on European Civilization', (iii) 'Muslim Democracy', and (iv) 'Islam and Reason' (cf. *Iqb«ln«mah*, II, 358). Abdullah Anwar Beg, however, speaks of Allama's extempore lecture on 'Certain Aspects of Islam' under the auspices of the Pan-Islamic Society, which, it is said, was reported verbatim in a number of leading newspapers the next day (ibid.).

19. Muhammad b. 'Abd al-Wahh«b's date of birth is now more generally given as 1115/1703; cf., however, Khair al-Dân al-Zikriklâ, *Al-A'l«m*, VII, 138 (note) and *A History of Muslim Philosophy*, ed. M. M. Sharif, II, 1446, in support of placing it in 1111/1700.

It is significant to note that whenever Allama Iqbal thought of modernist movements in Islam, he traced them back to the movement of Muhammad b. 'Abd al-Wahh«b cf. *Letters and Writings of Iqbal*, pp. 82 and 93. In his valuable article 'Islam and Ahmadism' Allama Iqbal observes: 'Syed Ahmad Khan in India, Syed Jamal-ud-Din Afghani in Afghanistan and Mufti Alam Jan in Russia. These men were probably inspired by Muhammad Ibn Abdul Wahab who was born in Nejd in 1700, the founder of the so-called Wahabi movement which may fitly be described as the first throb of life in modern Islam' (*Speeches, Writings and Statements*, p. 190). Again, in his letter dated 7 April 1932 to Muhammad Ahsan, Allama Iqbal, explaining the pre-eminent position of Jam«l al-Dân Afgh«nâ in modern Islam, wrote: 'The future historian of the Muslims of Egypt, Iran, Turkey and India will first of all mention the name of 'Abd al-Wahh«b Najadi and then of Jam«l al-Dân Afgh«nâ' (cf. *Iqb«ln«mah*, II, 231).

20. Cf. article 'Ibn Tëmart' in Encyclopaedia of Islam (New edition), III, 958-60, also in *Shorter Encyclopaedia of Islam* and R. Le Tourneau, *The Almohad Movement in North Africa in the Twelfth and Thirteenth Centuries*, chapter 4.

21. This is a clear reference to the well-known saying of the Prophet: *innamal-a'm«lu bi'nniyy«ti*, i.e. 'Actions shall be judged only by intentions'. It is to be noted that this *Áadâth* of great moral and spiritual import has been quoted by Bukh«râ in seven places and it is with this that he opens his *Al-J«mâ al-SaÁiÁ*.

22. For this Áadâth worded: '*al-arÁu kulluh«masjid-an*', see Tirmidhâ, *Sal«t*: 119; Nas«â, *Ghusl*: 26; *Mas«jid*: 3 and 42; Ibn M«jah, *Tah«rah*: 90, and D«rimâ, *Siyar*: 28 and *Sal«t*: 111. This superb saying of the Prophet also found expression in Allama's verse, viz. *Kulliy«t-i Iqb«l* (F«risâ), *Rumëz-i Bekhudâ*, p. 114, v. 3, and *Pas Chih B«yad Kard*, p. 817, v. 8:

Through the bounty of the ruler of our faith,
the entire earth became our mosque.
The King of the Faith said to the Muslims:
The whole earth is my mosque' (trans. B. A. Dar).

23. Cf. *The Muqaddimah*, trans. F. Rosenthal, I, 388-92.

24. For the Khawa`rij's view of the Caliphate, see Allama Iqbal's article 'Political Thought in Islam' (*Speeches, Writings and Statements of Iqbal*, pp. 119-20); also W. Thomson, 'Kharijitism and the Kharijites', *Macdonald Presentation Volume*, pp. 371-89, and E. Tyan, *Institutions du droit public musulman*, ii, 546-61.

25. Cf. F. A. Tansel (ed), Ziya Gö kalp kü lliyati 'i: Sü rler ve halk masallar, p. 129. On Allama's translation of the passages from Ziya G'kalp's kulliyati, Dr Annemarie Schimmel observes: 'Iqbal did not know Turkish, has studied his (Ziya Gö kalp's) work through the German translation of August Fischer, and it is of interest to see how he (Iqbal) sometimes changes or omits some words of the translation when reproducing the verses in the Lecture' (*Gabriel's Wing*, p. 242).

It may be added that these changes of omissions are perhaps more due to August Fischer's German translation as given in his *Aus der religiö sen Reformbewegung in der Tü rkei* (Religious Reform Movement in Turkey) than to Allama. The term 'esri', for example, has been used by Ziya Gö kalp for 'secular' and not for 'modern' as Fischer has put it. Again, a line from the original Turkish text is missing in the present passage, but this is so in the German translation.

For this comparative study of the German and English translations of passages from Gö kalp's *kü lliyati*, I am very much indebted to Professor S. Qudratullah Fatimi, formerly Director: Regional Cooperation for Development, Islamabad.

26. This is a reference to the Quranic verse 49:13.

27. Cf. *Ziya Gö kalp kü lliyati*, p. 112. According to the Turkish original, the second sentence in this passage should more fittingly have begun with 'in this period' rather than with 'in every period' as rendered by A. Fischer. Again the next, i.e. the third sentence, may be said to be not so very close to the text; yet it is quite faithful to its German version.

28. Cf. *ibid*., p. 113; also Uriel Heyd, *Foundation of Turkish Nationalism: The Life and Teachings of Ziya Gö kalp*, pp. 102-03, and Allama Iqbal's statement 'On the Introduction of Turkish Prayers by Ghazi Mustafa Kemal Pasha' published in the Weekly *Light* (Lahore), 16 February 1932, reproduced in Rahim Bakhsh Shaheen (ed.), *Memontos of Iqbal*, pp. 59-60.

29. On Ibn Tumart's innovation of introducing the call to prayer in the Berber language, cf. Ibn Abâ Zar', *Raud al-Qirt«s*, Fr. trans. A. Beaumier, *Histoire des souverains du Magreb*, p. 250; I. Goldziher, 'Materalien zur Kenntniss der Almohadenbewegung in Nordafrika', *ZDMG*, XLI (1887), 71, and D. B. Macdonald, *Development of Muslim Theology*, p. 249. This practice, according to Ahmad b. Kh«lid al-Sal«wâ, was stopped and call to prayer in Arabic restored by official orders in 621/1224; cf. his *Al-Istiqs«li Akhb«r Duwal al-Maghrib'l-Aqs«*, II, 212.

30. Cf. *Ziya Gö kalp kü lliyati*, p. 133. The word 'sun' in the second sentence of this passage stands for Gunum in Turkish which, we are told, could as well be translated as 'day'; some allowance, however, is to be made for translation of poetical symbols from one language into another.

31. Cf. *ibid*., p. 161. It is interesting to note how very close is late Professor H. A. R. Gibb's translation of this passage as well as of the one preceding it (Modern Trends in Islam, pp. 91-92), to that of Allama's even though

his first reference is to the French version of them in F. Ziyaeddin Fahri's *Ziya Gö kalp: sa vie et sa sociologie*, p. 240.

32. Cf. Bukh«râ, *I'tis«m*: 26; *'Ilm*: 39; *Jan« 'iz*: 32; *Marad«*: 17, and Muslim, *Jan« 'iz*: 23 and *Wasâyyah*: 22; see also last in *Sahih Muslim*, English translation by A. H. Siddiqi`, III 870, note 2077.

33. For further elucidation of Allama's observations on Luther and his movement here as also in a passage in his 'Statement on Islam and Nationalism in Reply to a Statement of Maulana Husain Ahmad' (*Speeches, Writings and Statements of Iqbal*, p. 254), see his most famous and historical 'All-India Muslim League Presidential Address of 29 December 1930', ibid., pp. 4-5. Cf. also the closing passages of the article: 'Reformation' in *An Encyclopedia of Religion*, ed. Vergilius Ferm, p. 642.

34. Cf. Subhâ Mahmas«nâ, *Falsafah-i Sharâ'at-i Isl«m*, Urdu trans. M. Ahmad Ridvâ, pp. 70-83.

35. This acute observation about the development of legal reasoning in Islam from the deductive to the inductive attitude in interpretation is further elaborated by Allama Iqbal on pp. 140-41. It may be worthwhile to critically examine in the light of this observation the attempts made by some of the well-known Western writers on Islamic law to analytically trace the historical development of legal theory and practice in early Islam, viz. N. J. Coulson, *A History of Islamic Law*, chapters 3-5; J. Schacht, *Introduction to Islamic Law*, chapters 7-9 and his earlier pioneer work: *Origins of Muhammadan Jurisprudence*, by General Index especially under 'Medinese and 'Iraqians'.

36. This is a reference to a passage in Lecture I, p. 7.

37. Cf. M. V. Merchant, *A Book of Quranic Laws*, chapters v-vii.

38. Cf. *Briefe ü ber Religion*, pp. 72 and 81. The passages translated here are as under:

"Das Urchristentum legte keinen Wert auf die Erhaltung von Staat Recht, Organisation, Produktion. Es denkt einfach nicht ü ber die Bedingungen der Existenz der menschlichen Gesellschaft nach."

Also entweder man wagt es, staatslos sein zu wollen, man wirft sich der Anarchie freiwillig in die arme, oder man entschliesst sich, neben seinem religiö sen Bekenntnis ein politisches Bekenntnis zu haben.

Joseph Friedrich Naumann (1860-1919), a passage from whose very widely read *Briefe ü ber Religion* ('Letters on Religion') has been quoted above in Lecture III, pp. 64-65, was a German Protestant theologian, socialist politician, political journalist and a champion of *Mitteleuropa* plan. He was one of the four ders and the first president of German National Socialist Party (1896) which both in its name and in its policy of according great importance to the agricultural and working classes in the development of the State adumbrated Hitler's Nazi Party (1920). His Mitteleuropa published in 1915 (English translation by C. M. Meredith in 1916) stirred up considerable discussion during World War I as it revived, under the impulse of Pan-Germanism, the idea of a Central European Confederation including Turkey and the Balkan States under Germany's cultural and economic control. It also contemplated the expansion of the Berlin-Baghdad railway into a grandiose scheme of empire extending from Antwerp in Belgium to the Persian Gulf.

Except for the year 1912-13, Naumann was the member of Reichstag (German Parliament) from 1907 to 1919. Shortly before his death, he was elected as the leader of Democratic Party. Naumann known for his wide learning, acumen and personal integrity was very influential with German liberal intellectuals of his day. For the life and works of Naumann, cf. the two articles: 'Naumann, Friedrich' and 'National Socialism, German' by Theodor Heuss in the *Encyclopaedia of Social Sciences*, XI, 310 and 225a; also *The New Encyclopaedia Britannica* (Micropaedia), VIII, 561. For some information given in the above note I am deeply indebted to the Dutch scholar the Reverend Dr Jan Slomp and his younger colleague Mr Harry Mintjes. Mr Mintjes took all the trouble to find out what he said was the oldest available edition of *Briefe ü ber Religion* (Berlin, Georg Reimer, 1916, sixth edition) by making a search for it in all the libraries of Amsterdam. Dr Jan Slamp was kind enough to mark the passages in *Briefe* quoted by Allama Iqbal in English and mail these to me for the benefit of all Iqbalian scholars.

39. Hence, The Introduction of Dissolution of Muslim Marriages Act or Indian Act VIII of 1939. Cf. Maul«n« Ashraf 'Alâ Th«nawâ, *Al-Hilat al-N«jizah lil-Halâlat al-'ÿjizah*, p. 99 and A. A. A. Fyzee, Outlines of Muhammadan Law, pp. 153-61.

40. See *Al-Muw«fiq«t*, II, 4: also Ghaz«lâ, *Al-Mustasf«*, 1, 140.

41. Cf. al-Marghin«nâ, *Al-Hid«yah*, II, *Kit«b al-Nik«h*, p. 328; English trans. *The Hedaya or Guide* by C. Hamilton, p. 66.

42. Cf. *Speeches, Writings and Statements of Iqbal*, p. 194, where, while making an appraisal of Ataturk's 'supposed or real innovations', Allama Iqbal observes: 'The adoption of the Swiss code with its rule of inheritance is certainly a serious error . . . . The joy of emancipation from the fetters of a long-standing priestcraft sometimes derives a people to untried courses of action. But Turkey as well as the rest of the world of Islam has yet to realize the hitherto unrevealed economic aspects of the Islamic law of inheritance which von Kremer describes as the supremely original branch of Muslim law.' For some recent accounts of the 'economic significance of the Quranic rule of inheritance', cf. M. A. Mannan, *Islamic Economics*, pp. 176-86 and Shaikh Mahmud Ahmad, *Economics of Islam*, pp. 154-58.

43. Marriage has been named in the Qur'«n as *mâth«q-an ghalâz-an*, i.e. a strong covenant (4:21).

44. Cf. M. V. Merchant, op. cit., pp. 179-86.

45. Cf. I. Goldziher, *Muhammedanische Studien*, English trans. C. R. Barber and S. M. Stern, *Muslim Studies*, II, 18f. This is the view held also by some other orientalists such as D. S. Margoliouth, *The Early Development of Mohammedanism*, pp. 79-89, and H. Lammens, *Islam: Beliefs and Institutions*, pp. 65-81.

46. This is the closing paragraph of chapter III of *Mohammedan Theories of Finance: With an Introduction to Mohammedan Law and a Bibliography* by Nicolas P. Aghnides published by Columbia University (New York) in 1916 as one of its *Studies in History, Economics and Public Law*. A copy of this work as reported by Dr M. 'Abdulla`h Chaghata`'i was sent to Allama Iqbal by Chaudhry Rahmat 'Ali`Kha`n (President: American Muslim Association) from the United States and was presented to him on the conclusion of the thirty-eighth annual session of Anjuman-i Àim«yat-i Isl«m (Lahore), i.e. on 31 March 1923 or soon after. Dr Chaghat«'âs essay: 'Khutuba`t-i Madra`s ka Pas-i Manzar' in his *Iqb«l kâ Àuhbat Men* and the section: 'Six Lectures on the Reconstruction of Religious Thought in Islam' with useful notes in Dr. Rafâ al-Dân H«shimâ's *TaÄ«nâf-i Iqb«l k« TaÁqâqâ-o Tauîâhâ MuÇ«la'ah* throw light on the immediate impact that Aghnides's book had on Allama's mind. It seems that Aghnides's book did interest Allama and did play some part in urging him to seek and study some of the outstanding works on *Usël al-Fiqh* such as those by ÿmidâ, Sh«Çibâ, Sh«h Walâ All«h, Shauk«nâ, and others. This is evident from a number of Allama's letters to Sayyid Sulaim«n Nadvâas also from his letters from 13 March 1924 to 1 May 1924 to Professor Maulavâ M. Shafâ' [*Oriental College Magazine*, LIII (1977), 295-300]. It is to be noted that besides a pointed reference to a highly provocative view of *Ijm«* ' alluded to by Aghnides, three passages from part I of *Mohammedan Theories of Finance* are included in the last section of the present Lecture, which in this way may be said to be next only to the poems of Ziya Gö kalp exquisitely translated from Fischer's German version of them.

47. This is remarkable though admittedly a summarized English version of the following quite significant passage from Sh«h Walâ All«h's magnum opus Hujjat All«h al-B«lighah (I,118):

This is the passage quoted also in Shiblâ Něm«nâ's *Al-Kal«m* (pp. 114-15), a pointed reference to which is made in Allama Iqbal's letter dated 22 September 1929 addressed to Sayyid Sulaim«n Nadvâ. There are in fact three more letters to Sayyid Sulaim«n Nadvâ in September 1929, which all show Allama's keen interest in and preceptive study of Hujjat All«h al-B«lighah at the time of his final drafting of the present Lecture (cf. *Iqb«ln«mah*, pp. 160-63).

From the study of these letters it appears that Allama Iqbal in his interpretation of at least the above passage from *Àujjat All«h al-B«ligah* was much closer to Shiblâ Něm«nâ than to Sayyid Sulaimân Nadvâ.

It is to be noted that Allama Iqbal was always keen to seek and study the works of Sha`h WalâAll«h, whom he considered to be 'the first Muslim who felt the urge of a new spirit in him' (Lecture IV, p. 78). Some of these works have been referred to by titles in Allama's more than 1200 letters and it is noteworthy that their number exceeds that of the works of any other great Muslim thinker; Ghazz«lâ, Fakhr al-Dân R«zâ, Jal«l al-Dân Rumâ, Ibn Taimiyyah, Ibn Qayyim; Sadr al-Dân Shâr«zâ, or any other. In his letter dated 23 September 1936 to Maulavi Ahmad Rid« Bijnârâ, Allama reports that he had not received his copies of Sh«h WalâAll«h's *Al-Khair al-Kathâr* and *Tafhâm«t* supposed to have been dispatched to him through some dealer in Lahore. He also expresses in this letter his keen desire to have the services on suitable terms of some competent Muslim scholar, well-versed in Islamic jurisprudence and very well-read in the works of Sh«h Walâ All«h.

48. Cf. Aghnides, *op. cit.*, p. 91. This is the statement which, according to Dr 'Abdullah Chaghat«'â (*op. cit.*, pp. 300-04) and Dr. Rafâ al-Dân H«shimâ occasioned Allama Iqbal's fiqhi discussions with a number of renowned religious scholars which finally led to his writing a paper on *Ijtih«d* in 1924; the present Lecture may be said to be only a developed form of that paper. On the impossible question of Ijm«'s repealing the Qur'«n one is to note Allama's two inquiring letters to Sayyid Sulaim«n Nadvâ and more importantly a letter also to Maul«n« Abul Kal«m Az«d (*Iqb«ln«mah*, 1, 131-35).

49. ÿmidâ, *Ihk«m fi Usël al-Ahk«m*, 1, 373.

50. Shauk«nâ, *Irsh«d al-Fuhël*, pp. 65-72.

51. *Mu'awwidhat«n* are the last two *sërahs* of the Qur'«n, i.e. 113 and 114; they are called so because they teach man how to seek refuge with God and betake himself to His protection.

52. This is summing up of Karkhi`'s somewhat longer statement as quoted by Aghnides, *op. cit.*, p. 106; cf. also Sarakhsâ, Usul «l-Sarakhsâ, II, 105.

53. For Allama's views on Persian constitutional theory see his articles: 'Political Thought in Islam' and 'Islam and Ahmadism', *Speeches, Writings and Statements of Iqbal*, pp. 118-19 and 195.

54. For Allama's practical guidelines to reform the present system of legal education in the modern Muslim world especially in the subcontinent, see his very valuable letter dated 4 June 1925 to Sahibzadah Aftab Ahmad Khan (*Letters of Iqbal*, p. 155); also the last paragraph of his Presidential Address at the All-India Muslim Conference on 21 March 1932 (*Speeches, Writings and Statements*, p. 43).

55. For Sh«fâ'â's 'identification' of Qiy«s and *Ijtih«d*, cf. M. Khadduri, *Islamic Jurisprudence Sh«fi'âs Ris«lah*, p. 288 and J. Schacht, *The Origins of Muhammadan Jurisprudence*, pp. 127-28.

56. Cf. Shauk«nâ, op. cit., p. 199; ÿmidâ, op. cit., IV, 42ff; and Mahmas«nâ, *op. cit.*, Urdu trans. M. A. Ridvâ, p. 188.

57. Cf. *Mohammedan Theories of Finance*, p. 125. This is the observation, in fact, of the Sh«fi'âjurist Badr al-Dân Muhammad b. Bah«dur b. 'Abd All«h al-Zarkashâ of eighth century and not of Sarkashâof tenth century of the Hijrah, as it got printed in the previous editions of the present work (including the one by Oxford University Press in 1934). 'Sarkashâ' is a palpable misprint for Zarkashâ'; Aghnides in the above-cited work spells it 'Zarkashi' but places him in the tenth century of the Hijrah. None of the Zarkashâs, however, given in the well-known biographical dictionaries, say, 'Umar Rid« Kahhalah's fifteen-volume *Mu'jam al-Mu'allifân* (V, 181; IX, 121; X, 22, 205, 239 and XI, 273) is reported to have belonged to tenth century - except, of course, Muhammad b. Ibra`hi`m b. *Lu'lu' al-Zarkashâ* mentioned in VIII, 214 who is said to be still living after 882/1477 or as al-Ziriklâ puts it to have died sometime after 932/1526 (*op. cit.*, V, 302); but this Zarkashâ, though he may be said to have made name as an historian of the Muwahhids and the Hafasids, was no jurist.

It is to be noted that the passage on the future prospects of *Ijtih«d* quoted by Allama Iqbal is only a more significant part of Zarkashâ's somewhat longer statement which Aghnides gives as under:

If they [i.e., the people entertaining this belief] are thinking of their contemporaries, it is a fact that they have had contemporaries like al-Qaff«l, al-Ghazz«lâ, al-Razâ, al-R«fi'â, and others, all of whom have been full mujtahids, and if they mean by it that their contemporaries are not endowed and blessed by God with the same perfection, intellectual ability and power, or understanding, it is absurd and a sign of crass ignorance; finally, if they mean that the previous writers had more facilities, while the later writers has more difficulties, in their way; it is again nonsense, for it does not require much understanding to see that *Ijtih«d* for the later doctors (*muta'akhirēn*) is easier than for the earlier doctors. Indeed the commentaries on the Koran and the sunnah have been compiled and multiplied to such an extent that the mujtahid of today has more material for interpretation than he needs.'

This statement on *ijtih«d* which Aghnides ascribes clearly to Zarkashâ, albeit of the tenth century of Hijrah, is in fact, as may be seen, translation of the following passage from Shauk«nâ's *Irsh«d al-Fuhēl* (p. 223):

From the study of the section of *Irsh«d al-Fuhēl* dealing with the 'possibility of there being a period of time without a mujtahid, it becomes abundantly clear that the views embodied in the above passage are those of the Sh«fi'â jurist Badr al-Dân Zarkashâ of the eighth century of Hijrah and not of Sarkashâ, nor of Zarkashâof the tenth century. For an account of the life and works of Badr al-Dân Zarkashâ, cf. Muhammad Abē'l-Fadl al-Rahâm's 'introduction' to Zarkashâ's well-known, *Al-Burh«n fi 'ulēm al-Qur'«n*.

It may be added that the Persian translator of the present work Mr. Ahmad ÿr«m considers 'Sarkashâ' to be a misprint for 'Sarakhsâ', i.e. the Hanafâ jurist Shams al-ÿimmah Abē Bakr Muhammad b. Abâ Sahl al-Sarakhsâ, the author of the well-known thirty-volume *al-Mabsēt*, who died in near about 483/1090. Referring to 'many errors and flaws' that have unfortunately crept into the Lahore edition of the present work, Mr. ÿr«m is inclined to think that 'tenth century' is another misprint for 'fifth century' (cf. *Ihy«-i Fikr-i Dânâ dar Isl«m*, pp. 202-03, note).

Ahmad ÿr«m admittedly takes his clue from a line in Madame Eva Meyerovitch's French translation: *Reconstruire la pensee religieus de l'Islam* (p.192) and perhaps also from the Urdu translation: *Tashkâl-i Jadâd Il«hiy«t-i Isl«mâyah* (p. 274) by the late Syed Nadhir Niy«zâ who corrects the name (Sarakhsâ) but not the date. This is, however, better than the Arabic translator who retains both the misprints without any comments (cf. 'Abb«s Mahmēd, *Tajdâd al-Tafkâr al-Dânâfi'l-Isl«m*, p. 206).

58. Cf. article 'Turkey' in *Encyclopaedia Britannica*, (1953) XXII, 606-08. The French writer alluded to by Allama Iqbal is Andre Servier whose work *L'Islam et la psychologie da Musulman* translated under the intriguing title *Islam and the Psychology of a Musulman* by A. S. Moss Blandell (London, 1924) aroused the curiosity of many. It is in the last chapter of his work dealing with French foreign policy that Servier makes some observations on Turkey such as the following:

(a) 'The Turks constitute *an element of balance* . . . they form a buffer State between Europe and the Asiatic ferment' (p. 267). (Italics mine.)

(b) 'Our interests, therefore, make it our duty to protect them, to maintain them as *an element of equilibrium* in the Musulman World' (p. 268). (Italics mine.)

59. This may profitably be compared with the following passage from Allama's famous 'Statement on Islam and Nationalism in Reply to a Statement of Maulana Husain Ahmad': 'The history of man is an infinite process of mutual conflicts, sanguine battles and civil wars. In these circumstances can we have among mankind a constitution, the social life of which is based upon peace and security? The Quran's answer is: Yes, provided man takes for his ideal the propagation of the Unity of God in the thoughts and actions of mankind. The search for such an ideal and its maintenance is no miracle of political manoeuvring: it is a peculiar greatness of the Holy Prophet that the self-invented distinctions and superiority complexes of the nations of the world are destroyed and there comes into being a community which can be styled ummat-am muslimat-al laka (a community submissive to Thee, 2:128) and to whose thoughts and actions the divine dictate shuhada'a 'al-an nas-i (a community that bears witness to the truth before all mankind, 2:143) justly applies' (*Speeches, Writings and Statements of Iqbal*, pp. 262-63).

Is Religion Possible?

by Dr. Muhammad Iqbal

Broadly speaking religious life may be divided into three periods. These may be described as the periods of 'Faith', 'Thought', and 'Discovery.' In the first period religious life appears as a form of discipline which the individual or a whole people must accept as an unconditional command without any rational understanding of the ultimate meaning and purpose of that command. This attitude may be of great consequence in the social and political history of a people, but is not of much consequence in so far as the individual's inner growth and expansion are concerned. Perfect submission to discipline is followed by a rational understanding of the discipline and the ultimate source of its authority. In this period religious life seeks its foundation in a kind of metaphysics - a logically consistent view of the world with God as a part of that view. In the third period metaphysics is displaced by psychology, and religious life develops the ambition to come into direct contact with the Ultimate Reality. It is here that religion becomes a matter of personal assimilation of life and power; and the individual achieves a free personality, not by releasing himself from the fetters of the law, but by discovering the ultimate source of the law within the depths of his own consciousness. As in the words of a Muslim Sufi - 'no understanding of the Holy Book is possible until it is actually revealed to the believer just as it was revealed to the Prophet.'[1] It is, then, in the sense of this last phase in the development of religious life that I use the word religion in the question that I now propose to raise. Religion in this sense is known by the unfortunate name of Mysticism, which is supposed to be a life-denying, fact-avoiding attitude of mind directly opposed to the radically empirical outlook of our times. Yet higher religion, which is only a search for a larger life, is essentially experience and recognized the necessity of experience as its foundation long before science learnt to do so. It is a genuine effort to clarify human consciousness, and is, as such, as critical of its level of experience as Naturalism is of its own level.

As we all know, it was Kant who first raised the question: 'Is metaphysics possible?'[2] He answered this question in the negative; and his argument applies with equal force to the realities in which religion is especially interested. The manifold of sense, according to him, must fulfil certain formal conditions in order to constitute knowledge. The thing-in-itself is only a limiting idea. Its function is merely regulative. If there is some actuality corresponding to the idea, it falls outside the boundaries of experience, and consequently its existence cannot be rationally demonstrated. This verdict of Kant cannot be easily accepted. It may fairly be argued that in view of the more recent developments of science, such as the nature of matter as 'bottled-up light waves', the idea of the universe as an act of thought, finiteness of space and time and Heisenberg's principle of indeterminacy[3] in Nature, the case for a system of rational theology is not so bad as Kant was led to think. But for our present purposes it is unnecessary to consider this point in detail. As to the thing-in-itself, which is inaccessible to pure reason because of its falling beyond the boundaries of experience, Kant's verdict can be accepted only if we start with the assumption that all experience other than the normal level of experience is impossible. The only question, therefore, is whether the normal level is the only level of knowledge-yielding experience. Kant's view of the thing-in-itself and the thing as it appears to us very much determined the character of his question regarding the possibility of metaphysics. But what if the position, as understood by him, is reversed? The great Muslim Sufi philosopher, Muhyaddin Ibn al-'Arabâ of Spain, has made the acute observation that God is a percept; the world is a concept.[4] Another Muslim Sufi thinker and poet, 'Ir«qâ, insists on the plurality of space-orders and time-orders and speaks of a Divine Time and a Divine Space.[5] It may be that what we call the external world is only an intellectual construction, and that there are other levels of human experience capable of being systematized by other orders of space and time - levels in which concept and analysis do not play the same role as they do in the case of our normal experience. It may, however, be said that the level of experience to which concepts are inapplicable cannot yield any knowledge of a universal character, for concepts alone are capable of being socialized. The standpoint of the man who relies on religious experience for capturing Reality must always remain individual and incommunicable. This objection has some force if it is meant to insinuate that the mystic is wholly ruled by his traditional ways, attitudes, and expectations. Conservatism is as bad in religion as in any other department of human activity. It destroys the ego's creative freedom and closes up the paths of fresh spiritual enterprise. This is the main reason why our medieval mystic techniques can no longer produce original discoveries of ancient Truth. The fact, however, that religious experience is incommunicable does not mean that the religious man's pursuit is futile. Indeed, the incommunicability of religious experience gives us a clue to the ultimate nature of the ego. In our daily social intercourse we live and move in seclusion, as it were. We do not care to reach the inmost individuality of men. We treat them as mere functions, and approach them from those aspects of their identity which are capable of conceptual treatment. The climax of religious life, however, is the discovery of the ego as an individual deeper than his conceptually describable habitual selfhood. It is in contact with the Most Real that the ego discovers its uniqueness, its metaphysical status, and the possibility of improvement in that status. Strictly speaking, the experience which leads to this discovery is not a conceptually manageable intellectual fact; it is a vital fact, an attitude consequent on an inner biological transformation which cannot be captured in the net of logical categories. It can embody itself only in a world-making or world-shaking act; and in this form alone the content of this timeless experience can diffuse itself in the time-movement, and make itself effectively visible to the eye of history. It seems that the method of dealing with Reality by means of concepts is not at all a serious way of dealing with it. Science does not care whether its electron is a real entity or not. It may be a mere symbol, a mere convention. Religion, which is essentially a mode of actual living, is the only serious way of handing Reality. As a form of higher experience is corrective of our concepts of philosophical theology or at least makes us suspicious of the purely rational process which forms these concepts. Science can afford to ignore metaphysics altogether, and may even believe it to be 'a justified form of poetry'[6], as Lange defined it, or 'a legitimate play of grown-ups', as Nietzsche described it. But the religious expert who seeks to discover his personal status in the constitution of things cannot, in view of the final aim of his struggle, be satisfied with what science may regard as a vital lie, a mere 'as-if'[7] to regulate thought and conduct. In so far as the ultimate nature of Reality is concerned, nothing is at stake in the venture of science; in the religious venture the whole career of the ego as an assimilative personal centre of life and experience is at stake. Conduct, which involves a decision of the ultimate fate of the agent cannot be based on illusions. A wrong concept misleads the understanding; a wrong deed degrades the whole man, and may eventually demolish the structure of the human ego. The mere concept affects life only partially; the deed is dynamically related to Reality and issues from a generally constant attitude of the whole man towards reality. No doubt the deed, i.e. the control of psychological and physiological processes with a view to tune up the ego for an immediate contact with the Ultimate Reality is, and cannot but be, individual in form and content; yet the deed, too, is liable to be socialized when others begin to live though it with a view to discover for themselves its effectiveness as a method of approaching the Real. The evidence of religious experts in all ages and countries is that there are potential types of consciousness lying close to our normal consciousness. If these types of consciousness open up possibilities of life-giving and knowledge-yielding experience, the question of the possibility of religion as a form of higher experience is a perfectly legitimate one and demands our serious attention.

But, apart from the legitimacy of the question, there are important reasons why it should be raised at the present moment of the history of modern culture. In the first place, the scientific interest of the question. It seems that every culture has a form of Naturalism peculiar to its own world-feeling; and it further appears that every form of Naturalism ends in some sort of Atomism. We have Indian Atomism, Greek Atomism, Muslim Atomism, and Modern

Atomism.[8] Modern Atomism is, however, unique. Its amazing mathematics which sees the universe as an elaborate differential equation; and its physics which, following its own methods, has been led to smash some of the old gods of its own temple, have already brought us to the point of asking the question whether the casualty-bound aspect of Nature is the whole truth about it? Is not the Ultimate Reality invading our consciousness from some other direction as well? Is the purely intellectual method of overcoming Nature the only method? 'We have acknowledged', says Professor Eddington,

'that the entities of physics can from their very nature form only a partial aspect of the reality. How are we to deal with the other part? It cannot be said that other part concerns us less than the physical entities. Feelings, purpose, values, made up our consciousness as much as sense-impressions. We follow up the sense-impressions and find that they lead into an external world discussed by science; we follow up the other elements of our being and find that they lead - not into a world of space and time, but surely somewhere.'[9]

In the second place we have to look to the great practical importance of the question. The modern man with his philosophies of criticism and scientific specialism finds himself in a strange predicament. His Naturalism has given him an unprecedented control over the forces of Nature, but has robbed him of faith in his own future. It is strange how the same idea affects different cultures differently. The formulation of the theory of evolution in the world of Islam brought into being Rëmâ's tremendous enthusiasm for the biological future of man. No cultured Muslim can read such passages as the following without a thrill of joy:

Low in the earth
I lived in realms of ore and stone;
And then I smiled in many-tinted flowers;
Then roving with the wild and wandering hours,
O'er earth and air and ocean's zone,
In a new birth,
I dived and flew,
And crept and ran,
And all the secret of my essence drew
Within a form that brought them all to view -
And lo, a Man!
And then my goal,
Beyond the clouds, beyond the sky,
In realms where none may change or die -
In angel form; and then away
Beyond the bounds of night and day,
And Life and Death, unseen or seen,
Where all that is hath ever been,
As One and Whole.

(Rëmâ: Thadani's Translation)[10]

On the other hand, the formulation of the same view of evolution with far greater precision in Europe has led to the belief that 'there now appears to be no scientific basis for the idea that the present rich complexity of human endowment will ever be materially exceeded.' That is how the modern man's secret despair hides itself behind the screen of scientific terminology. Nietzsche, although he thought that the idea of evolution did not justify the belief that man was unsurpassable, cannot be regarded as an exception in this respect. His enthusiasm for the future of man ended in the doctrine of eternal recurrence - perhaps the most hopeless idea of immortality ever formed by man. This eternal repetition is not eternal 'becoming'; it is the same old idea of 'being' masquerading as 'becoming.'

Thus, wholly overshadowed by the results of his intellectual activity, the modern man has ceased to live soulfully, i.e. from within. In the domain of thought he is living in open conflict with himself; and in the domain of economic and political life he is living in open conflict with others. He finds himself unable to control his ruthless egoism and his infinite gold-hunger which is gradually killing all higher striving in him and bringing him nothing but life-weariness. Absorbed in the 'fact', that is to say, the optically present source of sensation, he is entirely cut off from the unplumbed depths of his own being. In the wake of his systematic materialism has at last come that paralysis of energy which Huxley apprehended and deplored. The condition of things in the East is no better. The technique of medieval mysticism by which religious life, in its higher manifestations, developed itself both in the East and in the West has now practically failed. And in the Muslim East it has, perhaps, done far greater havoc than anywhere else. Far from reintegrating the forces of the average man's inner life, and thus preparing him for participation in the march of history, it has taught him a false renunciation and made him perfectly contented with his ignorance and spiritual thraldom. No wonder then that the modern Muslim in Turkey, Egypt, and Persia is led to seek fresh sources of energy in the creation of new loyalties, such as patriotism and nationalism which Nietzsche described as 'sickness and unreason', and 'the strongest force against culture[11]'. Disappointed of a purely religious method of spiritual renewal which alone brings us into touch with the everlasting fountain of life and power by expanding our thought and emotion, the modern Muslim fondly hopes to unlock fresh sources of energy by narrowing down his thought and emotion. Modern atheistic socialism, which possesses all the fervour of a new religion, has a broader outlook; but having received its philosophical basis from the Hegelians of the left wing, it rises in revolt against the very source which could have given it strength and purpose. Both nationalism and atheistic socialism, at least in the present state of human adjustments, must draw upon the psychological forces of hate, suspicion, and resentment which tend to impoverish the soul of man and close up his hidden sources of spiritual energy. Neither the technique of medieval mysticism, nor nationalism, nor atheistic socialism can cure the ills of a despairing humanity. Surely the present moment is one of great crisis in the history of modern culture. The modern world stands in need of biological renewal. And religion, which in its higher manifestations is neither dogma, nor priesthood, nor ritual, can alone ethically prepare the modern man for the burden of the great responsibility which the advancement of modern science necessarily involves, and restore to him that attitude of faith which makes him capable of winning a personality here and retaining it in hereafter. It is only by rising to a fresh vision of his origin and future, his whence and whither, that man will eventually triumph over a society motivated by an inhuman competition, and a civilization which has lost its spiritual unity by its inner conflict of religious and political values.

As I have indicated before,[12] religion as a deliberate enterprise to seize the ultimate principle of value and thereby to reintegrate the forces of one's own personality, is a fact which cannot be denied. The whole religious literature of the world, including the records of specialists' personal experiences, though perhaps expressed in the thought-forms of an out-of-date psychology, is a standing testimony to it. These experiences are perfectly natural, like our normal experiences. The evidence is that they possess a cognitive value for the recipient, and, what is much more important, a capacity to centralize the forces of the ego and thereby to endow him with a new personality. The view that such experiences are neurotic or mystical will not finally settle the question of their meaning or value. If an outlook beyond physics is possible, we must courageously face the possibility, even though it may disturb or tend to modify our normal ways of life and thought. The interests of truth require that we must abandon our present attitude. It does not matter in the least if the religious attitude is originally determined by some kind of physiological disorder. George Fox may be a neurotic; but who can deny his purifying power in England's religious life of his day? Muhammad, we are told, was a psychopath[13]. Well, if a psychopath has the power to give a fresh direction to the course of human history, it is a point of the highest psychological interest to search his original experience which has turned slaves into leaders of men, and has inspired the conduct and shaped the career of whole races of mankind. Judging from the various types of activity that emanated from the movement initiated by the Prophet of Islam, his spiritual tension and the kind of behaviour which issued from it, cannot be regarded as a response to a mere fantasy inside his brain. It is impossible to understand it except as a response to an objective situation generative of new enthusiasms, new organizations, new starting-points. If we look at the matter from the standpoint of anthropology it appears that a psychopath is an important factor in the economy of humanity's social organization. His way is not to classify facts and discover causes: he thinks in terms of life and movement with a view to create new patterns of behaviour for mankind. No doubt he has his pitfalls and illusions just as the scientist who relies on sense-experience has his pitfalls and illusions. A careful study of his method, however, shows that he is not less alert than the scientist in the matter of eliminating the alloy of illusion from his experience.

The question for us outsiders is to find out an effective method of inquiry into the nature and significance of this extraordinary experience. The Arab historian Ibn Khaldūn, who laid the foundations of modern scientific history, was the first to seriously approach this side of human psychology and reached what we now call the idea of the subliminal self. Later, Sir William Hamilton in England and Leibniz in Germany interested themselves in some of the more unknown phenomena of the mind. Jung, however, is probably right in thinking that the essential nature of religion is beyond the province of analytic psychology. In his discussion of the relation of analytic psychology to poetic art, he tells us that the process of artistic form alone can be the object of psychology. The essential nature of art, according to him, cannot be the object of a psychological method of approach. 'A distinction', says Jung,

'must also be made in the realm of religion; there also a psychological consideration is permissible only in respect of the emotional and symbolical phenomena of a religion, where the essential nature of religion is in no way involved, as indeed it cannot be. For were this possible, not religion alone, but art also could be treated as a mere sub-division of psychology.'[14]

Yet Jung has violated his own principle more than once in his writings. The result of this procedure is that, instead of giving us a real insight into the essential nature of religion and its meaning for human personality, our modern psychology has given us quite a plethora of new theories which proceed on a complete misunderstanding of the nature of religion as revealed in its higher manifestations, and carry us in an entirely hopeless direction. The implication of these theories, on the whole, is that religion does not relate the human ego to any objective reality beyond himself; it is merely a kind of well-meaning biological device calculated to build barriers of an ethical nature round human society in order to protect the social fabric against the otherwise unrestrainable instincts of the ego. That is why, according to this newer psychology, Christianity has already fulfilled its biological mission, and it is impossible for the modern man to understand its original significance. Jung concludes:

'Most certainly we should still understand it, had our customs even a breath of ancient brutality, for we can hardly realize in this day the whirlwinds of the unchained libido which roared through the ancient Rome of the Caesars. The civilized man of the present day seems very far removed from that. He has become merely neurotic. So for us the necessities which brought forth Christianity have actually been lost, since we no longer understand their meaning. We do not know against what it had to protect us. For enlightened people, the so-called religiousness has already approached very close to a neurosis. In the past two thousand years Christianity has done its work and has erected barriers of repression, which protect us from the sight of our own sinfulness.'[15]

This is missing the whole point of higher religious life. Sexual self-restraint is only a preliminary stage in the ego's evolution. The ultimate purpose of religious life is to make this evolution move in a direction far more important to the destiny of the ego than the moral health of the social fabric which forms his present environment. The basic perception from which religious life moves forward is the present slender unity of the ego, his liability to dissolution, his amenability to reformation and the capacity for an ampler freedom to create new situations in known and unknown environments. In view of this fundamental perception higher religious life fixes its gaze on experiences symbolic of those subtle movements of Reality which seriously affect the destiny of the ego as a possibly permanent element in the constitution of Reality. If we look at the matter from this point of view modern psychology has not yet touched even the outer fringe of religious life, and is still far from the richness and variety of what is called religious experience. In order to give you an idea of its richness and variety I quote here the substance of a passage from a great religious genius of the seventeenth century - Shaikh AÁmad of Sirhind - whose fearless analytical criticism of contemporary Sufism resulted in the development of a new technique. All the various system of Sufi technique in India came from Central Asia and Arabia; his is the only technique which crossed the Indian border and is still a living force in the Punjab, Afghanistan, and Asiatic Russia. I am afraid it is not possible for me to expound the real meaning of this passage in the language of modern psychology; for such language does not yet exist. Since, however, my object is simply to give you an idea of the infinite wealth of experience which the ego in his Divine quest has to sift and pass through, I do hope you will excuse me for the apparently outlandish terminology which possesses a real substance of meaning, but which was formed under the inspiration of a religious psychology developed in the atmosphere of a different culture. Coming now to the passage. The experience of one 'Abd al-Mumin was described to the Shaikh as follows:

'Heavens and Earth and God's Throne and Hell and Paradise have all ceased to exist for me. When I look round I find them nowhere. When I stand in the presence of somebody I see nobody before me: nay even my own being is lost to me. God is infinite. Nobody can encompass Him; and this is the extreme limit of spiritual experience. No saint has been able to go beyond this'.

On this the Shaikh replied:

'The experience which is described has its origin in the ever varying life of the *Qalb*; and it appears to me that the recipient of its has not yet passed even one-fourth of the innumerable 'Stations' of the *Qalb*. The remaining three-fourths must be passed through in order to finish the experiences of this first 'Station' of spiritual life. Beyond this 'Station' there are other 'Stations' know as *RëÅ, Sirr-i-Khafâ*, and *Sirr-i-Akhf«*, each of these 'Stations' which together constitute what is technically called '*ÿlam-i Amr* has its own characteristic states and experiences. After having passed through these 'Stations' the seeker of truth gradually receives the illuminations of 'Divine Names' and 'Divine Attributes' and finally the illuminations of the 'Divine Essence'.[16]

Whatever may be the psychological ground of the distinctions made in this passage it gives us at least some idea of a whole universe of inner experience as seen by a great reformer of Islamic Sufâsm. According to him this '*ÿlam-i Amr*, i.e. 'the world of directive energy', must be passed through before one reaches that unique experience which symbolizes the purely objective. This is the reason why I say that modern psychology has not yet touched even the outer fringe of the subject. Personally, I do not at all feel hopeful of the present state of things in either biology or psychology. Mere analytical criticism with some understanding of the organic conditions of the imagery in which religious life has sometimes manifested itself is not likely to carry us to the living roots of human personality. Assuming that sex-imagery has played a role in the history of religion, or that religion has furnished imaginative means of escape from, or adjustment to, an unpleasant reality - these ways of looking at the matter cannot, in the least, affect the ultimate aim of religious life, that is to say, the reconstruction of the finite ego by bringing him into contact with an eternal life-process, and thus giving him a metaphysical status of which we can have only a partial understanding in the half-choking atmosphere of our present environment. If, therefore, the science of psychology is ever likely to possess a real significance for the life of mankind, it must develop an independent method calculated to discover a new technique better suited to the temper of our times. Perhaps a psychopath endowed with a great intellect - the combination is not an impossibility - may give us a clue to such a technique. In modern Europe, Nietzsche, whose life and activity form, at least to us Easterns, an exceedingly interesting problem in religious psychology, was endowed with some sort of a constitutional equipment for such an undertaking. His mental history is not without a parallel in the history of Eastern Sufâsm. That a really 'imperative' vision of the Divine in man did come to him, cannot be denied. I call his vision 'imperative' because it appears to have given him a kind of prophetic mentality which, by some kind of technique, aims at turning its visions into permanent life-forces. Yet Nietzsche was a failure; and his failure was mainly due to his intellectual progenitors such as Schopenhauer, Darwin, and Lange whose influence completely blinded him to the real significance of his vision. Instead of looking for a spiritual rule which would develop the Divine even in a plebeian and thus open up before him an infinite future, Nietzsche was driven to seek the realization of his vision in such scheme as aristocratic radicalism.[17] As I have said of him elsewhere:

The 'I am' which he seeketh,
Lieth beyond philosophy, beyond knowledge.
The plant that groweth only from the invisible soil of the heart of man,
Groweth not from a mere heap of clay![18]

Thus failed a genius whose vision was solely determined by his internal forces, and remained unproductive for want of expert external guidance in his spiritual life,[19] and the irony of fate is that this man, who appeared to his friends 'as if he had come from a country where no man lived', was fully conscious of his great spiritual need. 'I confront alone', he says, 'an immense problem: it is as if I am lost in a forest, a primeval one. I need help. I need disciples: I need a master.[20] It would be so sweet to obey.' And again:

'Why do I not find among the living men who see higher than I do and have to look down on me? Is it only that I have made a poor search? And I have so great a longing for such.'

The truth is that the religious and the scientific processes, though involving different methods, are identical in their final aim. Both aim at reaching the most real. In fact, religion; for reasons which I have mentioned before, is far more anxious to reach the ultimately real than science.[21] And to both the way to pure objectivity lies through what may be called the purification of experience. In order to understand this we must make a distinction between experience as a natural fact, significant of the normally observable behaviour of Reality, and experience as significant of the inner nature of Reality. As a natural fact it is explained in the light of its antecedents, psychological and physiological; as significant of the inner nature of Reality we shall have to apply criteria of a different kind to clarify its meaning. In the domain of science we try to understand its meaning in reference to the external behaviour of Reality; in the domain of religion we take it as representative of some kind of Reality and try to discover its meanings in reference mainly to the inner nature of that Reality. The scientific and the religious processes are in a sense parallel to each other. Both are really descriptions of the same world with this difference only that in the scientific process the ego's standpoint is necessarily exclusive, whereas in the religious process the ego integrates its competing tendencies and develops a single inclusive attitude resulting in a kind of synthetic transfiguration of his experiences. A careful study of the nature and purpose of these really complementary processes shows that both of them are directed to the purification of experience in their respective spheres. An illustration will make my meaning clear. Hume's criticism of our notion of cause must be considered as a chapter in the history of science rather than that of philosophy. True to the spirit of scientific empiricism we are not entitled to work with any concepts of a subjective nature. The point of Hume's criticism is to emancipate empirical science from the concept of force which, as he urges, has no foundation in sense-experience. This was the first attempt of the modern mind to purify the scientific process.

Einstein's mathematical view of the universe completes the process of purification started by Hume, and, true to the spirit of Hume's criticism, dispenses with the concept of force altogether.[22] The passage I have quoted from the great Indian saint shows that the practical student of religious psychology has a similar purification in view. His sense of objectivity is as keen as that of the scientists in his own sphere of objectivity. He passes from experience to experience, not as a mere spectator, but as a critical sifter of experience, who by the rules of a peculiar technique, suited to his sphere of inquiry, endeavours to eliminate all subjective elements, psychological or physiological, in the content of his experience with a view finally to reach what is absolutely objective. This final experience is the revelation of a new life-process - original, essential, spontaneous. The eternal secret of the ego is that the moment he reaches this final revelation he recognizes it as the ultimate root of his being without the slightest hesitation. Yet in the experience itself there is no mystery. Nor is there anything emotional in it. Indeed with a view to secure a wholly non-emotional experience the technique of Islamic Sufâsm at least takes good care to forbid the use of music in worship, and to emphasize the necessity of daily congregational prayers in order to counteract the possible anti-social effects of solitary contemplation. Thus the experience reached is a perfectly natural experience and possesses a biological significance of the highest importance to the ego. It is the human ego rising higher than mere reflection, and mending its transiency by appropriating the eternal. The only danger to which the ego is exposed in this Divine quest is the possible relaxation of his activity caused by his enjoyment of and absorption in the experiences that precede the final experience. The history of Eastern Sufâsm shows that this is a real danger. This was the whole point of the reform movement initiated by the great Indian saint from whose writings I have already quoted a passage. And the reason is obvious. The ultimate aim of the ego is not to see something, but to be something. It is in the ego's effort to be something that he discovers his final opportunity to sharpen his objectivity and acquire a more fundamental 'I am' which finds evidence of its reality not in the Cartesian 'I think' but in the Kantian 'I can.' The end of the ego's quest is not emancipation from the limitations of individuality; it is, on the other hand, a more precise definition of it. The final act is not an intellectual act, but a vital act which deepens the whole being of the ego, and sharpens his will with the creative assurance that the world is not something to be merely seen or known through concepts, but something to be made and re-made by continuous action. It is a moment of supreme bliss and also a moment of the greatest trial for the ego:

Art thou in the stage of 'life.' 'death', or 'death-in-life.' Invoke the aid of three witnesses to verify thy 'Station.'

The first witness is thine own consciousness -
See thyself, then, with thine own light.
The second witness is the consciousness of another ego -
See thyself, then, with the light of an ego other than thee.
The third witness is God's consciousness -
See thyself, then, with God's light.
If thou standest unshaken in front of this light,
Consider thyself as living and eternal as He!
That man alone is real who dares -
Dares to see God face to face!
What is 'Ascension'? Only a search for a witness
Who may finally confirm thy reality -
A witness whose confirmation alone makes thee eternal.
No one can stand unshaken in His Presence;
And he who can, verily, he is pure gold.
Art thou a mere particle of dust?
Tighten the knot of thy ego;
And hold fast to thy tiny being!
How glorious to burnish one's ego.
And to test its lustre in the presence of the Sun!
Re-chisel, then, thine ancient frame; And build up a new being.
Such being is real being;
Or else thy ego is a mere ring of smoke!

J«vid N«mah

Lecture VII Notes: IS RELIGION POSSIBLE?

Lecture delivered in a meeting of the fifty-fourth session of the Aristotelian Society, London, held on 5 December 1932 with Professor J. Macmurray in the chair, followed by a discussion by Professor Macmurray and Sir Francis Younghusband - cf. 'Abstract of the Minutes of the Proceedings of the Aristotelian Society for the Fifty-Fourth Session', in *Proceedings of the Aristotelian Society* (New Series), XXXIII (1933), 341.

The Lecture was published in the said *Proceedings of the Aristotelian Society*, pp. 47-64, as well as in *The Muslim Revival* (Lahore), I/iv (Dec. 1932), 329-49.

1. This is a reference to Allama Iqbal's own father, who was a devout Sufâ; cf. S. Sulaim«n Nadvâ, Sair-i Afgh«nist«n, p. 179; also S. Nadhâr Niy«zâ, *Iqb«l ke Àëîur*, pp. 60-61. This bold but religiously most significant statement, I personally feel, is Allama's own; it has been attributed here to an unnamed 'Muslim Sufi' perhaps only to make it more presentable to the orthodoxy; see M. Saeed Sheikh, 'Philosophy of Man', *Iqbal Review*, XIX/i (April-June 1988), 13-16, found expression in Allama's verse, viz. *Kulliy«t-i Iqb«l* (Urdë), *B«l-i Jibrâl*, Pt. II, Ghazal 60, v. 4:

Unless the Book's each verse and part
Be revealed unto your heart,
Interpreters, though much profound,
Its subtle points cannot expound.

2. Cf. *Critique of Pure Reason*, Introduction, section vi, pp. 57-58; also Kemp Smith's *Commentary to Kant's 'Critique'*, pp. 68-70. Metaphysics, if it means knowledge of the 'transcendent', or of things-in-themselves, was rejected by Kant as dogmatic, because it does not begin with a critical examination of human capacity for such knowledge. Reference may here be made to one of the very significant jottings by Allama Iqbal on the closing back page of his own copy of Carl Rahn's *Science and the Religious Life* (London, 1928), viz. 'Is religion possible? Kant's problem'; cf. Muhammad Siddiq, *Descriptive Catalogue of Allama Iqbal's Personal Library*, pp. 21-22 and Plate No. 7.

3. The 'principle of indeterminacy' was so re-christened by A. S. Eddington in his *Nature of the Physical World*, p. 220. Now more often known as 'principle of uncertainty' or 'uncertainty principle', it was 'announced' by the physicist philosopher Heisenberg in *Zeitschrift fü r Physik*, XLIII (1927), 172-98. Broadly speaking, the principle states that there is an inherent uncertainty in describing sub-microscopic process. For instance, if the position of an electron is determined, there remains a measure of uncertainty about its momentum. As in a complete casual description of a system both the properties must needs be accurately determined, many physicists and philosophers took this 'uncertainty' to mean that the principle of causality had been overthrown.

4. Cf. *Fusës al-Hikam* (ed. 'Afâfâ), I, 108, II, 11-12 - the words of 'the great Muslim Sufâ philosopher' are: *al-khalqu ma'qël-un w 'al-Haqqu mahsës-un mashhëd-un*. It is noteworthy that this profound mystical observation is to be found in one of Allama Iqbal's verses composed as early as 1903; cf. *B«qây«t-i Iqbal*, p. 146, v. 2.

5. For the Sufi`doctrine of plurality of time and space stated in Lecture III, pp. 60-61 and Lecture V, pp. 107-10 on the basis of the then a rare Persian MS: *Gh«yat al-Imk«n fi Dir«yat al-Mak«n* (The Extent of Possibility in the Science of Space) ascribed by Allama Iqbal to the eminent Sufâ poet (Fakhr al-Dân) 'Ir«qâ, see Lecture III, note 34; cf. also Allama's letter to Dr M. 'Abdull«h Chaghat«'â in Iqbalnamah, II, 334.

6. Cf. John Passamore, *A Hundred Years of Philosophy*, p. 98. In fact both these pronouncements on metaphysics are to be found in Hans Vaihinger's work referred to in the next note. Vaihinger in his chapter on Nietzsche tells us that 'Lange's theory of metaphysics as a justified form of 'poetry' made a deep impression upon Nietzsche' (p. 341) and he also alludes to Nietzsche's patiently asking himself: 'Why cannot we learn to look upon metaphysics and religion as the legitimate play of grown ups?' (p. 346, note). Both these passages are underlined in Allama's personal copy of Vaihinger's work (cf. M. Siddiq, *op. cit.*, p. 6).

7. This is a reference to the title: The Philosophy of 'As If' (1924), translation of *Die Philosophie des Als Ob* (1911), a work of the German Kantian philosopher Hans Vaihinger (1852-1933). The 'as if' philosophy known as fictionism is an extreme form of James's pragmatism or Dewey's instrumentalism; it, however, traces its descent from Kant through F. A. Lange and Schopenhauer. It holds that as thought was originally an aid and instrument in struggle for existence it still is incapable of dealing with purely theoretical problems. Basic concepts and principles of natural sciences, economic and political theory, jurisprudence, ethics, etc., are merely convenient fictions devised by the human mind for practical purposes - practical life and intuition, in fact, are higher than speculative thought.

One meets quite a few observations bearing on Vaihinger's doctrine in Allama's writings, for example, the following passage in 'Note on Nietzsche': 'According to Nietzsche the 'I' is a fiction. It is true that looked at from a purely intellectual point of view this conclusion is inevitable; Kant's *Critique of Pure Reason* ends in the conclusion that God, immoratality and freedom are mere fictions though useful for practical purposes. Nietzsche only follows Kant in this conclusion' (*Thoughts and Reflections of Iqbal*, ed. S. A. Vahid, pp. 239-40).

Also in 'McTaggart's Philosophy': 'Not William James but Kant was the real founder of modern pragmatism' (ibid., p. 119).

8. For a comparative study of Indian, Greek, Muslim and modern theories of atomism, cf. *Encyclopaedia of Religion and Ethics*, II, 197-210, and for a more recent account of modern atomism Niels Bohr's article: 'Atom' in Encyclopaedia Britannica, II, 641-47.

9. A. Eddington, *The Nature of Physical World*, chapter: 'Science and Mysticism', p. 323.

10. N«nikr«m Vasanmal Thad«nâ *The Garden of the East*, pp. 63-64. Cf. *Mathnawi*, iii, 3901-06, 3912-14, for Rëmâ's inimitable lines on the theme of 'biological future of man' which *Thad«nâ* has presented here in a condensed form. Thada`ni`in the Preface to his book has made it clear that 'The poems . . . are not translations of renderings . . .; they are rather intended to recreate the spirit and idea of each master . . . .'

11. Cf. *The Joyful Wisdom*, Book V, where Nietzsche denounces 'nationalism and race-hatred (as) a scabies of the heart and blood poisoning', also The Twilight of the Idols, chapter viii where he pronounces nationalism to be 'the strongest force against culture'.

12. Cf. pp. 145-46.

13. Reference here is to the misguided observations of the orientalists to be found in such works as A. Sprenger, *Des Leben und die Lehre des Mohammed* (1861), 1, 207; D.S. Margoliouth, *Mohammed and the Rise of Islam* (1905), p. 46; R. A. Nicholson, *A Literary History of the Arabs* (1907), pp. 147-48; and D. B. Macdonald, *Religious Attitude and life in Islam* (1909), p. 46.

14. C. Jung, *Contribution to Analytical Psychology*, p. 225.

15. Idem, *Psychology of the Unconscious*, pp. 42-43.

16. Cf. Shaikh Ahmad Sirhindâ, *Maktëb«t-i Rabb«nâ*, vol. I, Letter 253, also Letters 34, 257 and 260. In all these letters there is listing of the five stations, viz. *Qalb* (the 'heart'), *Rëh* (the 'spirit'), *Sirr* (the 'inner'), *Khafiy* (the 'hidden'), and *Akhf«*; together they have also been named as in Letter 34 *Jaw«hir-i Khamsah-i ÿlam-i Amr* ('Five Essences of the Realm of the Spirit'). Cf. F. Rahman, *Selected Letters of Shaikh Ahmad Sirhindi*, chapter iii (pp. 54-55).

17. Cf. *Stray Reflections*, ed. Dr Javid Iqbal, p. 42, where Nietzsche has been named as a 'great prophet of aristocracy'; also article: 'Muslim Democracy' (*Speeches, Writings and Statements of Iqbal*, pp. 123-24), where a critical notice of Nietzsche's 'Aristocracy of Supremen' ends up in a very significant rhetorical question: 'Is not, then, the democracy of early Islam an experimental refutation of the ideas of Nietzsche?'

18. Cf. *Kulliy«t-i Iqb«l* (F«risâ), *J«vâd N«mah*, p. 741, vv. 4 and 3.

Compare this with Allama Iqbal's pronouncement on Nietzsche in his highly valuable article: 'McTaggart's Philosophy':

A more serious thing happened to poor Nietzsche, whose peculiar intellectual environment led him to think that his vision of the Ultimate Ego could be realized in a world of space and time. What grows only out of the inner depths of the heart of man, he proposed to create by an artificial biological experiment' (*Speeches, Writings and Statements of Iqbal*, p. 150).

Again in 'Note on Nietzsche': 'Nietzsche's Supreman is a biological product. The Islamic perfect man is the product of moral and spiritual forces' (*Thoughts and Reflections of Iqbal*, ed. S. A. Vahid, p. 242).

19. Allama Iqbal wished that Nietzsche were born in the times of Shaikh Ahmad of Sirhind to receive spiritual light from him see *Kulliy«t-i Iqb«l* (F«risâ), *J«vâd N«mah*, p. 741, v. 10:

Would that he had lived in Ahmad's time
so that he might have attained eternal joy. (trans. Arberry)

And he himself could be Nietzsche's spiritual mentor, were he be in Iqbal's times; see *Kulliy«t-i Iqb«l* (Urdë), *B«l-i Jibrâl*, Pt. II, Ghazal 33, v. 5.

If that Frankish Sage
Were present in this age

Him Iqbal would teach
God's high place and reach (trans. S. Akbar Ali Shah).

20. Cf. A. Schimmel, 'Some Thoughts about Future Studies of Iqbal,' *Iqbal*, XXIV/iv (1977), 4.

21. Cf. pp. 145-46.

22. Cf. Bertrand Russell, 'Relativity: Philosophical Consequences', Section: 'Force and Gravitation', Encyclopaedia Britannica, XIX, 99c.

23. Cf. *Kulliy«t-i Iqb«l* (F«risâ), *J«vâd N«mah*, p. 607, vv. 10-15 and p. 608, vv. 1-7.

Commenting on Allama's translation of this passage A. J. Arberry in the Introduction to his translation of *J«vâd Nam«h* observes that this 'affords a very fair example of how close and how remote Iqbal was prepared to make his own version of himself'. And he adds that for comparison, in addition to the translation of this passage offered by him, the reader may like to consider its verse-paraphrase by Shaikh Mahmud Ahmad in *Pilgrimage of Eternity*, II, 230-256.

Bibliography

by Dr. Muhammad Iqbal

I. **Works of Allama Iqbal**

(A) Works in Prose

Bedil in the Light of Bergson, ed. and annotated by Dr. Tehsin Firaqi, Lahore, 1988.*The Development of Metaphysics in Persia* (a contribution to the history of Muslim philosophy), London, 1908. Reprinted Lahore, 1954, 1959, 1964.

Ilm al-Iqtisad, Lahore, 1903. Rep. Karachi, 1962.

Six Lectures on the Reconstruction of Religious Thought in Islam, Lahore, 1930. 2nd edn., with revision at about six places and quite a few proof-reading corrections and changes, and more importantly with the addition of Lecture: 'Is Religion Possible?' and an Index, published under the title: *The Reconstruction of Religious Thought in Islam*, London, 1934. Reprinted Lahore, 1944, many later edns. Reprinted Delhi, 1974. French trans. by de Eva Meyerovitch: *Reconstruire la pensé e religieuse de l'Islam,* Paris, 1955. Arabic trans. by 'Abb«s Mahmëd: *Tajdâd al-Tafkâr al-Dân fi'l-Islam,* Cairo, 1955. Urdu trans. by Sayyid Nadhâr Niy«zâ: *Tashkâl-i Jadâd Il«hây«t-i Isl«mâyah*, Lahore, 1958. Persian trans. by Ahmad Aram, I*hya-i Fikr-i Din dar Islam*, Tehran, 1967. Also translated at least in five more languages.

The Reconstruction of Religious Thought in Islam, ed. and annotated by M. Saeed Sheikh, Lahore, 1986, reprinted Lahore, 1989; Spanish trans. by Jose Esteban Calderon: *La Reconstruccion del Pensamiento Religioso en el Islam*, Lahore 1989; *Stray Reflections, A Note-Book of Allama Iqbal* (1910), ed. by Javid Iqbal, Lahore, 1961.

T«râkh-i Tasawwuf (1916), ed. by S«bir Kalurvâ, Lahore, 1985.

(B) *Major Poetical Works* (With English Translation)

Asr«r-i Khudâ trans. by R. A. Nicholson: *The Secrets of the Self*, London, 1920; rev. edn., Lahore, 1940, many later edns.

B«l-i Jibrâl (1935), trans. of the earlier two Parts (16 + 61 Ghazals) by Syed Akbar Ali Shah: *Gabriel's Wing*, Islamabad, 1979; trans. of six quatrains and of twenty-three poems from the last part (as also of some poems from other works) by V. G. Kiernan: *Poems from Iqbal*, London, 1955 (Part II).

J«vâd N«m«h (1932), trans. by Shaikh Mahmud Ahmad: *The Pilgrimage of Eternity*, Lahore, 1961, 1977; also by Arthur J. Arberry: *Javid-Nama*, London, 1966; trans. of the concluding section: *Khit«b ba J«vâd* by B. A. Dar: *Address to Javid*, Karachi, 1971.

P«y«m-i Mashriq (1923), trans. by M. Hadi Hussain: *A Message from the East*, Lahore, 1977.

Rumëz-i Bekhudâ, trans. by Arthur H. Arberry: *The Mysteries of Selflessness*, London, 1953.

Zabër-i 'Ajam (1927), trans. by Arthur J. Arberry: *Persian Psalms*, Lahore, 1948; trans. of the all too important mathnawâ *Gulshan-i R«z-i Jadâd* (New Garden of Mystery) as well as *Bandagâ N«m«h* (Book of Servitude), the closing parts of this work, by Bashir Ahmad Dar, Lahore, 1964; also by M. Hadi Hussain: *The New Rose Garden of Mystery and the Book of Slaves*, Lahore, 1969.

Complete poetical works in Persian and Urdu published in 2 vols. *Kulliy«t-i Iqb«l*: F«risâ & *Kulliy«t-i Iqb«l*: Urdu, Lahore, 1973.

(C) *Addresses, Articles*, Letters, etc.

(i) Compilations in English

Discourses of Iqbal, ed. by Shahid Hussain Razzaqi, Lahore, 1979.

Iqbal by Atiya Begum, Bombay, 1947.

Letters and Writings of Iqbal, ed. by B. A. Dar, Karachi, 1967.

Letters of Iqbal, ed. by Bashir Ahmad Dar, Lahore, 1978.

Letters of Iqbal to Jinnah, with a Foreword by (Quaid-i-Azam) M. A. Jinnah, Lahore, 1942.

Mementos of Iqbal, compiled by Rahim Bakhsh Shaheen, Lahore, n.d.

Speeches, Writings and Statements of Iqbal ed. by Latif Ahmad Sherwani (3rd rev. and enlarged edn.), Lahore, 1977.

Thoughts and Reflections of Iqbal, ed. by Syed Abdul Vahid, Lahore, 1964.

(ii) *Major Compilations in Urdu*

Anw«r-i Iqb«l, ed. by Bashir Ahmad Dar, Karachi, 1967.

Guft«r-i Iqb«l, ed. by M. Rafâq Afîal, Lahore, 1969.

Iqb«ln«mah (Majmë'ah-i Mak«tâb-i Iqb«l), ed. by Shaikh 'At« Ull«h, 2 Parts, Lahore, 1945, 1951.

Khutët-i Iqbal, ed. and annotated by Rafâ'-ud-Dân H«shimâ, Lahore, 1976.

Maq«l«t-i Iqb«l, ed. by Sayyid 'Abdul V«hid Mu'ânâ, Lahore, 1963.

Rëh-i Mak«tâb-i Iqb«l, ed. by M. 'Abdull«h Quraishâ, Lahore, 1977 (a useful compendium of 1233 letters arranged chronologically).

(II) SECONDARY WORKS AND ARTICLES REFERRED

TO IN NOTES AND TEXT

(A) Works

'Abd al-Q«dir, 'Alâ Hasan, *Nazarah 'ÿmmah fi T«râkh al-Fiqh al-Isl«mâ*, Cairo, 1942.

'Abd al-Quddës Gangohâ, *Lat«'if-i Quddësâ*, ed. by Shaikh Rukn al-Dân, Delhi, 1311 A. H.

'Abd al-Sal«m Khurshâd, Dr, *Sargudhasht-i Iqb«l*, Lahore, 1977.

'Abdullah Anwar Beg, *The Poet of the East*, Lahore, 1939.

'Abdull«h Chaghat«'â, Dr, *Iqb«l ki Suhbat Men*, Lahore, 1977.

'Abë D«wëd, Sulaiman b. al-Ash'ath al-Sijist«nâ, *Kit«b al-Sunan*, 4 vols. in 2, Cairo, 1935; English trans. by Ahmad Hasan, *Sunan 'Abë D«wëd*, 3 vols., Lahore, 1984.

Abë Rashâd Sa'âd b. Muhammad b. Sa'âd al-Nais«bërâ, *Kit«b al-Mas«'il fi 'l-Khil«f bain Basriyyân wa 'l-Baghd«diyyân* ed. and trans. into German by Arthur Biram: *Die atomistische Substanzenlehre aus dem Buch der Streitfragen Basrensern und Baghdadensern*, Leyden, 1902.

Aghnides, Nicolas P., *Mohammedan Theories of Finance* (with an Introduction to Mohammedan Law and a Bibliography), New York, 1916; rep. 1969.

Ahmad b. Hanbal, *Musnad*, 6 vols., Beirut, n.d.

Ahmad Hasan, *The Doctrine of Ijm«' in Islam*, Islamabad, 1976.

Ahmad Nabi Khan, Dr (ed.), *Relics of Allama Iqbal (Catalogue)*, Islamabad, Ministry of Culture and Tourism, Government of Pakistan, 1982.

Ahmad Sirhindâ, Shaikh, *Maktëb«t-i Im«m-i Rabb«nâ*, Vol. I, Lahore, n.d.

'Ain al-Qud«t Hamad«nâ, *Gh«yat al-Imk«n fî Dir«yat al-Mak«n*, ed. by Rahâm Farmanish in his compilation *Ahw«l-o-Ath«r 'Ain al-Qud«t*, Tehran, 1338(S); Eng. trans. based on collation with Rampur Library MS by A. H. Kamali, Karachi, 1971.

Alexander, Samuel, *Space, Time and Deity* (The Gifford Lectures at Glasgow, 1916-1918), 2 Vols., London, 1920.

al-Amidâ, Saif al-Dân, *Al-Ihk«m fî UÄël al AÁk«m*, 4 Vols., Beirut, 1400/1980.

Arberry, A. J. (tr.) *Muslim Saints and Mystics: Episodes from the Tadhkirat al-Auliy«'* (Memorial of the Saints) by Farâd al-Dân al- 'AÇÇ«r, London, 1979.

---, *Revelation and Reason in Islam* (The Forwood Lectures for 1956), London, 1957.

Asad, Muhammad, *The Message of the Qur'«n*, Gibralter, 1980.

al-Ash'arâ, Abu'l-Hasan 'Alâb. Ism«'âl, *Maq«l«t al-Isl«miyân*, ed. by Muhammad Muhy al-Dân 'Abd al-Hamâd, 2 vols., Cairo, 1369/1950.

Ashnawi`, Shaikh T«j al-Dân Mahmëd b. Khud«d«d, *Gh«yat al-Imk«n fî Ma'rifat al-Zam«n wa'l-Mak«n*, ed. by Nadhr S«birâ, Campbellpur, 1401 A.H.

Ashraf 'Alâ Th«nawâ, Maul«n«, *Al-Hâlat al-N«jizah lil-Halâlat al-'ÿjizah*, Deoband, 1351 (1931).

Atiyeh, George N., *Al-Kindi: The Philosopher of the Arabs*, Rawalpindi, 1966.

'AÇÇ«r, Farâd al-Dân, *ManÇiq al-ñair*, Isfahan, 1334(S).

Augustine, Saint, *The Confessions of St. Augustine*, trans. by E. B. Pusey, New York, 1945.

Becon, Roger, *Opus Majus*, Eng. trans. by R. B. Burke, 2 vols., Philadelphia, 1928.

Bahiy, Muhammad al-, *Al-Fikr al-Isl«mi al-Àadâth wa Silat bi'l-Istâm«r*, Cairo.

al-Baqill«nâ, Abë Bakr Muhammad b. al-Tayyib, *Kit«b al-Tamhâd*, ed. by Richard J. McCarthy, Beyrouth, 1957.

Barstrow, Robbins Wolcott (ed.), *The Macdonald Presentation Volume*, Princeton, 1933.

Bergson, Henri Louis, *Creative Evolution*, trans. by Arthur Mitchell, London, 1911.

---, *Matter and Memory*, trans. by Nancy Margaret Paul & W. Scott Palmer (pseud), London, 1911.

---, *Time and Free Will: An Essay on the Immediate Data of Consciousness*, trans. by F. L. Pogson, London, 1910.

Berkes, Niyazi, *The Development of Secularism in Turkey*, Montreal, 1964.

al-Bârënâ, Abë Raih«n, *Al-Qanën al-Mas'ëdâ*, vol. I, Hyderabad (Deccan), 1373/1954.

Al-Bârënâ Commemoration Volume (A. H. 362-A.H. 1362), Calcutta, Iran Society, 1951.

Blavatsky, Helena Petrovna, *The Secret Doctrine: The Synthesis of Science, Religion and Philosophy*, 6 vols., Adyar (Madras), 1971.

de Boer, Tjitze J., *Geschichte der Philosophie im Islam* (Stuttgart, 1901), trans. by Edward R. Jones: *The History of Philosophy in Islam*, London, 1903.

Bonola, Roberto, *Non-Euclidean Geometry: A Critical and Historical, Study of Its Development*, Chicago, 1912.

Bradley, Francis Herbert, *Appearance and Reality: A Metaphysical Essay*, Oxford, 1930.

---, *Ethical Studies*, Oxford, 1927.

---, *The Principles of Logic*, 2 vols., Oxford, 1922.

Briffault, Robert, *The Making of Humanity*, London, 1923.

Brockelmann, Carl, *Geschichte der arabischen Litteratur*, 2 vols., Leiden, 1943, 1949; Supplementbä nde, 3 vols., Leiden, 1937, 1938, 1942.

Browne, Robert T., *The Mystery of Space (A Study of the Hyperspace Movement in the Light of the Evolution of New Psychic Faculties and an Inquiry into the Genesis and Essential Nature of Space)*, New York & London, 1919.

Brunschvig, R., *La Berberie orientale sous les Hafasides*, Paris, 1947.

al-Bukharâ, Abë 'Abd All«h Muhammad b. Ism«'âl, *ÂaÁâÁ al-Bukh«râ*, Arabic text with Eng. trans. by Dr. Muhammad Muhsin Khan, 9 vols., Lahore, 1979.

Burnet, John, *Greek Philosophy*: Thales to Plato, London, 1961.

Cajori, F., *A History of Elementary Mathematics*, New York, 1917.

Carr, W. Wildon, *The General Principle of Relativity in Its Philosophical and Historical Aspect*, London, 1920.

---, (ed.), *Life and Finite Individuality*, London, 1918.

---, *A Theory of Monads: Outlines of the Philosophy of the Principle of Relativity*, London, 1922.

Carra de Vaux, Baron Bernard, *Avicenne*, Paris, 1900.

Cornford, F. M., *Plato's Theory of Knowledge (The Theaetetus and the Sophist of Plato, trans. with a running commentary)*, London, 1946.

Coulson, N. J., *A History of Islamic Law*, Edinburgh, 1964.

D«rimâ, Abë Muhammad 'Abd All«h b. 'Abd al-Rahm«n, *Sunan al-D«rimâ*, 2 vols., Damascus, 1349/1930.

Daw«nâ, Jalal al-Dân, *Ris«lat al-Zaur«'*, Cairo, 1326/1908.

Denison, John Hopkins, *Emotion as the Basis of Civilization*, New York & London, 1928.

Descartes, Rene, *The Geometry*, trans. by D. E. Smith & M. L. Latham, Chicago, 1925.

---, *The Philosophical Works of Descartes*, trans. by E. S. Haldane & G.R.T. Ross, 2 vols., London, 1911, 1912.

Durant, Will, *The Age of Faith*, New York, 1950.

---, *Caesar and Christ*, New York, 1944.

Eddington, Arthur Stanley, *The Nature of the Physical World* (Gifford Lectures 1927), London, 1928.

---, *Space, Time and Gravitation: An Outline of the General Relativity Theory*, Cambridge, 1920.

Eliade, Mircea (Editor in Chief), *The Encyclopedia of Religion*, 16 vols, New York & London, 1987.

Encyclopaedia Britannica, 24 vols., Chicago, London & Toronto, 1953.

Encyclopaedia of Islam, The, 4 vols., Leiden & London, 1913-1934; Supplement (in 5 parts), 1934-1938.

Encyclopaedia of Islam, The, New Edition, Leiden & London, 1954 (in progress).

Encyclopaedia of Religion and Ethics, 13 vols., Edinburgh & New York, 1908-1927.

Encyclopaedia of the Social Sciences, 14 vols., in 8, New York, 1950.

Encyclopaedia of Philosophy, The, 8 vols. in 4, New York & London, 1967

Encyclopedia of Philosophy, The, 4 vols., New York, 1984.

Encyclopedia of Religion, An, ed. by Vergilius Ferm, New York, 1945.

Fahri, F. Ziyaeddin, *Ziya Gö kalp: sa vie et sa sociologie*, Paris, 1935.

Fakhry, Majid, *A History of Islamic Philosophy*, New York & London, 1970.

---, *Islamic Occasionalism and Its Critique by Averroes and Aquinas*, London, 1958.

Farnell, Lewis Richard, *The Attributes of God* (The Gifford Lectures delivered in the University of St. Andrews in the year 1924-25), London, 1925.

Feigel, Herbert & May Brodbeck (eds.), *Readings in the Philosophy of Science*, New York, 1953.

Fischer, August, *Aus der religiö sen Reformbewegung in der Tü rkei*, Leipzig, 1922.

Flint, Robert, *History of the Philosophy of History in France*, Belgium and Switzerland, Edinburgh, 1893.

Fu'«d 'Abd al-B«qâ, Muhammad, *al-Mu'jam al-Mufahras li Alf«z al-Qur'«n al-Karâm*, Cairo, 1364/1945.

Fyzee, Asaf A. A., *Outlines of Muhammedan Law*, London, 1955.

al-GhaZz«lâ, Abë H«mid Muhammad b. Muhammad, *Al-Munqidh min al-Dal«l*, trans. by Claud Field: *Confessions of al-Ghazali*, London, 1909, also in W. Montgomery Watt, *The Faith and Practice of al-GhazZ«lâ*, London, 1953, pp. 19-85.

---, *Al-Mustasf«min 'Ilm al-UÄël*, 2 vols., Cairo, 1937.

---, *Al-Qist«s al-Mustaqâm*, trans. with Intro. and Notes by D. P. Brewster: *The Just Balance*, Lahore, 1978.

---, *Tah«fut al-Fal«sifah*, trans. by Sabih Ahmad Kamali: *Incoherence of the Philosophers*, Lahore, 1958.

Ghul«m Mustaf« Kh«n, *Iqb«l aur Qur'«n*, Lahore, 1977.

Gibb, H. A. R., *Modern Trends in Islam* (The Haskell Lectures in Comparative Religion, 1945), New York, 1947, reprint 1978.

---, & J. H. Kramers (eds), *Shorter Encyclopaedia of Islam*, Leiden & London, 1953.

Gillispie, Charles Coulston (ed.), *Dictionary of Scientific Biography*, 16 vols., New York, 1970-80.

Goethe, Johann Wolfgang Von, *Conversation of Goethe with Eckermann and Soret*, trans. by John Oxenford, London, 1901.

Gökalp, Ziya, *Ziya Gökalp küllïyati'i: Sürler ve halk masallari*, ed. by F. A. Tansel, Ankara, 1952.

---,*Turkish Nationalism and Western Civilization: Selected Essays of Ziya Gökalp*, trans. & ed. by Niyazi Berkes, London & New York, 1959.

Goldziher, Ignaz, *Muhammadanische Studien*, 2 vols., (1889-90), Hildsheim, 1961; trans. by C. R. Barber & S. M. Stern, *Muslim Studies*, 2 vols., London, vol. I: 1967, vol. II: 1971.

---,*The Z«hirâs: Their Doctrine and Their History*, trans. by Wolfgang Behn, Leiden, 1971.

Gunn, J. Alexander, *The Problem of Time: A Historical and Critical Study*, London, 1929.

Gwatkin, H. M. & J. P. Whitney (eds.), *The Cambridge Medieval History*, 2 vols., London, 1911, 1913.

À«jâ Khalâfah, Mustaf«b. 'Abd All«h, *Kashf al-Zunën 'an al-As«mi'l-Kutub wa'l-Funën*, 2 vols., Istanbul, 1941-43.

al-Hajwâ, Muhammad b. al-Hasan, *Al-Fikr al-S«mâfâ T«râkh al-Fiqh al-Isl«mâ*, 4 vols., Rabat-Fez-Tunis, 1345-49/1926-31.

Haldane, Viscount Richard Burdon, *The Reign of Relativity*, London, 1921.

al-Hall«j, Husain b. Mansër, *Kit«b al-Taw«sin*, Arabic text and Persian version of Baqlâ, ed. by Louis Massignon, Paris, 1913; French translation by L. Massignon in *La passion d'al-Àall«j*, II, 830-93; Eng. trans. by Aisha Abd Ar-Rahman, Berkeley & London, 1974; also in Gilani Kamran: *Ana al-Haqq Reconsidered*, Lahore, 1398 A. H., pp. 55-108.

Hamidullah, Dr M. (ed.), *Sahifa Hammam-Bin-Munabbih* (Arabic text with Urdu trans.), Hyderabad (Deccan), 1956.

Hanâf Nadvâ, Muhammad, *'Aqliy«t-i Ibn-i Taimâyyah*, Lahore, 1981.

Hassan, Riffat, *The Sword and the Sceptre* (A collection of writings on Iqbal), Lahore, 1977.

Heath, Sir Thomas Little (tr.), *The Thirteen Books of Euclid's Elements*, vol. I, Cambridge, 1926.

Heyd, Uriel, *Foundations of Turkish Nationalism: The Life and Teachings of Ziya Gökalp*, London, 1950.

Hitti, Philip Khuri, *History of the Arabs*, London & New York, 1951.

Hocking, William Ernest, *The Meaning of God in Human Experience*, New Haven, 1955.

Hoernle, R. F. Alfred, *Matter, Life, Mind and God (Five Lectures on Contemporary Tendencies of Thought)*, London, 1923.

Holy Bible, The (Authorised King James Version), London & New York, n.d.

Horten, Max, *Die Hauptlehren des Averroes nach seiner Shrift: Die Widerlegung des Gazali*, Bonn, 1913.

Hourani, George F. (ed.), *Essays on Islamic Philosophy and Science*, Albany, 1975.

al-Hujwârâ, 'Alâb. 'Uthm«n, *Kashf al-Mahjëb* (Iran Pakistan Institute of Persian Studies, Publication no. 29), Lahore, 1398/1978; Eng. trans. by R. A. Nicholson, London, 1911.

Ibn AbâZar, Abu'l-Hasan 'Alâb. 'Abd All«h, *Raud al-Qirt«s* (Upsala, 1843); French trans. by A. Beaumier: *Histoire des souverains du Magreb* . . .' Paris, 1860.

Ibn al-'Arabâ, Muhy al-Dân, *Fusës al-Hikam*, ed. & annotated by Abu'l-'Al«'Afâfâ, 2 vols., Cairo, 1365/1946.

Ibn Hazm, 'Alâb. Ahmad, *Kit«b al-Fisal fi'l-Milal wa'l-Ahw«' wa'-l-Nihal*, 4 vols., Cairo, 1311-1312.

---, *Al-Taqrâb li-Hadd al-Mantiq*, ed. by Dr Ihsan Abbas (from the only MS 6814, al-Maktabat al-Ahmadâyah, Tunis), Beirut, 1959.

Ibn Jam«'ah, Badr al-Dân, *Tahrâr al-Ahk«m fi'l-Tadbâr Ahl al-Isl«m*, ed. & trans. into German by Hans Kofler in *Islamica*, VI (1934), 349-414 and VII (1935), 1-64.

Ibn Khaldën, *The Muqaddimah: An Introduction to History*, trans. by Franz Rosenthal, 3 vols., New York & London, 1958.

Ibn M«jah, Abë'Abd All«h Muhammad b. Yazâd, *Sunan*, ed. by Muhammad Fu'a`d 'Abd al-Ba`qi, 2 vols., Cairo, 1952-53.

Ibn Maskawaih, Abu 'Alâ Ahmad, *Al-Fauz al-Asghar*, Cairo, 1325 A.H.; Eng. trans. by Khwaja Abdul Hamid in Ibn Maskawaih: *A Study of His Al-Fauz al-Asghar*, Part I, Lahore, 1946.

Ibn Qutaibah, 'Abd All«h b. Muslim, *Kitab al-Ma'«rif*, ed. by Tharwat 'Uk«shah, Cairo, 1960 (Urdu trans. by Dr Zia-ul-Haq: Ph. D. Dissertation, University of the Punjab, Lahore, 1950).

---, *Kit«b Ta'wâl Mukhtalif al-Hadâth*, ed. by Faraj All«h Zaki`al-Kurdi`, et. al., Cairo, 1326 A.H.

Ibn Rushd, Averroes' *Tah«fut al-Tah«fut (The Incoherence of the Incoherence)*, trans. with Intro. and Notes by Simon van den Bergh, 2 vols., London, 1954.

Ibn Taimâyyah, *Kitab al-Radd 'al«al-ManÇiqiyân*, ed. by 'Abd al-Samad Sharaf al-Di`n al-Kurtubi, Bombay, 1949.

Ikram, S. M., *Modern Muslim India and the Birth of Pakistan*, Lahore, 1977.

Iqbal As A Thinker (Essays by Eminent Scholars), Lahore, Sh. Muhammad Ashraf, 1944.

Isfrâ'ânî, Abë Ish«q Ibrahâm, *Al-Tabsir fi'l-Din wa Tamâz al-Firqat al-N«jâyah 'an al-Firaq al-Halikân*, Cairo, 1374 A.H.

Isl«hâ, Amân Ahsan, *Tadabbar-i-Qur'«n* (1967-1980), Fourth reprint, 9 vols., Lahore, 1989.

James, William, *Human Immortality* (Ingersoll Lecture at Harvard University for 1898), London, 1917.

---, *The Principles of Psychology*, 2 vols. in 1, New York, 1950.

---, *The Varieties of Religious Experience: A Study in Human Nature* (Gifford Lectures, 1901-1902), London & New York, 1902.

J«mâ, 'Abd al-Rahm«n, *Law«ih (A Treatise on Sufâsm)* ed. & trans. by E. H. Whinfield and Mirza M. Kazwini, London, 1906. Rep., Lahore, 1978.

Jung, Carl Gustav, *Contribution to Analytical Psychology*, trans. by H. G. & Cary F. Baynes, London, 1928.

---, *Psychology of the Unconscious*, trans. by B. M. Hinkle, London, 1919.

Kahh«lah, 'Umar Riîa, *Mu'jam al-Mu'allifin: Tar«jim Musannifâ'l-Kutub al-'Arabâyyah*, 15 vols. in 8, Damascus, 1957-61.

Kant, Immanuel, *Critique of Pure Reason*, trans. by N. Kemp Smith, London, 1953.

Khuda Bukhsh, Salahuddin, *Politics in Islam (von Kremer's 'Staatsidee des Islam': enlarged and amplified)*, Lahore, 1948.

al-Khudarâ, Muhammad, *T«râkh al-Tashrâ' al-Isl«mâ*, (Cairo, 1926) Urdu trans. by 'Abd al-Salam Nadvâ: *Tarâkh-i Fiqh-i Islami*, A'zamgarh, 1346 A.H.

Kirkpatrick, F. (ed.), *Lectures on the History of the Nineteenth Century*, Cambridge, 1904.

Kohler, W., *The Mentality of Apes*, trans. by Ella Winter, London, 1924.

Lammens, H., *Islam, Beliefs and Institutions*, trans. by Sir E. Denison Ross, London, 1929.

Lane, Edward William, *An Arabic-English Lexicon*, Parts 1-8, 8 vols., ed. by Stanley Lane-poole, New York, 1950-56.

Lewes, George Henry, *The Biographical History of Philosophy*, London, 1857.

Macdonald, Duncan Black, *Development of Muslim Theology, Jurisprudence and Constitutional Theory*, New York, 1903; rep. Lahore, 1960.

---, *The Religious Attitude and Life in Islam* (The Haskell Lectures on Comparative Religion, 1906), Beyrouth, 1965.

McTaggart, John McTaggart Ellis, *Nature of Existence*, ed. by C. D. Broad, Cambridge, 1927.

---, *Philosophical Studies*, ed. by S. V. Keeling, London, 1934.

---, *Studies in the Hegelian Dialectic*, Cambridge, 1922.

Mahmansani, Sobhi (Mahmas«nâ, Subhâ), *Falsafat al-Tashrâ' fi'l-Isl«m* (Beirut, 1952); trans. by Farhat J. Ziadeh: *The Philosophy of Jurisprudence in Islam*, Leiden, 1961; Urdu trans. by M. Ahmad Rîîvâ: *Falsafah-i Shari'at- Islam*, Lahore, 1981.

Maimonides, Moses, *The Guide of the Perlexed*, trans. by Shlomo Pines, with introductory essay by Leo Strauss, Chicago, 1963.

al-Marghin«nâ, Burh«n al-Dân, *Al-Hidayah: Sharh Bid«yat al-Mubtadâ*, 4 vols., Cairo 1326-27 A.H., trans. by Charles Hamilton: *The Hedaya or Guide: A Commentary on the Mussulman Laws*, 2nd edn., London, 1870; rep. Lahore, 1957.

Margoliouth, David Samuel, *The Early Development of Mohammedanism*, London, 1914.

---, *Mohammed and the Rise of Islam*, New York, 1905.

Mas'ëd; Dr Kh«lid, *Iqb«l ka Tasawwur-i Ijtih«d*, Islamabad, 1985.

Merchant, Muhammad Valibhai, *A Book of Quranic Laws*, Lahore, 1947.

Metz, Rudolf, *A Hundred Years of British Philosophy*, trans. from German by J. W. Harvey, et. al., and ed. by J. H. Muirhead, London, 1938.

Monzavi, Ahmad, *A Catalogue of Persian Manuscripts*, vol. II, Pt. I, Tehran, 1934(S).

Morgan, C. L., *Emergent Evolution*, London, 1923.

Munk, Salomon, *Mé langes de philosophie Juive et arabe*, Paris, 1859.

Murphy, Gardner, *Historical Introduction to Modern Psychology*, London, 1949.

Muslim, Abu'l-Husain b. al-Hajj«j al-Nâs«bërâ, *Al-ÂahâÁ*, 8 vols., Cairo, 1334 A.H.; Eng. trans. by 'Abdul Hamâd Siddâqâ: *Sahih Muslim*, 4 vols., Lahore, 1976-81.

Nadhâr Niy«zâ, Sayyid, *Iqb«l ke Huîër*, Karachi, 1971.

Nas«'â, Ahmad b. Shu'aib, *Sunan*, Cairo, 1930.

al-Nashsh«r, 'Alâ S«mâ, *Man«hij al-Bahth 'inda Mufakkiri'l-Isl«m wa Naqd al-Muslimân lil-Mantiq al-Aristët«lâsâ*, Cairo, 1367/1947.

Nasr, Seyyed Hossein, *An Introduction to Islamic Cosmological Doctrines: Conceptions of Nature and Methods Used for the Study by the Ikhwan al-Safa', al-Biruni and Ibn Sina*, Cambridge (Mass.), 1964.

Naumann, Joseph Friedrick, *Briefe Ü ber Religion*, Berlin, 1916.

---, *Mitteleuropa*, trans. by C. M. Meredith: Central Europe, London, 1916.

New Encyclopaedia Britannica, The (Propaedia, Micropaedia and Macropaedia), 30 Vols., Chicago, London, Toronto, etc., 1973, 1985.

Newton, Sir Isaac, *The Mathematical Principles of Natural Philosophy*, trans. by Andrew Motte, 3 vols., London, 1803.

Nicholson, Reynold A., *A Literary History of the Arabs*, Cambridge, 1953.

Nietsche, Friedrich Wilhelm, *The Complete Works of Friedrich Nietzsche*, trans. by W. A. Haussmann, et. al., ed. by Oscar Levy, 18 Vols., Edinburgh, 1909-14.

Ouspensky, Peter Demianovich, *Tertium Organum: A Key to the Enigmas of the World*, (1912), trans. by Nicholas Bessaraboff & Claude Bragdon, London, 1926.

Passamore, John, *A Hundred Years of Philosophy*, Harmondsworth, 1975.

Rafâ' al-Dân Hashimâ, Dr. *Tas«nâf-i Iqb«l Ka Tahqâqi-o-TauîâÁâ MuÇ«la'ah*, Lahore, 1982.

al-Raghib, Abu'l-Q«sim al-Husain, *Al-Mufrad«t fî Gharâb al-Qur'«n*, Beirut, n.d.

Rahâm Bakhsh Sh«hân, *Aur«q-i Gumgashtah*, Lahore, 1975.

---, *Mementos of Iqbal*, Lahore n.d.

Rahm«n, Fazlur, *Selected Letters of Shaikh Ahmad Sirhindi*, Karachi, 1968.

---, *Major Themes of the Qur'«n*, Minneapolis, 1980.

Raschid, M. Salman, *Iqbal's Concept of God*, London, 1981.

R«zâ, Fakhr al-Dân, *Al-Mab«hith al-Mashriqâyyah*, vol. I, Hyderabad (Deccan), 1343 A.H.

---, *Al-Tafsâr al-Kabâr*, 8 vols., Cairo, 1307 A.H.

Renan, Ernst, *Averroes et l'averroisme: essai historique*, Paris, 1882; Urdu trans. by Ma'shë`q Husain: *Ibn-i Rushd wa Falsafah-i Ibn-i Rushd*, Hyderabad (Deccan), 1347/1929.

Rescher, Nicholas, *The Development of Arabic Logic*, Pittsburgh, 1964.

Rodwell, J. M. (tr.), *The Koran* (1861), London, 1948.

Ross, William David, *Aristotle*, London, 1923.

Rougier, Louis, *Philosophy and the New Physics: An Essay on the Relativity Theory and the Theory of Quanta*, authorised trans. by Morton Masius, Philadelphia, 1921.

Royce, Josiah, *The World and the Individual* (Gifford Lectures), 2 vols., London, 1900.

Rëmâ, Maul«n« Jal«l al-Dân, *Mathnawâ-i Ma'nawâ*, text ed. and trans. and commentary by Reynold A. Nicholson: *The Mathnawâof Jal«lu'ddân Rëmâ*, 8 vols., London, 1925-40.

Runes, D. D. (ed.), *The Dictionary of Philosophy*, New York, 1982.

Russell, Bertrand, *History of Western Philosophy*, London, 1949.

---, *Mysticism and Logic*, London, 1949.

---, *Our Knowledge, of the External World*, London, 1949.

Sa'âd Ahmad Akbar«badâ, *Khutab«t-i Iqb«l per ek Naïr*, Srinagar, 1983; reprinted, Lahore, 1987.

Sa'âd b. Ahmad al-Andalusi, *ñabaq«t al-Umam*, Beirut, n.d.

al-Sa'âdâ, 'Abd al-Muta'«l, *Al-Mujaddidën fi'l-Isl«m*, Cairo, n.d.

al-Sal«wâ, Ahmad b. Kh«lid al-N«sirâ, *Al-Istiqs«' li Akhb«r Duwal al-Maghrib al-Aqs«*, vol. II, al-D«r al-Baid«, 1954.

S«lik, 'Abd al-Majâd, *Dhikr-i Iqb«l*, Lahore, 1955.

Salâm Akhtar (ed.), *Fikr-i Iqb«l Ke Munawwar Goshay*, Lahore, 1973.

al-Sarakhsâ, Shams al-A'immah AbëBakr Muhammad b. Ahmad, *UÄël al-Sarakhsâ*, Cairo, 1373/1954.

Sarkhwush, Muhammad Afdal (ed.) *Kalim«t al-Shu'ar«'*, Lahore, n.d.

Sarton, George, *Introduction to the History of Science*, 3 vols. in 5, Baltimore, 1927-48.

Sayyid Sulaim«n Nadvâ, *Sair-i Afgh«nist«n*, Hyderabad (Deccan), 1945.

Schacht, Joseph, *The Origins of Muhammedan Jurisprudence*, Oxford, 1953.

---, with C. E. Bosworth (eds.), *The Legacy of Islam*, 2nd edn., Oxford, 1974.

Schilpp, P. A. (ed.), *Albert Einstein: Philosopher-Scientist*, New York, 1951.

Schimmel, Annemarie, *Gabriel's Wing (A Study in to the Religious Ideas of Sir Muhammad Iqbal)*, Leiden, 1963.

---, *Mystical Dimensions of Islam*, Chapel Hill, 1975.

Schmö lders, August, *Essai sur les Ecoles philosophiques chez les Arabes, et notament sur la doctrine d'Algazzali*, Paris, 1842.

Schopenhauer, Arthur, *World as Will and Idea*, trans. by R. B. Haldane & John Kemp, vol. I, London, 1923.

Servier, Andre, *Islam and the Psychology of Musulman*, trans. by A. S. Moss-Blandell, London, 1924.

Shabistarâ, *Mahmëd, Gulshan-i R«z*, ed. and trans. by E. H. Whinfield: *Gulshan-i R«z: The Mystic Rose Garden*, London, 1880; rep. Lahore, 1978.

Shafâ'â, Abë 'Abd Allah Muhammad, *Islamic Jurisprudence: Sh«fi'âs Ris«la*, trans. with intro. and notes by Majid Khadduri, Baltimore, 1961.

al-Shahrast«nâ, Muhammad b. 'Abd al-Karâm, *Kit«b al-Milal wa'l-Nihal*, ed. by W. Cureton, London, 1846.

Shams al-Haqq, *'Aun al-Ma'bëd li-Hall-i Mushkil«t Sunan AbëD«wëd*, 4 vols., Multan, 1399 A.H.

Sharâf, M. M. (ed.), *A History of Muslim Philosophy (with Short Accounts of Other Disciplines and Modern Renaissance in Muslim Lands)*, 2 vols., Wiesbaden, 1963, 1966.

al-Sh«tibâ, Abë Ish«q Ibr«hâm b. Mës«, *Al-Muw«fiq«t fi Usël al-Ahk«m*, 4 vols., Cairo, 1341 A.H.

al-Shaukanâ, Muhammad b. 'Alâ, *Irsh«d al-Fuhël*, Cairo, 1356 A.H.

Sheikh, M. Saeed, *A Dictionary of Muslim Philosophy*, Lahore, 1981.

Shiblâ Nu'm«nâ, *'Ilm al-Kal«m*, Agra, n.d.

---, *Al-Kal«m*, Cawnpore, 1904.

---, *Shi'r al-'Ajam*, vol. III, ÿzamgarh, 1945.

Shih«b al-Dân Suhrawardâ Maqtël, *Kit«b Hikmat al-Isr«q*, ed. by Henri Corbin, Tehran, 1952.

Siddâqâ, Dr Abu'l-Laith (ed. and annotator), *Malfëz«t-i Iqb«l*, Lahore, 1977.

Siddiqâ, Mazheruddân, *Concept of Muslim Culture in Iqb«l*, Islamabad, 1970.

Siddâq Hasan Kh«n, Muhammad, *Husël al-Ma'mël min 'Ilm al-UÄël*, Lucknow, 1298 A.H.

Siddiq, Muhammad, *Descriptive Catalogue of Allama Iqbal's Personal Library*, Lahore, 1983.

Smith, Norman Kemp, *A Commentary to Kant's 'Critique of Pure Reason'*, New York, 1923.

Spencer, Herbert, *First Principles: A System of Synthetic Philosophy*, London, 1911.

Spengler, Oswald, *The Decline of the West*, trans. by C. E. Atkinson, 2 vols. in one, London, 1954.

Sprenger, Aloys, *Das Leben und die Lehre des Mohammed*, 3 vols., Berlin, 1861-65.

Steinberg, S. H. (ed.), *Cassell's Encyclopaedia of Literature*, vol. I, London, 1953.

Stockl, Albert, *Geschichte der Philosophie des Mittelaters*, vol. II, Bonn, 1865.

al-Suyëtâ, Jal«l al-Dân, *Àusn al-Muhadarah fi Akhb«r Misr wa'l-Q«hirah*, vol. I, Cairo, 1299 A.H.

Tauq«n, Qadrâ H«fiz, *Tur«th al-'Arab al-'Ilmâ*, Cairo, 1382/1963.

Thadani, Nanikram Vasanmal, *The Garden of the East*, Karachi, 1932.

al-Tirmidhâ, Muhammad b. '¥s«, *Al-J«mi' al-Sahâh*, ed. by Ahmad Muhammad Sh«kir, 3 vols., Cairo, 1356/1937.

Tourneau, R. Le, *The Almohad Movement in North Africa in the Twelfth and Thirteenth Centuries*, Princeton, 1969.

Toynbee, A., *A Study of History*, Vol. III, London, 1934.

Tsanoff, Radoslav A., *The Problem of Immortality: Studies in Personality and Value*, London, 1924.

al-ñësâ, Nasâr al-Dân, *'Al-Ris«lat al-Sh«fiyah an al-Shakk fi'l-Khutët al-Mutaw«ziyah'* in (ñësâ's) *Ras« 'il*, vol. II, Hyderabad (Deccan), 1359 A.H.

Tyan, Emile, *Institutions du droit public musulman*, Tome II: Sultanat et califat, Paris, 1956.

Vaihinger, Hans, *The Philosophy of 'As If*, trans. by C. K. Ogden, London, 1924.

Wahâd-ud-Dân, Faqâr Sayyid, *Rëzg«r-i Faqâr*, Lahore, 1963.

Walâ All«h, Sh«h, *Àujjat All«h al-B«lighah*, Vol. I, Cairo, 1322 A.H., Urdu trans. by Maul«n«'Abd al-Rahâm, Lahore, 1961.

Whinfield, E. H. (tr.), *Masnavi-i Ma'navi (Spiritual Couplets of Maul«n« Jal«lud-Dân Muhammad Rëmâ*: trans. & abridged), London, 1898.

Whitehead, Alfred North, *The Concept of Nature*, Cambridge, 1920.

---, *Religion in the Making* (Lowell Lectures in Boston in 1926), New York & Cambridge, 1926.

---, *Science and the Modern World* (Lowell Lectures in Boston in 1925), New York, 1925.

Wolfson, Harry Austryn, *The Philosophy of the Kalam*, Cambridge, Mass., 1976.

Yënus Farangâ Mahallâ, Muhammad, *Ibn Rushd*, A'zamgarh, 1324 A.H.

Z«hid al-Kautharâ, *Husn al-Taq«dâfî Sârat al-Im«m Abi Yësuf al-Q«îâ*, Cairo, 1948.

al-Zarkashâ, Badr al-Dân Muhammad, b. Bah«dur, *Al-Burh«n fî 'Ulëm al-Qur'«n*, ed. by Muhammad Abë 'l-Fadl al-Rahâm, 2 vols., Cairo, 1391/1972.

al-Ziriklâ, Khair al-Dân, *Al-A'l«m: Q«mës Tar«jim li-Ashhar al-Rij«l wa'l-Nis«' min al-'Arab wa'l-Musta'ribân wa'l-Mustashriqân*, 10 vols. in 5, Cairo, 1373-78/1954-59; rev. edn., 8 vols., Beirut, 1979.

(B) Articles

Arendonk, C. van, 'Ibn Hazm', *The Encyclopaedia of Islam* (First edition), II, 384-86.

Arnaldez, Roger, & A. Z. Iskander, 'Ibn Rushd', *Dictionary of Scientific Biography*, XII, 1-9.

Arnheim, R., 'Gestalt', *Encyclopedia of Psychology*, II, 58-60.

Barker, Henry, 'Berkeley', section: 'Metaphysics of Immaterialism', *Encyclopaedia of Religion and Ethics*, II, 526b-528b.

Bassett, R., 'Ibn Tumart', *The Encyclopaedia of Islam*, II, 425-27; also *Shorter Encyclopaedia of Islam*, pp. 152-54.

Bausani, A., 'Concept of Time in the Religious Philosophy of Muhammad Iqb«l', *Die Welt des Islams*, N. S., III (1954), 158-86.

Beare, Mary, 'Faust' in S. H. Steinberg (ed.), *Cassell's Encyclopaedia of Literature*, I, 217-19.

de Boer, T. J., 'Atomic Theory (Muhammadan)', *Encyclopaedia of Religion and Ethics*, II, 202b-203b.

Bohr, Niels, 'Atom', *Encyclopaedia Britannica*, II, 642-47.

Broad, C. D., 'Time' *Encyclopaedia of Religion and Ethics*, XII, 334a-345a.

Browne, E. G., 'Pan–Islamism' in F. Kirkpatrick (ed.), *Lectures on the History of the Nineteenth Century*.

Bütler, R. A., 'Kit«b al-Taw«sân of al-Àall«j, *Journal of the University of Baluchistan*, 1/2 (Autumn 1981), 49-117.

Carr, H. Wildon, 'The Idealistic Interpretation of Einstein's Theory', *Proceedings of the Aristotelian Society*, N. S., XXII (1921-22), 123-27.

Carra de Vaux, B., 'Averroes, Averroism', *Encyclopaedia of Religion and Ethics*, II, 264-66; 'Ibn Rushd,' *The Encyclopaedia of Islam*, II, 410-13.

D«r, Bashâr Ahmad, 'Iqbal Aur Mas'alah-i Zam«n-o-Mak«n,' in Salim Akhtar (ed.) *Fikr-i-Iqb«l ke Munawwar Goshay* (Lahore, 1977), pp. 141-51.

Deussen, Paul, 'Atman', *Encyclopaedia of Religion and Ethics*, II, 195b-197b.

Diwald, Susanna, 'Kit«b al-Qist«s al-Mustaqâm', *Der Islam*, XXXVI (1961), 171-74.

Dray, W. H., 'Spengler, Oswald', *The Encyclopaedia of Philosophy*, VII, 527-30.

Dummet, Michael, 'A Defence of McTaggart's Proof of the Unreality of Time', *Philosophical Review*, LXIX (1960), 497-504.

Ehsan Elahie, Rana M. N., 'Iqbal on the Freedom of Ijtih«d,' *Oriental College Magazine* (Allama Iqbal Centenary Number), LIII (1977), 295-330. Contains facsimiles of Allama Iqbal's recently discovered four letters to Professor Maulavi Muhammad Shafâ' from 13 March 1924 to 1 May 1924.

Emmet, Dorothy M., 'Alexander, Samuel', *The Encyclopaedia of Philosophy*, I, 69-73.

Forster, E. M., 'The Secrets of the Self (Asr«r-i-Khudi)', *The Athenaeum* (10 December 1920), pp. 803-04; a book review reproduced in Dr Riffat Hasan (ed.), *The Sword and the Sceptre*, pp. 277-85.

Frank, Philipp, 'Philosophical Interpretations and Misinterpretations of the Theory of Relativity', in Herbert Feigel & May Brodbeck (ed.), *Readings in the Philosophy of Science*, pp. 212-31.

Gilman, Richard C., 'Hocking, William Ernest', *Encyclopaedia of Philosophy*, IV, 46-47.

Goldziher, Ignaz, 'D«wëd B. 'Alâ B. Khalf', *Encyclopaedia of Religion and Ethics*, V, 405-06 'Ibn Hazm', ibid., VII, 70-72.

---, 'Materialien zur Kenntniss der Almohadenbewegung', *Zeitschrift der Deutschen morgenlä ndischen Gesellschaft*, XLI (1887), 30-140.

Haldane, J.S., 'Are Physical, Biological and Psychological Categories Irreducible?', *Proceedings of the Aristotelian Society*, XVIII (1917-18), 419-36.

Halperin, D.J., 'The Ibn Sayya`d Traditions and the Legend of al-Dajj«l,' *Journal of the American Oriental Society*, XCII/ii (1976), 213-25.

Hanney, A. Howard (ed.), 'Abstract of the Minutes of the Proceedings of the Aristotelian Society for the Fifty-Fourth Session,' *Proceedings of the Aristotelian Society*, N.S., XXIII (1932-33), 341-43 (contains a brief report about Allama Iqbal's lecture: 'Is Religion Possible?' on 5 December 1932).

Haque, Serajul, 'Ibn Taimiyya's Conception of Analogy and Consensus', *Islamic Culture*, XVII (1943), 77-87; 'Ibn Taimiyyah' in M. M. Sharif (ed.), *A History of Muslim Philosophy*, II, 796-819.

H«shimâ, Rafâ'al-Dân, 'All«mah ke Chand Ghair-Mudawwan KhuÇëÇ', *Iqbal Review*, XXIII/iv (Jan. 1983), 41-59 (reproduces Allama Iqbal's letter dated 6 May 1937 addressed to

Professor Dr Syed Zafarul Hasan, which indicates that Allama had gathered 'material' for his proposed Rhodes Memorial Lectures on 'Space and Time in Muslim Thought').

Haydar Ali Dirioz, 'Tevfik Fikret', *Journal of the Regional Cultural Institute*, I/4 (Autumn 1968), 12-15.

Haynie, H. A., 'Helmholtz, Hermann von', *Encyclopedia of Psychology*, II, 103.

Heisenberg, W., 'Über den anschaulichen Inhalt der quanten theoretischen Kinematik und Mechanik', *Zeitschrift für Physik*, XLIII (1927), 172-98.

Hopkins, J. F. P., 'Ibn Tumart', *The Encyclopaedia of Islam* (New edition), III, 958-60.

Hourani, G. F., 'The Dialogue Between Al-Ghazz«li and the Philosophers on the Origin of the World', *The Muslim World*, XLVIII/iii and iv (1958), 183-91, 308-14.

Hussain, Riaz, '1910 men Dunya-i Isl«m ke H«l«t ('Political Conditions of the Islamic World in 1910)', *Iqbal Review*, XIX/2 (July 1978), 85-90 (focussed on Allama Iqbal's letter dated 22 August 1910 addressed to the Editor, *Paisa Akhb«r* - an Urdu daily of Lahore).

Imtiy«z 'Alâ Kh«n 'Arshâ, M., 'Zam«n-o Mak«n kâ Bahth ke Muta'allaq 'All«mah Iqb«l ka aik Ma'akhadh: 'Ir«qâya Ashnawâ', *Iqbal Centenary Papers Presented at the International Congress on Allama Mohammad Iqbal* (2-8 December 1977), vol. IV (Papers in Urdu), pp. 1-10.

Jacobi, Hermann, 'Atomic Theory (Indian)', *Encyclopaedia of Religion and Ethics*, II, 199a-202b.

Kazim, M. A., 'Al-Bârënâ and Trignometry', *Al-Bârënâ Commemoration Volume*, pp. 161-70.

Kennedy, E. S., 'Al-Bârënâ Abë Raih«n', *Dictionary of Scientific Biography*, II, 147-68 (bases al-Bârënâ's 'theory of function' on his 'Treatise on Shadows').

Koffka, K., 'Gestalt', *Encyclopaedia of the Social Sciences*, VI, 642-46.

Kofler, Hans, 'Handbuch des islamischen Staats und Verwaltungsrechtes von Badr-ad-Din ibn Gama'ah. Herausgegeben, abersetzt und mit Anmerkungen versehen', *Islamics* VI (1934), 349-414, VII (1935), 1-64 and Schlüssheft (1938), 18-129 (Arabic text with German trans. of Ibn Jam«'ah's *Tahrâr al-Ahk«m fî Tadbâr Ahl al-Isl«m*).

Kroll, Wilhelm, 'Atomic Theory (Greek)', *Encyclopaedia of Religion and Ethics*, II, 197a-99a.

Laoust, H, 'Ibn Taimâyya', *The Encyclopaedia of Islam* (New edition), III, 951-55.

McCarthy, R. J., 'Al-Bakill«nâ,' *The Encyclopaedia of Islam* (New edition), I, 958-59.

Macdonald, D.B., 'Continuous Re-creation and Atomic Time in Moslem Scholastic Theology', *Isis*, IX (1927), 326-44; reprinted in *The Moslem World*, XVIII/i (Jan. 1928), 6-28.

---, 'Ijtih«d,' *The Encyclopaedia of Islam*, II, 448-49; reproduced in the New edition, III, 1026-27.

McTaggert, J. M. E., 'The Unreality of Time', *Mind*, New Series, XVII (October 1908), 457-74.

Margoliouth, D. S., 'Al-Mahdâ', *Shorter Encyclopaedia of Islam*, pp. 310-13.

Marmura, Michael E., 'Ghaz«lâ's Attitude to the Secular Sciences and Logic', in George F. Hourani (ed.), *Essays on Islamic Philosophy and Science*, pp. 100-11.

---, 'Soul: Islamic Concepts', *The Encyclopedia of Religion*, XIII, 460-65.

Mas'ĕd, Kh«lid, 'Khutub«ti Iqb«l men Ijtih«d ki Ta'rif: Ijtih«d k« T«râkhâ Pas-i Manzar,' *Fikr-o-Nazar*, XV/vii-viii, (Islamabad, Jan., Feb. 1978), 31-53.

Namus, Dr M. S., 'Ibn al-Haitham: The Greatest Physicist of Islam', in Hakim Mohammad Said (ed.), *Ibn Haitham: Proceedings of the Celebrations of 1000th Anniversary* (1-10 Nov. 1969, Karachi), pp. 124-34.

Nasr, Seyyed Hossein, 'Shih«b al-Dân Suhrawardâ Maqtĕl' in M. M. Sharif (ed.), *A History of Muslim Philosophy*, I, 372-98.

---, 'Al-ñĕsâ Nasâr al-Dân', *Dictionary of Scientific Biography*, XIII, 508-14 (also gives an assessment of al-Tu`si`'s work on parallel postulate).

Nunn, T. Percy, 'The Idealistic Interpretation of Einstein's Theory', *Proceedings of the Aristotelian Society*, New Series, XXII (1921-22), 127-30.

Obermann, J., 'Political Theology in Early Islam, Hasan al-Basri's Treatise on Qadar', *Journal of the American Oriental Society*, LV (1935), 138-62.

Peyser, C. S., 'Kohler, Wolfgang (1887-1967),' *Encyclopedia of Psychology*, II, 271.

Planck, Wilhelm, 'Reformation', *An Encyclopedia of Religion*, ed. Vergilius Ferm, pp. 640-42.

Poynting, J. Henry, 'Atomic Theory (Medieval and Modern)', *Encyclopaedia of Religion and Ethics*, II, 203b-210b.

Plessner, M., 'Al-J«hiz', *Dictionary of Scientific Biography*, VII, 63-65 (focusses on Kit«b al-Hayaw«n).

Qureshi, I. H., 'Historiography', in M. M. Sharif (ed.), *A History of Muslim Philosophy*, II, 1195-1219.

Reyburn, 'Idealism and the Reality of Time', *Mind*, October 1913, pp. 493-508.

Reichenbach, Hans, 'The Philosophical Significance of the Theory of Relativity', in H. Feigel & M. Brodbeck (eds.), *Readings in the Philosophy of Science*, pp. 195-211; also in P. A. Schilpp (ed.), *Albert Einstein: Philosopher-Scientist*, pp. 287-311.

Russell, Bertrand, 'Relativity, Philosophical Consequences', *Encyclopaedia Britannica* (1953), XIX, 98d-100a.

Sabra, A. I., 'Ibn al-Haytham', *Dictionary of Scientific Biography*, VI, 189-210. (Also gives an exhaustive bibliography including up-to-date information about MSS of Kit«b al-Man«zir).

Schimmel, A., 'Some Thoughts About the Future Study of Iqbal', *Iqbal* (Iqbal Number), XXIV/4 (October 1977), 1-8.

Sharif, M. M., 'Influence of Muslim Thought on the West', Section D: 'Philosophical Influence from Descartes to Kant', idem (ed.), *A History of Muslim Philosophy*, II, 1381-87.

Sheikh, M. Saeed, 'Allama Iqbal's Interest in the Sciences' (Iqbal Memorial Lecture, University of the Punjab, Lahore, 1988), *Iqbal Review*, XXX/i (April-June 1989), 31-43.

---, 'Al-Ghazali: Metaphysics', section D: 'Attack on the Philosophers', in M. M. Sharif (ed.) *A History of Muslim Philosophy*, I, 592-616.

---, 'Al-Ghazali: Mysticism', *ibid.*, I, 617-24.

---, 'Philosophy of Man' (General Presidential Address, Pakistan Philosophical Congress, 1987), *Iqbal Review*, XXIX/i; (April-June, 1988), 3-16.

Siddiqi, Dr M. Razi-ud-Din, 'Iqbal's Conception of Time and Space', *Iqbal As A Thinker*, pp. 1-40.

---, 'Mathematics and Astronomy', in M. M. Sharif (ed.), *A History of Muslim Philosophy*, II, 1277-92.

Smuts, J. C., 'Holism', *Encyclopaedia Britannica*, XI, 640c-644a.

Stern, S. M., 'Ibn al-Samh', *Journal of the Royal Asiatic Society*, 1956, pp. 31-44.

Syrier, Miya, 'Ibn Khaldun and Mysticism', *Islamic Culture*, XXI/ii, (1947), 264-302.

Taylor, Alfred Edward, 'Continuity', *Encyclopaedia of Religion and Ethics*, IV, 89b-98a (inter alia Zeno of Elia's notion, 91-92 and Cantor's theory, 96b-98a).

Thomson, W., 'Kharijitism and the Kharijites' in R. W. Barstrow (ed.), *The Macdonald Presentation Volume*, pp. 371-89.

Vernet, Juan, 'Mathematics, Astronomy, Optics', in J. Schacht (ed.), *The Legacy of Islam*, pp. 461-89.

Watt, W. Montgomery, 'The Political Attitudes of the Mu'tazilah', *Journal of the Royal Asiatic Society*, 1962, pp. 38-54.

Yazd«ni, Dr Khw«jah Hamâd, 'Ris«lah dar Zam«n-o-Mak«n', *Al-M« 'arif*, XVII/7 (Lahore, July 1984), 31-42, 56 (Urdu trans. of Khwaja Muhammad P«rs«'s tractate on space and time based on the unique MS 707, M«j«mâ' Tal'at, D«r al-Kutub, Cairo).

Zedler, B. H., 'Averroes and Immortality', *New Scholasticism*, 1954, pp. 436-53.

CPSIA information can be obtained
at www.ICGtesting.com
Printed in the USA
LVHW081520210420
654200LV00031B/924